CENSORSHIP

A Threat to Reading, Learning, Thinking

John S. Simmons

Florida State University, Tallahassee

Editor

International Reading Association
Newark, Delaware 19714, USA

The International Reading Association attempts, through its publications, to provide a forum for a wide spectrum of opinions on reading. This policy permits divergent viewpoints without assuming the endorsement of the Association.

Director of Publications Joan M. Irwin
Managing Editor Anne Fullerton
Associate Editor Chris Celsnak
Assistant Editor Amy Trefsger
Editorial Assistant Janet Parrack
Production Department Manager Iona Sauscermen
Graphic Design Coordinator Boni Nash
Design Consultant Larry Husfelt
Desktop Publishing Supervisor Wendy Mazur
Desktop Publishing Anette Schuetz-Ruff
Cheryl Strum
Proofing David Roberts

Library of Congress Cataloging in Publication Data

Censorship: a threat to reading, learning, thinking/John S. Simmons, editor.
        p.   cm.
    Includes bibliographical references and indexes.
        1. Academic freedom—United States.   2. Public schools—Censorship—United States.   3. School libraries—Censorship—United States.   I. Simmons, John S.
    LC72.2.C46   1994   94-20203

    025.213—dc20   CIP
    ISBN 0-87207-123-5

Contents

Contributors

Hugh Agee
The University of Georgia
Athens, Georgia

Rodney F. Allen
Florida State University
Tallahassee, Florida

Robert Cormier
Leominster, Massachusetts

Ken Donelson
Arizona State University
Tempe, Arizona

Donald R. Gallo
Central Connecticut State
University
New Britain, Connecticut

Linda S. Grantham
Bay County School District
Panama City, Florida

C. Jane Hydrick
National Council of Teachers
of English
Urbana, Illinois

Edward B. Jenkinson
Indiana University
Bloomington, Indiana

Robert J. Marzano
Mid-Continent Regional
Educational Laboratory
Aurora, Colorado

Ruth A. McClain
Paint Valley High School
Bainbridge, Ohio

Jack L. Nelson
Rutgers University
New Brunswick, New Jersey

Anne Levinson Penway
American Library Association
Chicago, Illinois

Marc Ravel Rosenblum
formerly, National Coalition
Against Censorship
New York, New York

Lawrence C. Scharmann
Kansas State University
Manhattan, Kansas

Robert E. Shafer
Arizona State University
Tempe, Arizona

John S. Simmons
Florida State University
Tallahasee, Florida

Rebecca Bowers Sipe
Anchorage Public School District
Anchorage, Alaska

Robert C. Small, Jr.
Radford University
Radford, Virginia

Malcolm E. Stern
Evanston Township High School
Evanston, Illinois

Carl M. Tomlinson
Northern Illinois University
DeKalb, Illinois

Michael O. Tunnell
Brigham Young University
Provo, Utah

James Anthony Whitson
University of Delaware
Newark, Delaware

Foreword

Censorship: A Threat to Reading, Learning, Thinking is a milestone in the battle against censorship. Intellectual freedom defenders will be forever grateful for this work put together by John Simmons. I know how active he has been in trying to preserve intellectual freedom, so he is the ideal person to have compiled this volume. Simmons has been pursuing the dream of publishing this book at least since 1989, when he succeeded me as chair of the National Council of Teachers of English Standing Committee Against Censorship. His help with "Common Ground," the joint publication of IRA and NCTE on intellectual freedom, is also well known to me.

As the years have sped by since the 1979 publication of *Dealing with Censorship*, which I edited for NCTE, I have often wished someone would put together an updated work to help in the battle against those who attack intellectual freedom in the schools. Often, teachers, administrators, and library media specialists do not know much about how to fight back. In the 25 years or so that I have been actively involved in defending intellectual freedom, I have found that much more information and advice is needed to help win the battle.

- Written policies and procedures are of the utmost importance. The first case I was officially involved in was lost on procedural grounds because firm policies were not in place.
- Teachers must always know why a particular work is being used, and the rationale should be written.
- Alternate textbook and literature selections are always necessary. In case after case I have discovered teachers who believe that their selections are sacred and that deviations are not allowed. This is often an impossible position to take. Teachers need to be more flexible. If a challenge does come along, it is better sometimes to concede to the use of another piece of literature for an individual student.

- Forming coalitions and alliances is often the only way to win. Teachers, administrators, and others must have a strong united front.
- Professional organizations and activist groups are extremely helpful. Often such groups as the International Reading Association, the National Coalition Against Censorship, the People for the American Way, the American Library Association, and the National Council of Teachers of English can make a difference.
- Those involved in defending books or materials in schools must have knowledge of legal procedures.
- School personnel and concerned citizens should be aware of the power of the professional censors. These well-financed, well-organized, zealous groups have strategies intellectual freedom defenders must know about and learn how to deal with.

Censorship: A Threat to Reading, Learning, Thinking provides useful information on all these matters and many others concerning the right to read, learn, and think. All defenders of the right to know should find the book a rich source for help.

James E. Davis
Past President
National Council of Teachers of English

Preface

It seems altogether timely and fitting that a collection of essays on censorship should be published by the International Reading Association now, when the problem of challenges to materials used in curricula in all grades and across content areas throughout the literate world has grown in both scope and intensity. It is time—in fact, past time—that educators, concerned parents, and thoughtful citizens recognize the pervasiveness of the issue of censorship in schools.

In its annual report, *Attacks on the Freedom to Learn*, the People for the American Way organization provides testimony to the fact that challenges to reading materials have been on the upswing over the past two decades coast to coast in the United States. In other English-speaking countries, notably Canada, Australia, and the United Kingdom, challenges and complaints are also on the increase. The same is true in the newly united Germany, where the difficulties of reconciling two disparate political, social, economic, and cultural philosophies are being faced, and xenophobic attitudes toward the presence of immigrants are being voiced. Such transitions have an inevitable impact on curricula, and German educators are confronting questions today never envisaged by their predecessors. Such philosophical and curricular confrontations will undoubtedly arise in countries of Central Europe and the former Soviet Union as their citizens struggle to institute a more democratic way of life for themselves and their children—a natural consequence of the assumption of freedom in any society.

It is easy—but dangerous—to underestimate the universal but idiosyncratic nature of censorship challenges: they can occur in virtually any community, at any time, in any classroom, and over any selection. Who would have thought, for instance, that

- school dictionaries would be barred from secondary school classrooms because they contained "dirty and suggestive" words?

- reference to Ralph Bunche—an African American civil rights leader—in a high school history text would be challenged, and citizens would demand that his name be removed?

- clergy of a community would lead an assault on a language arts program that had recently introduced instruction in U.S. regional and social dialects?

- Harper Lee's *To Kill a Mockingbird*, along with many other classics, would be challenged in numerous secondary schools for containing "racist language"?

- a beginning reading series would be challenged by several districts in California because its contents were "satanic and un-Christian" in nature?

- a big-city superintendent and widely respected educator would lose his job over his support of a contemporary, multicultural program of studies?

- a Miss America would be prevented from using the terms "AIDS" or "condoms" in her remarks to the school population of a large city?

- *all* paperback books would be prohibited from use in the classrooms of several communities because of their "potentially obscene" nature?

- children's fairy tales, including *Snow White* and *Sleeping Beauty*, would be challenged in elementary schools because of their "negative stereotyping of women"?

- the legislatures of three states would pass statutes requiring that the study of creationism be given equal time with that of evolution in all science classes?

- modern health and safety texts would be banned in several communities because of their consistently "filthy and objectionable" content?

- a public library would be accused of taking the lead in promoting homosexuality because its collection included two children's books—*Heather Has Two Mommies* and *Daddy's Roommate*—about tolerance for families where parents are gay or lesbian couples?

- the Holocaust would be excluded from history courses in several communities because of its "mythological basis"?
- discussion of Franklin Delano Roosevelt and the New Deal would be excluded from any U.S. history course in a large school district because of their "socialistic overtones"?
- *The Diary of a Young Girl* by Anne Frank would be removed from an entire school district because the protagonist meditates briefly on her first menstrual period?

These examples of extremely varied and widespread censorship represent only a few of the vast number of incidents. Moreover, as this anthology is being readied for publication, many more notorious challenges to school material and courses will be recorded.

The purpose of this collection is to provide a comprehensive view of the current censorship scene. It is only as comprehensive as the essays included will permit and only as current as was the situation when the authors sat down to compose. That it is either is debatable; that it is germane to the real world of today's curriculum conflicts is undeniable.

JSS

Some Dimensions of the Problem

C ensorship in schools is unquestionably only one element of worldwide controversy over who decides what people should see, hear, or read. From the fundamentalist Muslim denunciation of *The Satanic Verses* and the death sentence imposed by Iranian religious leaders on its author, Salman Rushdie, to the U.S. Congress' hearings on TV violence, efforts to place a cap on what all of us should be allowed to experience are being made in every corner of the globe by many different groups and individuals. Section One focuses on some of the larger aspects of such efforts as they relate to school curriculum materials.

Simmons' opening essay offers some perspectives on that broad, and often misused, term *critical reading*. He then describes strategies used for critical reading instruction and relates them to the concerns of book banners. Whitson investigates the necessary place of critical reading across the curriculum. He rejects the demands of several ultraconservative pressure groups that reading instruction focus on factual knowledge, and he develops his thesis that all reading is inevitably critical in nature—making it as untenable as it is unwise to attempt to prohibit young people from practicing it.

Jenkinson describes a variety of strategies used by those individuals and groups who seek to obstruct teachers' right to choose texts and students' right to read and react to them. Marzano analyzes a series of challenges to "New Age" thinking; he then considers the content and value of the "questionable" New Age materials, stressing their potential use in courses of study for young people. Rosenblum describes three book-banning attempts, ranging across the grades. He then recounts how the National Coalition Against Censorship has responded to each of them.

In a second essay, Simmons outlines the issue from the other side of the political spectrum: he discusses the origins of the "political correctness" movement and details its impact on the public school curriculum. Finally, Cormier, whose young adult novels have been attacked as often as they have been honored, offers a unique perspective on the problem. He reacts first as a writer to the several complaints and challenges his novels have provoked. Then, at greater length, he expresses his concern as a parent, describing ways in which he has seen children react when they are denied either the right to read or the opportunity to participate in classroom discussions of a book.

Chapter 1

Dimensions of Critical Reading: Focus on Censorship Elements

John S. Simmons

In the foreword to *Preface to Critical Reading* (1969), Richard Altick states,

> Of course everybody knows how to read, in one sense. From newspapers to novels, cartoons to captions, we absorb a daily barrage of printed words. In general we know what is being said; and we believe that we could report the gist of any passage of writing.
>
> But reading—*critical* reading—is far more than this. (It is) generated by the critical spirit which...is one's determination to see...everything for what it *really is* (p. xi).

My years of teaching English language arts and reading at the secondary level have led me to believe that the promotion of critical reading ability must be at the core of any curriculum; this is especially true in secondary programs of study in which we are preparing young people for entry into the "real world" of a free-enterprise, democratic society.

In the university-level education course I continue to teach, "Teaching Reading in Secondary Schools," I have always emphasized the element of purpose in establishing effective comprehension instruction. Further, I have stressed the difference between *basic* comprehension purposes (finding facts or details) and *critical* understanding (separating fact from opinion in propaganda, for example). My interest in this aspect of the reading process was stimulated in 1977 when I was invited by the then Florida education commissioner Ralph D. Turlington to prepare some instructional modules on reading comprehension. The purpose of these modules was to provide assistance for Florida's high school teachers as they attempted to ready their students for the first administration of the Florida Functional Literacy Test. To prepare suitable materials, I previewed the test and found that of the 77 questions asked, 28 depended on critical reading abilities. These questions were divided equally among the following stated objectives: (1) infer an idea from a selection; (2) identify a fact or opinion, or distinguish between facts and opinions; (3) infer a cause or effect of an action; and (4) identify an unstated opinion (Turlington & Williams, 1975). With these objectives in mind, I developed a four-phase instructional component that culminated in a series of sequential strategies aimed at teaching pertinent critical reading capacities. From these modules, I eventually created an introduction to critical reading worktext, *Reading by Doing* (Simmons & Palmer, 1994).

The connection between that work and the issue of challenges to school materials did not occur to me at that time. During the late 1970s, however, I became aware of an increase in such challenges in the United States, spurred on by the founding of several right-wing political action groups. These groups include the Moral Majority (later named the Liberty Foundation) founded by Jerry Falwell; Mel and Norma Gabler's Educational Research Analysts; the Eagle Forum led by Phyllis Schlafly; Concerned Women for America headed by Beverly La Haye; Citizens for Excellence in Education founded by Robert Simonds; and Pat Robertson's Christian Coalition.

During the 1980s, the focus of attacks by these groups—as well as by individual citizens—shifted from "dirty" words and descriptions of explicit sexual activity to any topic that, to them, represented a criticism, explicit or otherwise, of free-enterprise, patriotic, or fundamentalist Christian dogma. Also during the 1980s and '90s, groups and individuals from the opposite side of the political spectrum began attacks on school materials and curricula for "politically correct" reasons: noninclusion of specific minority groups, racist or sexist language, and so on.

My ongoing concern with challenges—from both the political right wing and left wing—to teachers' and students' right to read and discuss led me to review several critical reading strategies, many of which would be diluted or eliminated from school curricula were the efforts of the censors to prove successful. The following critical reading strategies are taught across the content areas and through the curriculum, kindergarten to college; and they are protested continually.

Reader Response Approaches

Many years ago, Richards, in his renowned text *Practical Criticism* (1929), contended that a writer's work was done when he or she finished the text. It was then that the reader took over the job of creating meaning by superimposing his or her background, experiences, perspectives, and value system on that text. This theory of active reader involvement in comprehension was further developed by Rosenblatt in *Literature as Exploration* (1938), a text that has been the object of renewed pedagogical interest over the past 15 years or so.

The reader response philosophy, which allows—indeed encourages—each reader to identify personally with the text to create its meaning, is suspect to many challengers who would prefer that factual knowledge be emphasized and authoritarian explanation of texts be passively accepted by student readers. Ironically, support for reader response theory—the creation of individually perceived meaning in texts—is evident in some notorious censorship cases:

- In Wrenshall, Minnesota, in 1961, citizens asked for the removal of "The Ant and the Grasshopper" fable from all elementary schools, claiming it taught communist doctrine.

- In 1969, parents in Nacogdoches, Texas, objected to the inclusion of John Hersey's *Hiroshima* in an anthology because it raised questions about U.S. motives in dropping the bomb and evoked "too much sympathy" for the victims.

- In Panama City, Florida, in 1989, some parents demanded the removal of Robert Cormier's novel *I Am the Cheese* from schools because they claimed it attacked the Central Intelligence Agency of the United States.

- A small group of citizens in Clay County, Florida, caused the "Little Red Riding Hood" fairy tale to be taken off all elementary school library shelves in 1989, on the grounds that the grandmother's expressed enjoyment of wine was immoral.

In all these cases, students were prohibited from reading books because of the censors' interpretations of and eventual actions against them.

Of course, any reader's response has both a cognitive and an affective dimension, and these work together as the reader creates meaning in the text. Students at virtually all levels read materials in and out of school that offer ideas, concepts, issues, and propositions. Some of these are explicit; others are implicit. In either case, the process of detecting central meaning demands that readers use their cognitive skills. When students reading a text can identify expressed main ideas, their cerebral activity is cognitive; when students come to a conclusion about main ideas they feel to be implied in a text, they are also performing a cognitive activity—one that I would label as critical reading. Because implicit ideas are present in texts in varying degrees of subtlety, students need critical reading skills to draw inferences, arrive at conclusions, separate relevant from irrelevant and fact from opinion, test hypotheses, and make comparisons and contrasts.

Few materials read by young people, however, are entirely cognitive at their core. Most main ideas considered in content area reading have an affective dimension as well. When readers encounter a main idea, expressed or implied, that promotes any degree of emotional response, then such material has led those readers into the *affective* domain. It's not that they have found or determined what has been expressed or implied; it's that they have *felt* something about that proposition. In realizing those responses, thoughtful readers recognize their own biases—the attitudes, experiences, and values that have influenced their positive or negative responses to what those texts have said to them. Thus, one most positive dimension of critical reading is that it can contribute to a reader's awareness of self.

Perhaps an example of this two-way, cognitive-affective happening can be found in the classroom assignment of Shirley Jackson's famous short story "The Lottery." From following the relatively abbreviated sequence of events in the story, readers may infer that in the annual, random stoning to death of a fellow citizen, the author is implying a skeptical, if not critical, attitude toward the mindless pursuit of ritual, custom, and tradition. While the story doesn't express this in so many words, it has been interpreted thus by innumerable readers. That's *cognition*. When the reading and evaluating of the story leads readers to examine their own rituals, customs, and traditions, and to view them in a new light, that's *affective*. If those individuals reaffirm their commitment to ritual or begin to question them, that's affective also.

Those who challenge the reading going on in public school classrooms protest both kinds of thinking activities and responses. Implied ideas are often perceived as dangerous to such people; that "young and impressionable" minds would even be exposed to the notions implicit in the Jackson story—let alone contemplate them—is highly objectionable to these would-be censors. Better that students be offered only texts containing factual knowledge. That way, they will not be confused by the possibly negative presentation of orthodox notions (see also Whitson's following chapter on critical literacy). Texts that lead students to examine their own value systems are even more repugnant to the dedicated book banners who feel that such evaluative experiences are best left to the home and the church.

Using Hayakawan (General) Semantics

Few textbooks offer more direct, clearly defined, and practical ideas on how to foster students' critical reading abilities than Hayakawa's *Language in Thought and Action* (1972). There are useful suggestions in every chapter, those on contexts, symbols, and the language of social control being excellent examples. The chapter titled "Reports, Inferences, and Judgments," however, serves here as a reflection of how critical reading can be delineated and applied to significant types of written discourse.

The author identifies *reports* as texts containing statements that are thoroughly factual and able to be verified—or disproved (Hayakawa, 1972). He succinctly denotes an *inference* as "a statement about the unknown made on the basis of the known" (p. 36), and a *judgment* as "an expression of the writer's approval or disapproval" (p. 6). As students learn to separate statements into these three categories, they become discriminating readers; as they learn to sense that some writers disguise inferential or judgmental statements as reports, they become more aware of how persuasive linguistic techniques are used. In the development of these categories of discourse, Hayakawa reveals a number of specific and familiar linguistic tricks used by writers to convince their audiences that what they are offering is true and sometimes profound (see, for example, the following section in this chapter, "Detecting Semantic Devices"). Also, Hayakawa's chapter "Discovering One's Bias" (pp. 42–43) provides a disturbing insight into how some of us talk ourselves into believing that some clearly judgmental statements are "really true."

Distinguishing among reports, inferences, and judgments can be vexing to many would-be book banners: in their sometimes fanatical commitment to particular beliefs, they present their judgments and inferences as reports. Conversely, they are eager to brand any discourse that appears to refute *their* version of the truth as distorted, dangerous, or maliciously judgmental. In their rigid support of a concept or dogma, they eschew any analysis of their position that is based on the Hayakawan (1972) categories; a vivid example of this lies in the creation versus evolution debate on the origin of the human species, a debate that found its way into state law in Arkansas and Louisiana during the 1980s (see Scharmann's chapter in Section Two of this work, "Teaching Evolution: Past and Present").

Assimilating procedures for seeking the true, the logical, and the verifiable as well as the biased elements within written discourse can assist teachers in their efforts to develop critical readers in their classes. But, as they create lessons to convey these procedures to students, teachers need to keep in mind that there will be some members of their communities who will undoubtedly protest.

Detecting Semantic Devices

There are several types of devices used by politicians, bureaucrats, advertisers, and promoters that carefully and deliberately manipulate language to evoke desired responses from the reader or listener. A few examples follow.

- **Glittering generalities:** "This peerless product is made in the United States by patriotic, dedicated Americans to meet the basic need of truly committed American citizen consumers who want to help preserve the American way of life."
- **Card-stacking:** "Every progressive, involved organization in this community—the Chamber of Commerce, the Boy Scouts, the Girl Scouts, the Salvation Army, among many others—supports this drive. So should you."
- **Testimonial:** "Michael Jordan eats *Whispies* with fruit and milk every morning. And just look at the scoring records he's broken on the basketball court! So can you."
- **Plain folks:** "Now, my friends, I'm just an everyday, down-to-earth working stiff like you, and I learned to read by studying *McGuffey's Reader*. Why can't our kids be taught the same way?"

To help students recognize the uses of emotion, ad hominem, and faulty logic in these devices is a goal of many reading and content area teachers. Would-be censors object to this goal on the grounds that such critical reading activities may lead students to question views the censors would like to promote.

Reading as Questioning What Is

In the opening chapter of the penetrating and once-controversial book *Teaching as a Subversive Activity,* Postman and Weingartner (1969) assert the need for schools to promote questioning skills among all students in order to affect change in society. The authors see two types of people as defenders of the status quo:

> In our society, as in others, we find that there are influential men at the head of important institutions who cannot afford to be found wrong, who find change inconvenient, perhaps intolerable, and who have financial or political interests they must conserve at any cost. Such men are, therefore, threatened in many respects by the theory of the democratic process and the concept of an ever-renewing society. Moreover, we find that there are obscure men who do *not* head important institutions who are similarly threatened because they have identified themselves with certain ideas

and institutions which they wish to keep free from either criticism or change (p. 2).

For Postman and Weingartner, few social or political agencies are constituted to oppose or even question this leadership. Schools, they believe, are the best-suited institutions for such confrontation: "The schools must serve as the principal medium for developing in youth the attitudes and skills of social, political, and cultural criticism" (p. 2). They continue to argue,

> What is the necessary business of the schools? To create eager consumers? To transmit the dead ideas, values, metaphors, and information of three minutes ago? To create smoothly functioning bureaucrats? *These* aims are truly subversive since they undermine our chances of surviving as a viable, democratic society (p. 15).

If students are to promote needed changes in society, they must be encouraged to commit themselves to continual questioning of school policies and customs, but it is the curriculum, and most particularly the textbooks that manifest the curriculum, that must be the constant object of their inquiry, skepticism, even attack. Students must voice the dissent that parents, political leaders, and teachers often avoid.

Thus, to Postman and Weingartner, critical reading is a relentless questioning by students of what is. Censorship is any attempt by school officials to deflect, obfuscate, or suppress that questioning.

> As Paul Goodman has pointed out, there are many forms of censorship, and one of them is to deny access to "loudspeakers," to those with dissident ideas, or even *any* ideas (p. 9).

We need to take our students into consideration as we grope for a policy that guarantees them the right to read. In the school board meetings I have attended that focused on the censorship issue, young people who wished to speak were often denied that right. If we honestly support the preservation and improvement of a democratic society, those whom we purport to be initiating into that society certainly deserve to be heard.

Critical Reading as It Should Be

In my local newspaper recently, I came across an essay by a high school student about her reading of a thought-provoking text in English class. Here are some of the key comments this student made:

> The *Fountainhead* is, in fact, 695 pages of the glorification of man. Rand beats this theme down the book spine. And although I absolutely loved reading this book, I differ on almost everything the author advocated.
>
> Rand celebrated man. She seemed to believe in order to build man, you have to tear down God. I believe in just the opposite. I look at life as a dark tunnel and God as a torch—people have a choice to use the torch and see in front of them and avoid traps. But Rand thought people could rely on just themselves—that they don't need the torch....
>
> Not only does altruism not exist in Rand's eyes, but compromise is bad. Can you imagine life without compromise? Rand seemed to have confused compromise with conformity. If individuals never compromised, then the world would be in greater turmoil than it already is. Many choices are neither right or wrong, but based on personal preference.
>
> The *Fountainhead* is a philosophical melodrama. Passion, treachery, deception, rape, conflict—the whole shazam—are in this novel. Many nights I lay curled up in my bed reading late into the night. Although I strongly disagree with Rand's philosophies, I encourage anyone who is looking for something to think about to swing by a bookstore and pick up a copy (Hsieh, 1993, p. 4B).

Here is education at its best. A student reads a sophisticated book. She infers its philosophical argument and relates it to her own position on a personally significant matter. She discusses the thesis she finds in the text and, despite her appreciation of its expression, explains why it is not acceptable to her. Maybe most important, she exercises the right and the desire to state her thoughts and feelings to all who are readers of the local newspaper. That's the way it ought to be.

References
Altick, R.D. (1969). *Preface to critical reading* (5th ed.). New York: Holt, Rinehart.

Hayakawa, S.I. (1972). *Language in thought and action.* New York: Harcourt Brace.

Hsieh, E. (1993, March 16). Novel has interesting ideas, even if you disagree with them. Teen Democrat section, *Tallahassee Democrat,* p. 4B.

Postman, N., & Weingartner, C. (1969). *Teaching as a subversive activity.* New York: Dell.

Richards, I.A. (1929). *Practical criticism.* New York: Harcourt Brace.

Rosenblatt, L.M. (1938). *Literature as exploration.* New York: Modern Language Association of America.

Simmons, J.S., & Palmer, B.C. (1994). *Reading by doing* (3rd ed.). Lincolnwood, IL: National Textbook.

Turlington, R.D., & Williams, E. (1975). *Education policy for the state of Florida.* Tallahassee, FL: Florida Department of Education.

Chapter 2

Critical Literacy Versus Censorship Across the Curriculum

James Anthony Whitson

Despite all that we know about the prevalence of censorship, I find that most preservice teacher education students, and even many experienced teachers, believe that censorship is not a problem they should be concerned about. One of the primary assumptions operating here is that censorship involves only a few areas of the curriculum (for example, advanced high school courses in literature and social studies), so that reading, writing, mathematics, and science teachers have no need to be concerned. Another assumption is that censorship is something that a teacher can avoid, without educational loss to the students; teachers who become embroiled in controversies are often thought to be the kind who were looking for such trouble. (Those familiar with the actual incidents will know how often they involve the most conservative of teachers, who are themselves astonished at demands to censor what they regard as unobjectionable curriculum materials.)

Why are there such discrepancies between the alarming reality of censorship in schools and the perception that censorship is only marginally problematic for the curriculum? I believe that this gap between perception and reality reflects the superficiality with which incidents of censorship have been reported and discussed. Too often, censorship issues are dealt with simply as

Research for this work was supported by the Council on Research at Louisiana State University.

issues of determining whether this or that particular poem, short story, or textbook will be provided to students. This focus on inclusion or exclusion of specific items not only masks the pervasive reach of censorship in schools today, but also reinforces the more fundamental, but generally unexamined, theory of education on which censorship depends. When opponents of censorship argue only for the students' right to read specific items, their defense of the materials that are being attacked by censors often implicitly supports the theory that portrays education as a process of transmitting specific bits of information to the students. Curricular and teaching practices conforming to this view—which is implicit in such arguments both for and against censorship of specific items—could reinforce metacognitive ideas about knowledge, learning, and literacy that will hamper the students' ability to learn in all areas of the curriculum, including subjects that have not been targeted for censorship. These educationally crippling ideas are essential elements of the implicit theory that is necessary to support the position that censorship need not pose any threat to literacy.

Consider this example: in his book *The Culture and Politics of Literacy* (1989), Winterowd reports that a school board member once told him and a group of his colleagues to "teach the children to write, but leave their minds alone" (p. 204). As Winterowd points out, this directive presupposes necessarily a theory of literacy in which reading and writing can be taught as skills that can be learned and practiced without engaging students' minds—at least not engaging them in any intellectual activities in which their minds might grow, change, or develop beyond learning the mechanics of transcription and word recognition.

This theory of literacy and learning is obviously indefensible, but it does not need to be defended as long as it remains unchallenged while the public is led to focus on the value of including this or that specific item in the curriculum. Yet, because the rationalization of censorship relies on this underlying theory, the persistence and pervasiveness of such unexamined assumptions might do more damage to the students' education than the exclusion of any one specific text. It is clear that there are serious implications for development of critical literacy across the curriculum.

The Scope of Censorship in the Curriculum

First, we need to recognize how failure to comprehend the rationales supporting censorship contributes to an underestimation of the extent to which censorship can pose a threat to learning across all areas of the curriculum. For example, many science education students express a belief that censorship may be a problem for English or social studies teachers, but not for them. Prospective chemistry and physics teachers tend to think that censorship encroaches on the science curriculum only when evolution comes up as a topic in biology. Even prospective biology teachers often discuss evolution as one item in a long list of topics that may or may not be covered in a given course. Hence, evolution is regarded as the one topic that might, but need not, concern biology teachers—leaving other science teachers free from any need to be concerned with censorship.

It is a grave mistake to think that the censors are treating evolution as but one objectionable topic for courses in which, otherwise, the science of biology should be taught. Consider, for example, the terms of Louisiana's "Balanced Treatment for Creation-Science and Evolution-Science Act." Before it was ruled unconstitutional by the U.S. Supreme Court in 1987, this law required all public schools to provide the "information and instruction in both creation and evolution models" that would provide "balanced treatment of these two models...in classroom lectures taken as a whole for each course, in textbook materials taken as a whole for each course, in library materials taken as a whole for the sciences and taken as a whole for the humanities, and in other educational programs in public schools, to the extent that such lectures, textbooks, library materials, or educational programs deal in any way with the subject of the origin of man, life, the earth, or the universe" (quoted by Justice Powell, concurring in Edwards v. Aguillard, 1987). (For a detailed discussion, see Scharmann's chapter in Section Two.)

Although this statute has been annulled, it spells out the scope of censorship demanded by its advocates. This is not limited to the biology class: the demand here is that nowhere in the curriculum, from prekindergarten through grade 12, from elementary reading to Advanced Placement history and literature courses, can there be any mention or reference to anything that implies, suggests, or presupposes evolution, unless it is "balanced" with the "equal treatment" of "creation science."

Science teachers—even chemistry and physics teachers—need to recognize that this involves more than just one topic in some courses in biology. What is at stake here is the ability to teach any kind of *scientific literacy* at all. Even the most ardently religious scientists would agree that scientific thought and understanding are preempted by the practice of acquiescing to a state legislature as the authority on the validity or the "equality" of theories, or even on what constitutes a scientific theory. Even prior to such concerns, however, is the obliteration of the very distinction between science and other modes of thought and inquiry, which must be the most basic concern of any real science class.

In actual complaints and cases, there is apparent evidence of the censors' impact on all areas of the curriculum. For example, materials in reading and in language arts curricula have been challenged simply for referring to dinosaurs as having lived in a time before the first human beings. In one incident, Mel and Norma Gabler—founders of Educational Research Analysts, which supports other groups and individuals in various censorship efforts—objected to one such reference in a reader for grade seven, explaining that "trilobites and dinosaurs lived side by side with man" (Jenkinson, 1986, p. 58). That was one of the beliefs that led a group of fundamentalist Christian parents to launch a legal challenge of the elementary reading series that had been adopted by the conservative, predominantly Baptist school authorities in Church Hill, Tennessee. In that case the trial judge initially ruled in favor of the challengers, acknowledging their fear that children exposed to the reading series "might adopt the views of a feminist, a humanist, a pacifist, an anti-Christian, a vegetarian, or an advocate of 'one-world government'" (647 Federal Supplement, p. 1199; *reversed on appeal,* see <u>Mozert v. Hawkins County Board of Education,</u> 1987).

Instead of aiming to develop and expand the students' intellectual abilities, the curriculum demanded by these censors would be designed deliberately to thwart the possibility of such development. The censors are demanding that the public schools provide a curriculum that will teach their children how to read and write, but without challenging the students' minds with anything that might prompt their children to think critically about their beliefs. Where this approach is implemented to appease the censors, the implicit theories of reading and thinking that are necessary to rationalize such an approach must not only be adopted tacitly, but also be implicitly communicated to the students, as a potentially debilitating "metacognitive" ideology of reading, thought, and meaning.

One aspect of the censors' theory with enormous implications for all teachers of all subjects at any grade level is the insistence that knowledge consists of absolute truths and meanings that cannot be questioned, as Simmons mentioned. Activities with more than one possible answer are condemned. For example, when a textbook suggested that students might engage in a panel discussion on the proposition that "computers are incapable of creative thinking and cannot replace man," the Gablers raised the objection that this "infers [*sic*] that there can be more than one answer" (Jenkinson, 1979/1982, p. 89). And we all know where that can lead: discussing math curricula, the Gablers warn that "when a student reads in a math book that there are no absolutes, every value he's been taught is destroyed. And the next thing you know, the student turns to crime and drugs" (Jenkinson, 1986, p. 57).

Proscriptions against classroom activities involving critical evaluation of multiple responses to a question or problem are not limited to protests against specific curricular *contents* in certain subjects, but extend to calls for banning a broad range of instructional *methods* from use in all classes. With a form letter widely disseminated by Phyllis Schlafly's Eagle Forum, for example, parents were directed to put teachers and principals on notice that the parents would exercise what they claimed as legal and constitutional rights to forbid classroom use of a long list of curriculum topics and instructional methods. These methods included "role-playing or open-ended discussions of situations involving moral issues," and "log books, diaries, and personal journals" (Jenkinson, 1986, pp. 82–83).

The censors are demanding a curriculum in which (1) students are actively prevented from knowing about anything that might prompt them to think critically about their beliefs or the beliefs presented to them as having unquestionable authority; (2) the insistence on absolute, unquestionable authority is reinforced by the deliberate exclusion of any questions or problems that might be open to more than one possible answer or response; and (3) a broad prohibition is imposed against methods or activities in which students might reflect critically on beliefs, values, or experiences. We have seen that any teacher, even the most unlikely math teacher, can be targeted for censorship. The more pervasive impact of censorship, however, is apparent when we consider the effects resulting when the censors' ideological theory of reading, literacy, knowledge, thought, and meaning is implicitly passed on to students, who carry it with them as metacognitive baggage that impedes their learning even in courses and subjects that have not specifically been targeted for censorship. The math teacher, for example, cannot teach successfully in professionally responsible and effective ways (as represented, for example, by the standards of the National Council of Teachers of Mathematics in the United States) without overcoming the ideology of unique, absolute, directed, and unquestionable authoritative answers, which is a necessary basis for rationalizing censorship. Teachers of mathematics, no less than teachers of reading and other subjects, are all too familiar with the kind of mindless rote learning of procedures and techniques that is so arduously achieved by students laboring under the burden of such ideologies.

Ideology and Criticism

I believe that this underlying ideological theory of curriculum and instruction (which might be motivated also by other factors besides censorship and accords with a good deal of traditional—but uninformed—common-sense thinking about education, as well) has become widespread in recent discourse about education—both publicly and within professional education circles. One consequence has been a recent change in attitudes toward the "critical" aspect of critical literacy and critical thinking in general.

Not long ago, it seemed that many educators and others were calling for more critical thinking and critical reading in the schools. Formal and informal surveys identified "critical thinking" as a preferred objective for curriculum, and many listed this as a priority for educational reform. Recently, however, there appears to have been a quiet retreat from the "critical." Educators who once advocated various means for the development of "critical thinking" are now writing instead about development of "higher order thinking," or simply "thoughtfulness." Even Barry Beyer (1987), who has made a career of developing methods for teaching "critical thinking" as a set of generic skills, has now conceded that "the term 'critical thinking' probably ought to be replaced by a more precise and less inflammatory term, such as, perhaps, 'evaluative thinking'" (p. 32). As he explains the problem,

> The term "critical" has negative connotations...reflected by a National Association of Elementary School Principals' wall plaque (often found in many school buildings) displaying a statement entitled *Children Learn What They Live* that starts
> > If a child lives with criticism,
> > He learns to condemn....
> When the word "critical" is attached to the term "thinking," as in "critical thinking,"...such thinking is assumed to consist of harsh criticism, fault-finding, carping negativism. Use of this term to describe important skills of analytical/evaluative thinking thus frequently evokes suspicion and, at times, even open hostility. Such hostility often finds expression in open opposition to efforts to teach these skills in schools (p. 32).

I believe that this retreat from the critical is a defensive reaction to recent ideological attacks on the curriculum, attacks premised on an idea of literacy and education as things that can be accomplished without engaging students in any genuinely critical thinking. This ideology is enlisted in support of allegations that the curriculum has become sidetracked by "critical" social or personal agendas that allegedly have nothing to do with education (which is construed as a nonpersonal, nonsocial, and noncritical process of attaining factual information and procedural skills). From this perspective, higher standards of literacy can be realized only if we rid ourselves of the distracting "critical" and, hence, the non-"educational" agendas. This presumes, in turn, that noncritical literacy is in fact a possibility, and that critical literacy is at best an option to be chosen for social, personal, political, or other noneducational purposes (Whitson, 1988). Instead of recognizing censorship as a threat to real literacy, this ideology limits the definition of literacy to such a degree that censorship is no longer an issue; it can pose no threat to the restricted kinds of learning recognized within the censors' own theory of education.

I believe that there is no real literacy that is not critical, and that for the sake of real education and real literacy we cannot afford to sacrifice the critical and replace it with some sanitized notion of "analytical evaluative thinking skills." I believe that the noncritical curriculum will necessarily produce illiteracy (rather than some kind of noncritical literacy) and that this illiteracy can be seen in the discourse advocating censorship and in the judicial opinions upholding censorship as a legitimate activity for school authorities.

Judicial Theories and Judicial Readings

When the courts in the United States have upheld censorship actions by school officials, they have generally argued that judges should not impose their own ideas on education but should defer to educators' expertise and allow them broad discretionary authority (Whitson, 1991). Ironically, the courts have used this rationale to justify judicial doctrines used to support political authorities who have limited the extent to which teachers and sometimes even school administrators use their judgment in censorship cases (Whitson, 1993). Even more ironical, despite the pretense of deferring to the expertise of educators, is that the rationale of these judges is based on their own ideas of education. In Board of Education, Island Trees (New York) Union Free School District No. 26 v. Pico (1982), for example, U.S. Supreme Court Justice William Rehnquist simply declared that "education consists of the selective presentation and explanation of ideas" (p. 914). If this were true, then it would follow that the question for curriculum development is primarily one of deciding who has the authority to choose which ideas the students should be taught.

This is the approach taken in Mercer v. Michigan State Board of Education, a 1974 case in which the plaintiffs were challenging a Michigan law against teaching about birth control. The court ruled in favor of the legislature's action, explaining that it is "the authorities" who "must choose which portions of the world's knowledge will be included in the curriculum's programs and courses, and which portions will be left for grasping from other sources, such as the family, peers, or other institutions" (379, Federal Supplement, p. 586).

The fallacy in this notion of the curriculum—as a meal served up especially for students with selectively prescribed "portions" of knowledge—can be seen in one point of contention that emerged in Island Trees v. Pico (1982), where the school board members justified removal of school library books in part because they found some of the books to be "anti-American." Justice William Brennan noted that when they were asked for an example of anti-Americanism in the banned books, two school board members identified Alice Childress's novel *A Hero Ain't Nothin' But a Sandwich* because it "notes at one point that George Washington was a slaveholder" (p. 873). Although we can certainly argue, as Justice Brennan did, that the students in this case should be recognized as having First Amendment rights to receive such information under the U.S. Constitution, this argument does not reveal the problem with regarding such issues as questions of simply choosing "portions" from a vast world of discrete bits of information of that kind. The fact that Washington owned slaves is incidental to the more complex and ironic passage in question, which deals with role and identity conflicts in the life of an African American teacher in a contemporary urban school. The passage would not be complete without the conflicted teacher's comment that "Washington owned a slave woman whose cookin was so fine that he freed her while he was still livin. She musta really known how to barbecue!" To understand that comment, the student needs to be reading at a level far more complex than mere reception of factual information. Yet judges have focused on the propositional content in such texts, and have argued that texts can be banned without impairing students' education because the same information can still be presented to them in lectures or in other texts free of the offending language.

I would argue that the authentic language of such texts is necessary for developing the literacy required for social understanding. Alice Childress (1989) herself has spoken about the way that censorship—even when its purported aim is only to exclude nonstandard language and sexual references—has the effect of excluding the language, lives, and voices of racial and cultural minorities. Indeed, it does seem difficult, if not impossible, to imagine how the experience of African Americans could be portrayed without the language of Childress's works or the works of Maya Angelou, James Baldwin, Langston Hughes, Alice Walker, or Richard Wright—to name just a few highly acclaimed writers and poets whose representations of the African American experience have been attacked by censors.

We must clearly understand, however, that when Childress has one of her characters tell us the story about Washington and his cook, it is as much a story about George Washington and white America as it is about the slave woman and black America. It is also important to recognize that the use of such texts is not a matter of burdening the curriculum with a social or political agenda at the expense of literacy—but rather that the development of literacy itself depends on the ability to understand such texts, just as social understanding depends on such literacy.

Realistic Texts as Necessary for Real Literacy

We have begun to see how rationales for censorship depend on politically motivated ideologies of literacy and learning, ideologies that can harm students' education not only by depriving them of pedagogically effective materials and activities but also by trivializing the curriculum that survives the censors' scrutiny and reducing it to the selective transmission of unquestionably authoritative bits of factual and procedural knowledge. Although this seems to be a clear case of sacrificing education to the censors' own political agenda, the censors' ideology projects the opposite scenario—a scenario in which the censors are the ones defending education by eliminating texts that they regard as being contaminated with noneducational social, personal, and "critical" concerns. We have seen how this ideology can operate to deprive students of access to authentic social understanding— and not just to objectionable expressions of factual information or abstract conceptual ideas that might be conveyed to students equally well through less objectionable forms of expression, as the censors would have us believe.

To counter this ideology, we need to go beyond the relatively obvious implications of such examples, and to articulate in more general terms how it is that literacy *requires* incorporation of the social, personal, and critical aspects that the censors would exclude. This articulation can only be accomplished through substantial theoretical work collaboratively undertaken by researchers and practitioners—including teachers in all subjects—with expertise in cognition, learning, language, and literacy. At this point, I can only raise a couple of suggestive aspects of the real literacy, which must be addressed within that larger collaborative effort.

Real literacy requires the ability to understand a textual discourse in the full range of its linguistic functions. Take one example: the cognitive psychologist Jerome Bruner has been most emphatic on the educational importance of the metalinguistic function (1986, pp. 125–127) that makes possible a reflective awareness of how meaning is determined by language that is "infinitely rich in devices at all levels for marking stance" (1982, p. 843). Readers need to understand the nuanced uses of such language devices, including "lexical elements and syntactic rules that have as virtually their sole object to make the speaker's perspective and stance clear," for example, in "the use of such words as *even, only,* and *just*" (1986, p. 85). Bruner describes "stance" as "the process of distancing oneself from one's thoughts" (1986, p. 129), which is textually signified in that aspect of meaning which is constituted by discursive implications "about the referent, about the speech act being performed, about one's own posture toward what is being said" (1982, p. 843). From this, he concludes,

> I do not for a minute believe that one can teach mathematics or physics without transmitting a sense of stance toward nature and toward the use of mind. One cannot avoid committing oneself, given the nature of natural language, to a stance as to whether something is, say, a "fact" or the "consequence of a conjecture" (1982, pp. 846–847).

Bruner's point helps to articulate how the censors' theory of curriculum as selective transmission of authoritative propositional or procedural knowledge deprives students of the opportunity to develop key elements of literacy and how this affects all areas of the curriculum: for example, even when math and science classes have not been targeted, students' ability to construe the "stance" markings of texts—to read critically—in these subjects will be impaired if their literacy has been stunted by restrictions on their language arts and social studies classes, especially if the students have absorbed the metacognitive ideology with which restrictions on those classes have been rationalized.

The Alice Childress novel *A Hero Ain't Nothin' But a Sandwich* provides an excellent example. Censors have condemned this book for exactly those textual features that provide students with an opportunity for learning to understand the "stances" that help constitute the meaning in linguistic discourse. The book comprises chapters narrated from the viewpoints of a broad range of extremely different characters who use their own voices and idioms to represent their widely diverse perspectives on events and circumstances surrounding the central character, a black male student in an inner-city middle school. The passage mentioning George Washington is a perfect example, in which the fact that Washington owned slaves is merely incidental to the text's value *as* a text that is especially useful for promoting students' ability to understand the meaning of the character's ironic remarks *on the basis of* the social and metalinguistic features of the text.

Bruner (1986) argues that for schooling to promote students' ability to recognize stance and develop other aspects of the metalinguistic competence that is so crucial for literacy, the curriculum must not be designed to prevent students from encountering controversial expressions that might challenge their beliefs and values:

> If one does not choose, as a vehicle for teaching this form of "human distancing," something that touches the bone in some way or other (however one characterizes the psychological processes involved), one creates another nonsense. For what is needed is a basis for discussing not simply the content of what is before one, but the possible stances one might take toward it (p. 129).

The ability to recognize stance markings in a text is only one element of reading that requires the use of socially and linguistically realistic texts for the development of real literacy. Thus, we see that the use of such texts does not represent a social or political agenda imposed at the expense of education; rather, it is the censors who do injury to students' learning in their efforts to exclude such texts for political reasons.

Bruner's discussion also helps explain why issues relevant to students' lives must not be excluded. Students will not learn how language is used in stance taking and in stance recognizing unless they learn to see how texts can address matters in which someone could be interested enough to take a stance. Speaking more directly from his experience as an inner-city high school English teacher, Welsh (1985) explains how dealing with issues relevant to students is not an unworthy substitute for teaching real literary competence (as the censors allege), but is, to the contrary, an important key to teaching even the most technical elements of reading literary works:

> By starting the study of poetry with works dealing with value issues that are important in the lives of the students, I feel I have a much stronger chance of engaging them with the literature, of getting them to experience ownership in the works. Once they are engaged, once they experience poems that speak to them about their lives, students see poetry— and, by extension, all literature— as having worth and meaning. They become much more eager to study and discuss the technical and historical aspects of literature and to tackle poems that at first may not seem accessible. At that point, I feel comfortable moving to more challenging poetry—that of Donne, Keats, Arnold, Yeats, Eliot—with one eye always on the values inherent in the poems and how those values relate to and illumine the students' world (p. 151).

Defining Literacy *as* "Critical" (Against the False Alternatives)

Bruner and Welsh have given us examples of how we need to articulate the necessity of including in the curriculum socially, linguistically, and personally relevant texts for the sake of students' real critical literacy. This brings us back to the problem of how to understand critical literacy in relation to censorship and the censors' ideology of education.

The censors' ideology presumes an opposition between educational and social or political concerns. I believe that this exploits an unfortunate dichotomy that can be observed in discussions of how "literacy" ought to be defined. Some progressive educators argue for comprehensive definitions of literacy that include the full range of basic competencies needed for social or political empowerment; others protest such a broadening of the term and insist on preserving the more restricted definition of "literacy" as "just the ability to read and write" (see, for example, Woodring, 1987). The same dichotomy is reflected in interpretations of the word "critical" as applied to critical literacy, critical thinking, and critical pedagogy (for example, in Beyer's suggestion, noted earlier, that the word should be abandoned altogether). When "critical" is taken to mean negative, adversarial, or rebellious, it follows that appeals for critical literacy might be rejected or embraced on the basis of political orientations that are not necessary for the development of students' intellectual abilities.

I believe that the dichotomy between literacy as political empowerment and literacy as "just reading and writing" presents us with a choice of false alternatives. While I agree that there is value in restricting "literacy" to reading and writing—when reading and writing are adequately understood in their full dimensions—the abilities required for literacy extend far beyond the notion of "*just* reading and writing," which is what censors (among others) presume when they claim that there is no threat to literacy when students are denied the use of realistic texts. When we say that our computers "read" or "write to" floppy disks, this in no way suggests that we think of our computers as being literate; "reading" and "writing," as they relate to literacy, mean something else.

Without going beyond the real sense of *literate* reading and writing, I believe we have begun to see that there is no such thing as literacy that is not critical. Literacy requires the competence to construe the meaning of linguistic utterances, and this requires abilities to understand such things as the socially situated linguistic stance markings described by Bruner and exemplified by Childress's *Hero* text as well as many other texts that have been censored specifically because of socially inflected linguistic elements. Such competence is necessarily "critical" in the most fundamental sense of the word, which signifies judgment and discernment. It involves all of the discriminations between genuine and phony, sincere and insincere, direct and ironic, or the more or less ideologically distorted or epistemologically biased—as well as the much more subtle distinctions involved in the mental and linguistic stance taking that enables us to "entertain" ideas that we may not necessarily want to claim as our own.

There is no real literacy that is not critical literacy, and critical literacy is necessarily threatened at the deepest level by the censors and their ideology of education. When we are told to teach students how to read and write but to "leave their minds alone," we need to be able to explain in the most specific and convincing terms why this is not possible; for there is no way for students to attain literacy without a critical, and potentially transformative, engagement of their minds.

References

Beyer, B.K. (1987). *Practical strategies for the teaching of thinking.* Boston, MA: Allyn and Bacon.

Board of Education, Island Trees Union Free School District No. 26 v. Pico, 457 U.S. 853 (1982).

Bruner, J.S. (1982). The language of education. *Social Research, 49*(4), 835–853.

Bruner, J.S. (1986). *Actual minds, possible worlds.* Cambridge, MA: Harvard University Press.

Childress, A. (1989, November). Black authors, banned books. *Newsletter on Intellectual Freedom, 212,* 241–243.

Edwards v. Aguillard, 482 U.S. 598 (1987).

Jenkinson, E.B. (1982). *Censors in the classroom.* New York: Avon. (Original work published 1979 by Southern Illinois University Press)

Jenkinson, E.B. (1986). *The schoolbook protest movement: 40 questions and answers.* Bloomington, IN: Phi Delta Kappa Educational Foundation.

Mercer v. Michigan State Board of Education, 379 F. Supp. 580; *affirmed by memorandum,* 419 U.S. 1081 (1974).

Mozert v. Hawkins County Board of Education, 847 F.2d 1058 (6th Cir. 1987).

Welsh, P. (1985). The role of values in teaching literature in the high school. In C.E. Finn, D. Ravitch, & P.H. Roberts (Eds.), *Challenges to the humanities* (pp. 147–148). New York: Holmes & Meier.

Whitson, J.A. (1988). The politics of "non-political" curriculum: Heteroglossia and the discourse of "choice" and "effectiveness." In W.F. Pinar (Ed.), *Contemporary curriculum discourses* (pp. 279–330). Scottsdale, AZ: Gorsuch Scarisbrick.

Whitson, J.A. (1991). *Constitution and curriculum: Hermeneutical semiotics of cases and controversies in education, law, and social science.* London: Falmer.

Whitson, J.A. (1993). After *Hazelwood:* The role of school officials in conflicts over the curriculum. *The ALAN Review, 20*(2), 2–6.

Winterowd, W.R. (1989). *The culture and politics of literacy.* New York: Oxford University Press.

Woodring, P. (1987). Let's go back to the dictionary definition: Illiteracy is the inability to read and write. *The Chronicle of Higher Education, 33*(34), 48.

Chapter 3

Tactics Used to Remove Books and Courses from Schools

Edward B. Jenkinson

Over the past 20 years, I have read about, analyzed, and written about more than 300 incidents of schoolbook protest throughout the United States. I have also been asked to serve as a consultant to more than 40 school systems that have experienced attempts to remove books and courses. As mentioned earlier, these attempts to remove textbooks, library books, films, courses, and teaching methods can occur anywhere—in every state or province, in every size city and town, in schools at every socioeconomic level. No community is immune.

Very early in my study of this protest movement, I grew tired of hearing teachers and administrators who read about the occasional censorship incident say, "It can't happen here." The "never in my community" syndrome leaves educators not only unaware of the pervasiveness of censorship, as Whitson stressed, but also ill-prepared to cope with even a mild protest. And I believe more and more protesters understand that a surprise attack on an unsuspecting community might result in victory or at least division within the community, as the incidents summarized following illustrate.

Nearly 20 years ago, the battle over English textbooks that was waged in West Virginia captured much attention and set the stage for hundreds of future skirmishes. Newspapers throughout the United States reported that schools were dynamited, that people were shot, that a sniper fired at a schoolbus filled with children, and that coal mines were closed by miners enraged by the book controversy. One writer called the events in Kanawha County "a class war, a cultural war, a religious war. It is a struggle for power and authority that has sundered a peaceful community into rigid and fearful factions" (Egerton, 1975, p. 13).

A five-member teacher committee submitted a list of 325 state-approved books for adoption in Kanawha County in March 1974. The school board voted unanimously in April to adopt the texts "but to delay purchase until they could be studied more thoroughly" (Parker, 1975, p. 8). Alice Moore, a member of the board who called for the delay, made several telephone calls to Mel and Norma Gabler to request copies of their reviews of the books (Hefley, 1976). Through Educational Research Analysts, the Gablers provide copies of their "Bills of Particulars"—detailed lists of objections, line-by-line, page-by-page, to textbooks submitted for adoption—to potential schoolbook protesters. According to the Gablers, their reviews have been used in schoolbook protests throughout the United States as well as in 25 other countries (Jenkinson, 1986).

In June, Moore launched a vigorous campaign against the textbooks. Ten ministers announced their support of the texts; twenty-seven declared the books to be immoral and indecent. Several of the ministers proposed "private fundamentalist schools" as one answer for parents who did not want their children to study the objectionable books (Jenkinson, 1979).

Angry parents kept their own children home during the first week of school, and more than 4000 miners showed their displeasure with the books by not reporting for work. Pickets closed construction sites, bus depots, and grocery stores. The board of education building, also closed by pickets, had several windows blown out by shotgun blasts. At least four men were shot, and the violence continued through October and November.

Moore invited the Gablers to Charleston in October to conduct a "whirlwind six-day speaking campaign" throughout the county (Hefley, 1976, p. 166). Finally the superintendent resigned, and a new superintendent asked the board to approve all the books for classroom use, with the exception of the D.C. Heath Communicating series. The board called for parental consent if children were asked to study the "most controversial" books.

The Kanawha County book war did not end with the restoration of most of the textbooks to classrooms; the divided community suffered long after. In *Storm in the Mountains* (1988), published 14 years after the protest, James Moffett records an interview with a board of education member:

> Textbooks weren't the issue. No one will ever convince me. The major issue was a political one and had to do with the black-and-white issue.... Part of it was a desire to set up a different *kind* of school system. The whole movement for a voucher system started in the Anaheim area. I think all those things are part of it, along with the black-and-white thing. I think it's a marriage of the conservative forces and the fundamentalist Christians.... The whole experience was so traumatic for me. I'm not over it yet and never will be (p. 94).

The Book Burning in Warsaw, Indiana

A power struggle over control of the public schools also divided the community of Warsaw, Indiana. In 1977 a newly appointed member of the school board, William Chapel, fired the first shot in a yearlong book and course war. At his first board meeting, he called for evaluation of the Individually Guided Education program, an individualized instruction program which had been brought to Warsaw years before by the superintendent and which was used in one elementary school. Outraged by the call for the evaluation, the superintendent resigned. The board dropped IGE, hired a new superintendent, and launched a campaign to rid Warsaw's high schools of elective courses (special areas in English that students wanted to study including women in literature, creative writing, and so forth) and books (Jenkinson, 1979, pp. 1–16).

Throughout the year, the local newspaper printed inflammatory news stories and editorials about schoolbooks and courses. The new superintendent discontinued elective English courses that covered gothic literature, science fiction, African American literature, and folklore and legends. One teacher was dismissed for writing a letter to the newspaper editor protesting the actions of the school board. Another teacher's contract was not renewed because of alleged insubordination when she refused to stop teaching a book in an elective course. A third teacher left the school system when the school board gave copies of *Values Clarification,* parts of which she used with troubled students, to several 12th grade students for burning in the city parking lot. Like the battle in Kanawha County, the one in Warsaw left long-lasting scars. So did a skirmish in southern Indiana even though it ended much differently.

The Tell City, Indiana, Incident

Secular humanism allegedly invaded the Ohio River town of Tell City during the 1981–82 academic year. A minister declared that the high school's English department was teaching "garbage" and that Christians in the community needed "to take a stand against Satan's attack upon the minds of our youth" (Jenkinson, 1990, pp. 66–69). In a guest column published in the local newspaper, a minister from nearby Kentucky raised the specter of secular humanism. Although he never defined the philosophy, he expressed grave reservations about "humanistic teachings" in the public schools. He equated humanists with atheists, who, he wrote, are more dangerous than rattlesnakes (*Tell City News,* 1982).

The Tell City incident began when a mother objected to her son's reading John Steinbeck's *Of Mice and Men* in English class. The boy was given an alternate assignment, but the mother talked about the novel with her minister, who asked the minister from Kentucky to serve as a spokesperson in the fight against "anti-God teachings." For three months, the two ministers and their followers also attacked a book taught in an elective sex education course as well as Dungeons & Dragons, a fantasy and role-playing game a few students played during an activity period. The ministers conducted a rally and invited Mel Gabler to be the featured speaker. At the rally, which I tape recorded, Gabler attacked secular humanism, sex education, Dungeons & Dragons, and textbooks in general. He cited passages from textbooks—only one of which was used in Tell City—to reinforce his argument that many textbooks are dangerous because they promote evolution, situation ethics, sex education, world citizenship, and socialism. He accused the school system of teaching "frills, not skills," and he declared that standardized test scores had declined dramatically in Tell City.

The school board responded: at its next meeting, the president refuted the charges leveled by Gabler and the ministers. The school board, the superintendent, and the teachers stood firmly together. One minister left the community. The charges were dropped, but the division in the community remained.

Common Strategies Used by Protesters

These three incidents contain some of the most common ways protesters attempt to remove materials from schools. Some of the other strategies are described as follows:

Petitions. Within one year after the publication of Phyllis Schlafly's *Child Abuse in the Classroom* (1984), the petition she included in the book was submitted to school boards in at least 17 U.S. states. People circulating the petition demanded that courses and teaching strategies be removed from the schools. Included in the objectionable parts of the curriculum were values clarification, death education, alcohol and drug education, globalism, human sexuality, guided fantasy techniques, discussions of witchcraft and the occult, and autobiography assignments. Similar petitions have been used by critics of the schools for more than 20 years.

Trial by newspaper. In dozens of incidents, protesters have used letters-to-the-editor campaigns and radio talk shows to attack courses and materials, as a case in Rosenblum's Chapter 5 describes. Frequently, protesters will studiously avoid following the

> **"It is imperative for educators and parents to recognize protestors' tactics and realize censorship can happen in any community."**

procedures that school systems have adopted for dealing with complaints; rather, they might use door-to-door campaigns, call press conferences, publish excerpts of "objectionable" materials, and urge their followers to call school board members, teachers, and administrators.

Organizations. National and state organizations in the United States advise protesters on how to form their own local organizations. Local organizations do not always identify themselves as part of a national movement; many, however, openly refer to their affiliation with the Eagle Forum, Concerned Women for America, or Citizens for Excellence in Education. CEE gives its members detailed strategies for getting members elected to school boards. In one of his recent undated newsletters, Robert Simonds—president of CEE—announced that more than 3500 members have been elected to school boards.

Lawsuits. In June 1992, Pat Robertson announced on the TV show *700 Club* that his American Center for Law and Justice would enter 500 complaints in federal courts to help return the schools to their "Christian heritage." On a later program, he announced that ACLJ had already entered 50 complaints about school prayer alone.

"Bills of Particulars." As noted earlier, Norma and Mel Gabler provide copies of their Bills of Particulars to their followers. Although the Gablers insist that concerned parents do their own homework by searching for objectionable passages in text-

---

Resource Books for Protesters

William M. Bowen, Jr. (1984). *Globalism: America's Demise.* Lafayette, LA: Huntington House.

Eric Buehrer (1990). *The New Age Masquerade: The Hidden Agenda in Your Child's Classroom.* Brentwood, TN: Wolgemuth & Hyatt.

James Dobson and Gary L. Bauer (1990). *Children at Risk: The Battle for the Hearts and Minds of Our Kids.* Dallas, TX: Word.

Homer Duncan (1983). *The Religion of Secular Humanism and the Public Schools.* Lubbock, TX: Missionary Crusader.

Mel Gabler and Norma Gabler, with James C. Hefley (1985). *What Are They Teaching Our Children?* Wheaton, IL: Victor.

Tim LaHaye (1983). *The Battle for the Public Schools: Humanism's Threat to Our Children.* Old Tappan, NJ: Fleming Revell.

Elliot Miller (1989). *A Crash Course on the New Age Movement.* Grand Rapids, MI: Baker.

Phyllis Schlafly (1984). *Child Abuse in the Classroom.* Westchester, IL: Crossway.

---

books, some protesters simply present the Gablers' objections to school boards as if they had written them themselves.

Books. Books calling attention to the problems of public schools and to the "alien" religions being promoted in them abound. The figure on page 34 lists just a few.

Errors in textbooks. Norma and Mel Gabler also search for errors in textbooks submitted for adoption in Texas and call them to the attention of the Texas State Textbook Committee. In two of their recent newsletters, the Gablers (1993) have reported that their error detection, among that of others, has resulted in publishers having to pay more than US$1 million in fines to the state of Texas.

Educational quackery. In June 1993, the Gablers sent a flier to their followers requesting funds to help them "bash" educational quackery:

> Whether it's factual errors in textbooks or bad teaching methods, no one galls the antieducation establishment like Mel and Norma Gabler. Bigger blows are coming. If you'd like to see the Gablers soon prove academic corruption or incompetence that should smash educrats as textbook errors crushed publishers...please send your contributions now...and watch the antieducation establishment really squirm.

Many of the strategies used by schoolbook protesters are no different from propaganda techniques and strategies used by individuals and groups to accomplish a variety of objectives—both in and out of public schools. It is imperative for educators and parents to recognize these tactics and realize censorship can happen in any community.

References

Egerton, J. (1975, June). The battle of the books. *The Progressive*, 13.

Hefley, J.C. (1976). *Textbooks on trial*. Wheaton, IL: Victor.

Jenkinson, E.B. (1979). *Censors in the classroom: The mind benders*. Carbondale, IL: Southern Illinois University Press.

Jenkinson, E.B. (1986). *The schoolbook protest movement*. Bloomington, IN: The Phi Delta Kappa Educational Foundation.

Jenkinson, E.B. (1990). Lessons learned from three schoolbook protests. In A.S. Ochoa (Ed.), *Academic freedom: To teach and to learn* (pp. 66–69). Washington, DC: National Education Association.

Moffett, J. (1988). *Storm in the mountains: A case study of censorship, conflict, and consciousness.* Carbondale, IL: Southern Illinois University Press.

Parker, F. (1975). *The battle of the books: Kanawha County.* Bloomington, IN: The Phi Delta Kappa Educational Foundation.

Tell City News. (1982, January). Guest Column. p. 5B.

Chapter 4

Censorship and the "New Age"

Robert J. Marzano

Would-be censors usually have a two-fold purpose: they want to stop what they consider is *not* in the public interest, and they want to proclaim or maintain what they consider *is* in the public interest. It is only from the perspective of this dual intent that some of the current attempts at censorship of school materials can be understood.

At the heart of many efforts at censorship in public education in the United States is the desire to preserve the country's religious heritage as it is perceived by ultrafundamentalist Christians. As Saperstein (1990) notes, a basic assumption of the religious right is that "the United States was founded on certain traditional values—specifically, Christian values. The purpose of government is to secure those values, even if it means determining when we pray in school, what we study in biology (scientific creationism), what we read in our libraries" (p. 218). Mel and Norma Gabler (1985) cite judicial evidence supporting this position:

> In 1892...the Supreme Court made an exhaustive study of the connections between Christianity and U.S. history. The court concluded that we are "a religious people" and the United States is a "Christian nation." In 1932 Justice George Sutherland looked at the 1892 decision and reiterated the belief that we are a "Christian people" (p. 34).

On the surface, this assertion appears to contradict the principle of separation of church and state. However, the religious right asserts that the doctrine is misunderstood by the American public. Kennedy (1987), an author who specializes in mailers about religious liberty, explains:

> We have a dominant view in this country which is supported by 99 percent of the people of the relationship between church and state that is almost diametrically opposed to what was taught by the Founding Fathers.... Does the First Amendment teach the separation of church and state? Probably 99 percent of the people in America today have been brainwashed into saying "Yes." But, it does not (p. 6).

As described in the next section of this Chapter, the misconception about the true Christian nature of America is perceived as no accident. Rather it is believed to be part of a well-orchestrated plot to seduce people in the United States to embrace a satanically based, new religion.

To many educators, sentiments such as those expressed by Kennedy, the Gablers, and others are a curious phenomenon. However, sociologist and anthropologist Shupe (1989) explains that these sentiments and the actions that result from them are a manifestation of "Christian reconstructionism" that began in the early 1960s. He explains that reconstructionism is a "movement within a movement within a movement, a splinter group in the uneasy alliance of charismatics, fundamentalists, and miscellaneous evangelicals who make up the Christian right" (p. 880). Six major tenets characterize the movement, according to Shupe:

1. Christ's kingdom was ushered in 2000 years ago and will culminate at his second coming.

2. Meanwhile, every institution of every nation—starting with the United States—needs to be reclaimed for Christ from the grip of Satan and his humanist minions.

3. Christian reconstructionism is a self-generated phenomenon rather than a top-driven phenomenon imposed by a religious denomination.

4. Politics is a major tool in the reconstructionist movement. Christians should be involved in politics, even if it is dirty. Who else has the means to clean it up?

5. God has entered into a covenant with the United States and will shower blessings on the country only if it stays obedient to God's will. Otherwise, the blessings will be showered on some other nation.

6. The Bible offers a perfect blueprint for what the reconstructed society must be like (p. 880).

Although the religious right's efforts at school censorship are not directly tied to Christian reconstructionism, the powerful movement of the 1960s certainly provided the foundation for more recent censorship efforts.

What Must Be Stopped?

Just as some protesters involved in the current censorship movement are adamant about preserving the Christian heritage of U.S. culture, so too are they adamant about stopping the spread of an anti-Christian religion referred to as the *New Age*. Although the emergence of the New Age religion is rather recent, it has its roots in secular humanism.

The Gablers (1985) explain that humanism can be traced to the Renaissance, but it received a foothold in the United States in the early 1900s when it infiltrated the thinking of the educational elite:

> Within so-called intellectual circles, it became fashionable to reject theism and the Bible for the "natural belief" that man must be his own savior. This set the stage for the humanists to seize the helm in public education (p. 28).

What is particularly dangerous about humanists, say the Gablers, is that they will stop at little to achieve their goals:

> Humanists are aggressive and evangelistic. They are adept at tearing down traditional faith, even if it means permitting the occult to enter the classroom. They are skilled at pouring their anti-God dogmas into the void (p. 44).

The anti-God, anti-Christian philosophy of humanism seemed to be well suited to the New Age religion. As Pat Robertson (1990), leader of the powerful Christian Coalition, explains: "The premises of the New Age are so radical and subversive of everything Christ taught us, it seems to be tailor-made for a secular elite looking for a philosophy" (p. 74). However, although humanism was best described as a philosophy, the New Age is a bonafide religion with clergy and printed scripture. Marrs (1987), author of a number of particularly dramatic books on the New Age, contends that this religion has a well-defined and evil agenda:

> The New Age appears to be the instrument that Satan will use to catapult his Antichrist to power. Once he is firmly entrenched, he will unite all cults and religions into one: the New Age world religion. When Christians refuse to be initiated into this satanic religious system, they will be dealt with very harshly. Many will be put to death. The New Age is working hard today to set up an environment of hatred toward Christians and what they stand for, so the public mood will be ready when the Antichrist begins his brutal anti-Christian programs (p. 262).

Perhaps what its critics find most disturbing about the New Age is that it is believed to have infiltrated the public schools. As Robertson (1990) notes,

> You can't put the Ten Commandments on the classroom wall, but apparently there's nothing wrong with having gurus come in to lecture or having seances and meditations. These practices are going on right now in many schools. We know of schools where they are teaching astral projection in the classroom. Students are taught that they are going out of their bodies into space, meeting with creatures in space, and bringing spirits back to earth with them (p. 64).

The battle lines are clear when the religious right considers the nature and intent of the New Age. In fact, Robert Simonds (1983) of Citizens for Excellence in Education, which focuses on electing right-minded Christians to local school boards (as Jenkinson explained in the previous chapter), warns his followers:

> Get organized for battle. This is a spiritual battle. What we most often call "political" are purely moral and spiritual issues. In fact, it can accurately be said that every law, rule, or statute passed by public officials is a moral issue of right and wrong (p. 4).

As illustrated, some of the current censorship efforts are not so much aimed at curtailing the freedom of educators and students as they are at protecting the United States from the perceived threat of a supposedly satanically inspired new religion.

Dealing with the New Censors

How can educators deal with these new censors—with their strong intensity and their intent—in a way that is productive? First and foremost, educators must understand the reasoning behind their efforts. Although the basic tenets of that reasoning have been outlined, the following books offer a more thorough description of the ultrafundamentalist point of view: *Inside the New Age Nightmare* (Baer, 1989); *The Hidden Dangers of the Rainbow* (Cumbey, 1983); *Unmasking the New Age* (Groothuis, 1988); *Dark Secrets of the New Age* (Marrs, 1987); *New Age Cults and Religions* (Marrs, 1990); *Understanding the Times* (Noebel, 1991); and *The New Millennium* (Robertson, 1990) (see also Jenkinson's chapter for a list of references).

Second, educators must realize and acknowledge that there is, in fact, a New Age movement in the United States and that it has had an impact on our culture. In her scholarly analysis of the New Age, O'Hara (1988) describes it in the following way:

> "**S**ome of the current censorship efforts are not so much aimed at curtailing the freedom of educators and students as they are at protecting the United States from the perceived threat of a supposedly satanically inspired new religion."

> People who hold New Age beliefs tend to be interested in extraordinary human capabilities like ESP, psychic phenomena, and mediumship. They embrace and go far beyond Maslow's ideal of a fully actualized person, or Rogers's "person of tomorrow," believing that enormous new powers—especially of the mind—are about to become manifest as humankind makes a large evolutionary leap. New Agers tend to hold a combination of religious beliefs, such as reincarnation, karma, Taoism, Zen, spiritism, ani-

mism, and shamanism, yet they reject Christian fundamentalism, Catholicism, and Judaism. Books and authors recently influential among New Agers include Marilyn Ferguson's *The Aquarian Conspiracy,* Shirley MacLaine's *Out on a Limb,* Fritjof Capra's *Tao of Physics* and *The Turning Point,* Gary Zukav's *Dancing Wu Li Masters,* Ken Keyes's *The Hundredth Monkey,* Rupert Sheldrake's *New Science of Life,* Ken Wilbur's *Up from Eden,* and Jean Houston's *The Possible Human,* among many others (pp. 162–163).

The use of these texts within the curriculum and the promotion of the basic concepts underlying them can be legitimately characterized as the promotion of religious beliefs. Although these texts are certainly not the standard fare in education, they are not totally absent from the curriculum. I am aware of specific situations in which each of the texts listed by O'Hara has been used as basic reading material in secondary classrooms. In addition, some of the basic concepts that underlie these texts have infiltrated educational practice. When a well-intentioned teacher asks students to seek out the advice of an "inner guide" before practicing a "left brain" activity, he or she is dangerously close to promoting New Age beliefs. When a teacher encourages students to repeat an affirmation that asserts that they can "do anything," he or she is also close to crossing the line between instructional practice and religious philosophy.

Third, educators must realize the breadth of people, institutions, and practices that have been directly or indirectly linked to the "New Age" by the religious right. A partial list includes acupressure, Blue Cross/Blue Shield, the Chrysler Corporation, Norman Cousins, and Pope John XXIII (identified by Cumbey, 1983); acupuncture, holistic health practices, and stress management (Baer, 1989); the American Civil Liberties Union, Alcoholics Anonymous, the fight to end world hunger, *Life* magazine, the NBC television network, the "Save the Whales" movement, the U.S. Social Security Administration, and Yale University (Marrs, 1990); biofeedback (Hunt, 1983) and creative visualization (Hunt, 1982); the movie *Cocoon,* the novel *The Grapes of Wrath,* and the Polaroid and Westinghouse corporations (Robertson, 1990); the "information revolution," the

Muppet movie *The Dark Crystal,* yoga, quantum physics, the human potential movement, networking, pluralism, and the United Nations (Groothuis, 1988). (For a more comprehensive listing, see Marzano, 1993.) Obviously, these items have no connection to religious practices. However, the list serves as a warning to educators that ultrafundamentalist groups have cast a broad net in their efforts to identify and eradicate New Age practices. What is even more disturbing is that more noneducators appear to be accepting the allegation that individuals, organizations, and practices like those listed are part of a religious conspiracy. To illustrate, an elementary school principal in Colorado recently confided in me that he recommended to the school's teachers that they cease using any instructional techniques involving visualization because some members of the community were convinced that visualization in any form was a tool of the New Age and would expose children to the influence of spirits.

On a much larger scale, the South Carolina legislature received a bill in March 1991 to "prohibit the use of New Age religious and occult philosophies and methods of instruction in the public schools in South Carolina" (Fair, 1991, p. 1). The bill provided that "a public school employee who violates the provisions of this section is subject to disciplinary procedure up to and including dismissal" (p. 2). Specific New Age practices that would have been banned had the bill passed included guided imagery, visualization, and deep processing (p. 1). In short, a teacher who asked children to imagine that they were snowflakes to prepare for a creative writing assignment could have been subject to dismissal for using alleged New Age practices. Although the bill was defeated, the fact that it reached the level of a legislative vote attests to the success of ultrafundamentalist groups in convincing the public that New Age practices permeate our culture.

Armed with an understanding of the reasoning of ultrafundamentalists, an awareness of the true nature of the New Age, and a healthy fear of what can be lost in students' education if ultrafundamentalists' claims are allowed to progress unchecked, educators must seek ways to engage ultrafundamentalist parents, community members, and organizations in productive dialogue regarding the changes that can and should be made in public education.

References

Baer, R.N. (1989). *Inside the New Age nightmare*. Lafayette, LA: Huntington House.

Cumbey, C. (1983). *The hidden dangers of the rainbow*. Lafayette, LA: Huntington House.

Fair, M. (1991, March 7). Council\Legis\Bills\DKA\3179.AL. South Carolina State Legislature.

Gabler, M., & Gabler, N. (1985). *What are they teaching our children?* Wheaton, IL: Victor.

Groothuis, D.R. (1988). *Unmasking the New Age*. Downers Grove, IL: InterVarsity.

Hunt, D.L. (1983). *Peace, prosperity and the coming holocaust*. Eugene, OR: Harvest House.

Kennedy, J. (1987). *No establishment or restrictions*. Fort Lauderdale, FL: Coral Ridge Ministries.

Marrs, T. (1987). *Dark secrets of the New Age*. Westchester, IL: Crossway.

Marrs, T. (1990). *New Age cults and religions*. Shiloh Court, TX: Living Truth.

Marzano, R.J. (1993). When two worldviews collide. *Educational Leadership, 51*(4), pp. 6–11.

Noebel, D.A. (1991). *Understanding the times*. Manitou Springs, CO: Summit.

O'Hara, M. (1988). Science, pseudoscience and mythmongering. In R. Basil (Ed.), *Not necessarily the New Age* (pp. 145–164). Buffalo, NY: Prometheus.

Robertson, P. (1990). *The new millennium*. Dallas, TX: Word.

Saperstein, D. (1990). Fundamentalist involvement in the political scene: Analysis and response. In N.J. Cohen (Ed.), *The fundamentalist phenomenon* (pp. 214–229). Grand Rapids, MI: William B. Eerdmans.

Shupe, A. (1989, October 4). The reconstructionist movement in the new Christian right. *The Christian Century,* pp. 880–882.

Simonds, R. (1983). *How to elect Christians to public office*. Costa Mesa, CA: National Association of Christian Educators/Citizens for Excellence in Education.

Chapter 5

Censorship in Schools: Three Case Studies

Marc Ravel Rosenblum

As Ken Donelson succinctly writes later in this work, the book has not been written that will not offend somebody for some reason. Indeed, almost every reason imaginable has been offered to support attacks on thousands of school and library books. Although these attacks on the freedom to read may at times come from the political left, as detailed in Simmons' following chapter, it is the religious right that has to date mounted most attacks.

In all three of the following cases describing attacks from the right, local activists have worked with the National Coalition Against Censorship to fight efforts to ban school books and programs. NCAC and other organizations encourage U.S. school districts to have written policies establishing objective, professional criteria for selecting materials and for reviewing them when they are challenged (see also Section Three, "Some Plans for Action"). Once an actual challenge arises, it is critical that school boards strictly enforce their procedures. NCAC also encourages community members to play an active role in supporting the right to read, teach, learn, and educate others about the dangers of censorship.

The Case Against *The Floatplane Notebooks*

In March 1992, listeners of radio evangelist J.B. Lineberry's regular biweekly show "Hour of Deliverance" were informed, "They are teaching smut" in the Carroll County, Virginia, schools. These were the opening shots of a five-month battle in Hillsville, Virginia, centered around Clyde Edgerton's novel *The Floatplane Notebooks*. Objections to the book were first raised by a parent whose child attended the 11th grade honors English class where it was used as a supplemental text. The parent objected to references to sex and masturbation and to the use of the words "piss" and "damn" in the novel. When the principal informed the parent that the class had already finished reading the book, the parent took his complaint to Lineberry.

Lineberry agreed that there were six different passages containing "offensive" material in the 200-page novel; he made it his mission to see that the book "be burned in the fireplace" and that any teacher or administrator who had approved it be removed from the school district (Lineberry, 1992). Lineberry focused on Marion Goldwasser, the 11th grade teacher who used the book in her class, calling for her immediate dismissal. Goldwasser had taught in the Carroll County schools for 20 years and was the "Teacher of the Year" in 1991. *The Floatplane Notebooks,* widely and favorably reviewed, had been chosen and paid for by the students to supplement the curriculum. The book was of particular interest to Goldwasser's class because it is about a rural North Carolina family with two sons the students' age. When the school offered to buy these books back from students, they all refused to part with their copies.

Lineberry launched his campaign by recruiting a dozen supporters in Hillsville to circulate petitions urging that the book be banned and Goldwasser be dismissed. Many local stores posted these petitions and distributed copies of the six pages of the book—completely out of context—to which Lineberry objected. (Many of the supporters admitted to never having read the book and to basing their complaints only on these pages.)

A week later Lineberry scheduled a demonstration in front of the school, again to demand that *The Floatplane Notebooks* be banned, Goldwasser be fired, and an investigation be conducted to find others who approved of the blasphemous book so that they too could be fired (Snow, 1992).

The Carroll County School District did have standing policies for selecting curriculum materials and reviewing them in the event of objections. But because no formal complaint had been filed against the book, no action was called for according to district policy. Likewise, the only appropriate action for the school board to take regarding Goldwasser—a tenured and respected teacher—was to support her and reject Lineberry's attacks. When threatened with Lineberry's public demonstration, however, the superintendent announced that he would unilaterally ban the book—disregarding the district's review procedures—and that the district would be more responsive to parents' concerns in the future (Dellinger, 1992).

This solution satisfied no one. There were reports that the superintendent agreed to ban the book forever if Lineberry ceased his attacks on Goldwasser, but Lineberry expressed dissatisfaction that Goldwasser and others had not been fired. Equally dissatisfied, Goldwasser and supporters were unwilling to allow *The Floatplane Notebooks* to be arbitrarily banned.

By this time Goldwasser was working closely with NCAC, which recruited community members to write letters and make phone calls to the school board in support of the freedom to teach and learn. Teachers and others demanded that the book go through the formal review procedure that (1) allowed the superintendent's decision to be appealed to the school board and (2) required a formal complaint to be filed. Instead, the board issued a statement at its next meeting supporting the right of teachers to choose their own materials but allowing the ban of *The Floatplane Notebooks* to stand.

Goldwasser continued to work with NCAC and the Virginia National Education Association and collected signatures from 67 of the 71 teachers in the district on a petition demanding that the book not be banned without a proper review. When the district still refused to reinstate the book, Goldwasser filed a grievance against the school for violating the freedom of expression clause in her contract. At this point Goldwasser got results: the book was subjected to a formal review and eventually reinstated, though at the 12th grade level.

Censorship of *Forever* in Rib Lake, Wisconsin

In March 1993, Rib Lake (Wisconsin) High School principal Paul Peterson strolled into the school cafeteria and, for no apparent reason, picked up Judy Blume's *Forever* from a table near a student. He flipped through it, found graphic descriptions of sex acts, and asked the ninth grade student where she got the novel (*Marshfield News-Herald*, 1993). When she said that it came from the school library, he told her to bring it to his office at the end of the day. Peterson later went to the library and removed other copies of the book.

When head librarian Ruth Dishnow confronted Peterson about his breach of district policy, he said that he had already talked to the district administrator, who had approved his action. The district administrator, Ramon Parks, told Dishnow later, "I don't have to follow the rules...the book is filth" (R. Dishnow, personal communication, March 1993). He warned Dishnow that if she brought the issue up before the school board at its next meeting, hundreds of other books would be banned.

Judy Blume's *Forever* is one of the most read young adult books published in the last two decades and has been placed on the American Library Association's "Best of the Best" list. It is also one of the most frequently censored books of all time. The book's story is of a high school senior who is in love and decides to have sexual intercourse for the first time. The novel deals with that difficult decision and then with the girl's sad realization that her love for her boyfriend will not last "forever" after all. *Forever* is often attacked for its frankness about the young woman's sexual desires and decision-making process and for an explicit love scene.

Both sides of the controversy prepared for a battle in the days leading up to the school board meeting. Knowing that the district had policies that prohibited administrators from unilaterally banning books, Parks showed the book to some like-minded parents and then filled out the complaint form himself, starting the review procedure (Lake, March 9, 1993). Meanwhile, Dishnow called NCAC and together they developed a two-pronged strategy to block the effort to censor *Forever*: they began grassroots organizing to keep the book in the library, and at the same time they explored legal ways to block the school board in case it decided to ban the book. (Litigation was considered in Rib Lake, though it is a very difficult means for fighting school censorship because the U.S. Supreme Court's 1987 Hazelwood v. Kuhlmeier ruling gave school boards broad powers to limit curricula. No lawsuit was ever filed.)

Over 100 people showed up for the school board meeting, and the majority of them opposed the removal of the book. One parent collected over 100 signatures on a petition supporting *Forever.* Many students wore homemade "Judy Blume for President" and "Judy Blume for Principal" buttons. Similar slogans were posted on students' lockers as well, but school officials removed them after deciding that one poster saying "censorship sucks" was obscene.

The board followed its standing procedures for reviewing materials, which called for a committee to review the book and make a recommendation to the board. However, Rib Lake's procedures called for the board and the principal at the school where the complaint arises—Paul Peterson in this instance, not an objective participant—to choose the review committee. Although a list soliciting volunteer committee members was circulated at the meeting, Peterson and the board eventually selected the committee in a closed session and included no one from the list of volunteers. The board also decided not to disclose to the public when or where the committee meetings were to take place. At this point the *Wausau Daily Herald*, a local newspaper, filed a complaint against the board with the district attorney based on Wisconsin's open-meeting laws (Lake, March 31, 1993). The board hastily publicized the first committee meeting.

Fifteen people attended the meeting in mid-March and planned to speak in favor of keeping the book, but only committee members were allowed to speak. The committee declared that community members could submit written testimonies, but that the committee would not be obliged to read them. Two weeks later, after committee members had a chance to read *Forever* (and ignore community input), they voted 7–4 to ban the book (*Milwaukee Sentinal*, 1993).

Acting on the complaint filed by the Wausau paper, the district attorney announced that the open-meeting law may have been violated. She obtained an injunction against the school board that prevented them from acting on the committee's recommendation and from discussing the *Forever* controversy at board meetings. As of June 1, 1993, the injunction against the board stands while

---

a judge considers whether to block the recommendation of the existing review committee. The book will remain in the Rib Lake High School library until a ruling is made.

The Case of the PUMSY Program

Two years after the Oconee County School District in South Carolina began using the *PUMSY in Pursuit of Excellence* elementary guidance program, complaints about it prompted the school board to discontinue its use pending a review by a committee of teachers, clergy, parents, and others in the community. This review committee began debating PUMSY in September 1992, and the program quickly became a political issue throughout the county.

Those attacking PUMSY in Oconee County were supported by Citizens for Excellence in Education and the Christian Coalition. These two groups are active around the United States in school board politics. Their primary areas of interest include guidance programs like PUMSY, sex education, and funding for public schools; their primary tactic seems to be to gain seats on school boards in order to pressure other board members (as Jenkinson and Marzano mentioned in the previous two chapters).

The objections to PUMSY voiced in Oconee County were the same as those heard in at least 30 other places where it has been attacked: the program "promotes Eastern religions," "promotes New Age philosophy," and "undermines parental and church authority." Some parents claimed that the PUMSY handpuppet was being used to hypnotize children and that the program, in encouraging kids to make decisions, taught that there were no absolutes and therefore no God. The school district had offered to allow children of parents who objected to the program to be excused from classes when it was taught, but these parents wanted to eliminate the program altogether.

A coalition of citizens formed Oconee County Citizens Against Censorship (OCAC) and rallied around the slogan "The issue is censorship; it is not PUMSY." Their position was that the PUMSY program should not be removed, because professional educators had chosen it and still supported its educational merit.

Both camps saw that the battle over PUMSY would be fought at the school board level because the board would decide what to do with the program after the review committee made a recommendation. With this in mind and with the knowledge that four school board seats were to open in the November elections, the local CEE group quietly ran a slate of candidates opposed to the PUMSY program. Because most people in the community opposed censorship on principle, the CEE candidates were not vocal about their hostility to the program. Nevertheless, CEE supporters aggressively campaigned for their candidates, primarily in local churches and community groups.

Working with NCAC, the Oconee County anticensorship group endorsed their own slate of candidates who were opposed to all censorship. They also forced school board candidates to take a public position on the PUMSY controversy. In candidate forums and through local newspapers, OCAC members called attention to the role new board members would play in resolving the PUMSY controversy and any future curriculum challenges.

The campaign path and the subsequent election results sent a clear anticensorship message to members of the school board and the community: of the four seats open, three went to incumbents and one to an OCAC candidate. In letters to the school board and newspaper during the campaign and in their votes during the school board election, members of the community rejected censorship of the PUMSY program. This community opposition to the censorship of the guidance program undoubtedly influenced the new board, which voted 6–3 in January 1993 to accept the review committee's recommendation that the program be returned to the district.

Common Traits and Tactics of Censors

Attacks on the freedom to teach and learn come from an array of sources, in these cases an individual from the community, an administrator from the school system, and a well-organized group in the community. The specific complaints about books and programs also vary in each instance. One characteristic all censors share by definition, though, is the desire to control what others read, see, and think.

J.B. Lineberry in Hillsville was furious when *The Floatplane Notebooks* was reinstated, asserting that Marion Goldwasser was able to "run over the school superintendent and tell him what to do" (*Galax* (Va.) *Gazette*, p. 1). Lineberry may have been particularly angry because *he* had not been able to assume control, for this was surely the goal of his planned demonstration and his biweekly radio broadcasts. In Rib Lake, Ramon Parks and Paul Peterson clearly stated their desire to censor books without answering to the school board. After Peterson confiscated copies of *Forever* from the library, Parks threatened additional censorship if librarian Ruth Dishnow resisted. As the controversy wore on over the next months, Dishnow and her husband, a teacher in the district, faced continual harassment from administrators. The CEE group in Oconee County wanted to make sure not only that their children were "protected" from the PUMSY program, but that other students were protected as well. By attempting to gain seats on the school board, the group hoped to make even more decisions about the information available to others.

> "**O**ne characteristic all censors share by definition is the desire to control what others read, see, and think."

Tactics of the would-be censors varied in these three cases. Lineberry's campaign was aggressive and typical of attacks by individual community members, like those described in Chapter 3. By circulating petitions, generating letters to the school board and to local papers, and planning a public demonstration, Lineberry created an exaggerated impression of opposition to *The Floatplane Notebooks* in Hillsville, thereby placing a good deal of pressure on the school board. As administrators, Peterson and Parks chose not to recruit community support for censoring *Forever*, but when attacks come from leadership within the school system, community support is often unnecessary. As they did in Rib Lake, school boards frequently close ranks around administrators who call for censorship. More important, because administrators and others within the school system are responsible for reviewing and selecting materials, the line between censorship and a normal review of materials can become unclear. When normal procedures are bypassed in the interest of banning books, however, it is clearly a case of censorship. Tactics used by the CEE and Christian Coalition in Oconee County are probably the most effective, and they are increasingly common. The CEE in particular runs school board campaigns all over the United States. When there is no organized opposition, few people learn about the issues or bother to vote, and the CEE candidates often win. In fact, the religious right has gained some notoriety recently for their "stealth" campaigns in which candidates hide their affiliations and their agendas, but they have not yet lost ground as a result.

Efforts by the religious right to gain seats on school boards deserve special attention from anticensorship activists because in most school-censorship cases, it is the board that has the final say. Unfortunately, school boards frequently fall into the same trap as the boards in Hillsville and Rib Lake and decide to give in to censors' demands "just this once" so that the controversy will end. This option is especially tempting to boards when, as in Rib Lake, the complaint comes from a school administrator.

But giving in to one demand for censorship inevitably invites others. When the superintendent surrendered to Lineberry's demand that *The Floatplane Notebooks* be censored, Lineberry immediately intensified his campaign to have Goldwasser fired. And, because Parks had already threatened to censor other books, there is no reason to think he would have stopped if the board had quickly banned *Forever.*

In all these cases the would-be censors eventually took up campaigns against the individuals who defended free expression. In Hillsville, Goldwasser was consistently the focus of radio broadcasts as Lineberry urged people to "burn the book, but most important get rid of the evil mind that brought it into the school." He warned his listeners that, because she made Teacher of the Year, that does not make her an angel, if all she wants to do is teach students blaspheming and garbage (*Galax* (Va.) *Gazette*, 1992). Rib Lake librarian Ruth Dishnow and OCAC leader Patricia Lightweis, who later received a PEN/Newman's Own First Amendment award for her work, were both labeled "immoral." Dishnow and her husband received threatening notes in their mailboxes. Lightweis found dead birds in front of her bookstore, and New Age books from the store were stolen and defaced. She also received threatening phone calls and was harassed while walking on the street.

Would-be censors often have a missionary-like zeal that stems from their firm belief that they are right. As mentioned earlier, they frequently receive financial and strategic support from large organizations. In seeking to impose their views on others, they rarely see themselves as censors. For all these reasons, the censors have had an alarming success rate in recent years. But anti-censorship activists can counter their efforts. The best defense against censorship is for groups and individuals to speak up against it and promote an honest discussion of the issues. Members of the community do not always understand that efforts to impose a single viewpoint necessarily restrict alternate views; we must strive for a plurality of views, especially in our educational system.

References

Dellinger, P. (1992, March 26). Book flap over, but dispute isn't. *Roanoke* (VA) *Times & World-News*, pp. A1, A8.

Galax (Va.) *Gazette*. (1992, May 4, 5). Evangelist wants CCHS teacher fired, p. 1.

Lake, M. (1993, March 9). Rib Lake residents object to book ban. *Wausau Daily Herald*, p. 1A.

Lake, M. (1993, March 31). Rib Lake board may have violated meeting law. *Wausau Daily Herald*, p. 3A.

Lineberry, J.B. (1992, March 20). Hours of deliverance. WHHV Radio, Hillsville, Virginia.

Marshfield (Wis.) *News-Herald*. (1993, March 9). Book issues attract a crowd, pp. 4A.

Milwaukee Sentinel. (1993, March 31). Removal of book is backed, p. 3.

Snow, S. (1992, March 23, 24). Carroll group seeks dismissal of teacher. *Galax* (Va.) *Gazette*, pp. 1, 3.

Chapter 6

Political Correctness—The Other Side of the Coin

John S. Simmons

Time was when challenges or complaints about what was being taught—and read—in the schools were fairly predictable. As the authors of the previous chapters have illustrated, certain groups and individuals--generally associated with the right wing of the political spectrum—took umbrage at the assignment of any book or material that included "dirty" words, explicit sexual descriptions, or "unpatriotic" language. Over the past 25 years, these people have come to be known as the book banners in contemporary society. But another force has been gaining ground in the movement to influence the choice of curricular materials in state education departments and local school districts throughout the United States. This faction displays an unmistakably politically left leaning. Consider, for example, an excerpt from an education bill passed by the 1978 California legislature:

> No instructional materials shall be adopted by any governing
> board for use in the schools which, in its determination, contains
> (a) any matter reflecting adversely upon persons because of their
> race, color, creed, national origin, ancestry, sex, or occupation.
> (b) any sectarian or denominational doctrine or propaganda con-
> trary to law (Simmons, 1981, p. 19).

During the past ten years or so, this type of influence on what students are assigned—or even permitted—to read has intensified. "Political correctness" is the all too familiar label associated with those who are aggressively liberal in their opposition to anything "offensive" in school curricula.

The Rise of Political Correctness

Who are these politically correct critics? What do they want? And how have they influenced U.S. culture in general and students' right to read in particular?

Probably the most clearly discernible antecedents of today's left-wing challengers are the civil rights activists of the 1950s and '60s. In those ranks were a large number of college-age individuals whose goal was to expose, to question, to attack, and ultimately to dispose of the status quo in the United States at the time. Their most heralded struggles suggest that these young, liberal-minded crusaders viewed U.S. education as a significant item on their agenda. And, in the wake of the John F. Kennedy assassination, the passage of the Civil Rights Act of 1964 and the Voting Rights Act of 1965 provided formidable levers for these activists.

Eventually they were joined in the late '60s and '70s by other groups with similar agendas, including the "hippies" who wanted also to reform the United States. These groups all shared a view of the white males of the "Establishment" as their most prominent opponents and as scapegoats for what seemed to them to be the cause of the country's most distinctive problems: the perpetuation of the Vietnam War, the deterioration of the environment, the miserable living conditions in the inner cities, and the oppression of minorities. This expanded focus in the movement appealed to additional individuals and groups including consumer rights advocates, environmentalists, and minority and women's rights advocates.

The equal rights movement has had a marked effect on curricular choices in all content areas and grades. For example, in 1964 the Illinois chapter of the National Association for the Advancement of Colored People forced the removal of *The Adventures of Huckleberry Finn* from the state's schools, citing as its rationale the negative image of Nigger Jim. The same objection was raised by a number of parents in Bucks County, Pennsylvania, some 20 years later, also causing the renowned

Twain novel to be temporarily removed. And, at roughly the same time, the National Organization for Women forced the cancellation of a Broadway production of *Lolita,* citing the sexual exploitation of girls as their rationale.

Spokespersons for other minority groups, chief among them Latinos, Native Americans, and Asians, joined forces with the groups noted earlier and began to question the choice of texts used in schools—particularly those that ignored minority considerations or placed representative characters from such groups in pejorative roles. This burgeoning concern with the status and image of women, minorities, and citizen's groups such as the environmentalists resulted in attempts by these groups to influence the inclusion or exclusion of certain materials and authors from the curriculum. They also urged the addition of new selections to revised anthologies. Harried publishers, long confronted by censorship from the right wing, now began to experience it from the new left coalition. In an *English Journal* piece (Simmons, 1981) titled "Proactive Censorship: The New Wave," I took note of these doings:

> Today, when writing a book for use in public schools, an author must be aware of
> 1. how many black faces appear in proportion to the number of white faces;
> 2. the use of names such as Carlos and Juanita in proportion to those of Billy and Sue;
> 3. the use of pronouns that *negate* sex bias;
> 4. putting anyone in a stereotypical role;
> 5. paying obeisance to the mandates of the consumer enlightenment moguls;
> 6. excluding materials that imply the rape of our natural beauty;
> 7. any vaguely humorous, satiric, and/or critical treatment of anyone's religious preference;
> 8. any allusion to stereotypes of ethnic or national origins;
> 9. statements that may contain political bias;
> 10. references to the use of drugs, tobacco, alcohol, nonnutritious food, etc. (p. 19).

It has been in the past eight to ten years that the full impact of political correctness has been felt by educators at all levels. E.D. Hirsch, Jr., got this message three years after the publication of his best-selling book *Cultural Literacy: What Every American Needs to Know* (1987), which advocated a core of knowledge that should be taught in the public schools. In the book Hirsch included a list of this core knowledge, expanded in the 1988 publication *The Dictionary of Cultural Literacy*. The immediate and widespread influence of the texts led Hirsch, with both private and public financial support, to form the Cultural Literacy Foundation in Charlottesville, Virginia. In March 1990 he organized a meeting of 100 educators and interested citizens on the University of Virginia campus to review the cultural literacy movement and make recommendations for its modification and expansion. The foremost criticism of his original paradigm was directed against its heavily Eurocentric, "dead white male" orientation. Thus Hirsch significantly modified the original text in the second edition of the *Dictionary* to include many more minority and female authors; he also added four major consultants to the Foundation roster—an African American literature scholar, a women's studies authority, an Hispanic literature scholar, and a Native American studies spokesperson. The Hirsch curriculum, now being tried out in several U.S. elementary schools, is far more multicultural than was the 1987 required readings counterpart.

Concurrent with the rapid increase in the multicultural overtones being placed in the curriculum is the rising demand that gay and lesbian studies be added as well. At present, this demand has mainly centered on college and university programs of study, but who is to say what future demands of this group will be? In any event, there can be no doubt that the effects of political correctness are being felt across the United States.

The Current Scene

To identify political correctness with a specific group or a clearly supportive organization is not really possible. It is a movement contributed to by a relatively large number of minorities who generally function independent of one another in their advocacy of or opposition to other aspects of contemporary society. In an academic sense, they have found common ground in opposing those traditional elements that have a white-male, Anglo-Saxon orientation. On another front, they seem to oppose individual freedoms and prerogatives when exercise of those freedoms and prerogatives denies particular groups their rights or derogates those groups in any way. Ironically, political correctness advocates would deny freedom of expression under certain circumstances: they would willingly suspend the right to free speech of those who—in the exercise of that right—offend some race, ethnic group, class, or sex.

Specific Impact on Schools

While the main influence of the politically correct activists has been on college and university curricula, the movement has begun to affect programs of study at elementary, middle, and high school levels. The active censorship of what is "objectionable" in literature anthologies is an excellent example of such influences; the censors' attempt to force publishers to reconstruct history texts along multicultural, feminist lines is another. More specifically, in literature study, politically correct censors have made an obvious attempt to add to, and often replace, the "traditional" canon of works with works by those authors who represent their culture and philosophy of life.

For example, some feminist groups demand more attention to female authors such as Jane Austen, the Brontë sisters, and Emily Dickinson, and the addition of selections by more contemporary writers such as Gwendolyn Brooks, Doris Lessing, Flannery O'Connor, Anne Tyler, and Alice Walker. They also protest the anthologized selections that place women in stereotypic, sexist roles. In the same sense, certain African Americans proclaim the need for the works of Maya Angelou, James Baldwin, Ralph Ellison, Langston Hughes, Toni

> **"In literature study, politically correct censors have made an obvious attempt to add to, and often replace, the 'traditional' canon of works with works by those authors who represent their culture and philosophy of life."**

Morrison, Richard Wright, and others to be given equal time with authors who are traditionally included—Hawthorne, Melville, Hemingway, Faulkner, and Frost—in American literature study. They, too, are often outraged at the use of selections from the canon (*The Adventures of Huckleberry Finn*) or the popular media (Amos 'n' Andy) that demean the image of black people past and present. Ironically, black males often are critical of black female writers such as Alice Walker and Toni Morrison for what they perceive to be the negative image of black men portrayed in their works.

Some Native Americans are also proponents of more inclusion of their authors. Their main concern, however, seems to be eliminating the image so often bestowed on them by writers and filmmakers—the image of the "noble savage" or, alternatively, of lazy, ill-educated, drunken, violent, often reclusive individuals who are most often a drain on mainstream society and contribute little of quality to its arts, commerce, research, or development.

Another minority group that has sought restitution for unfair treatment is disabled persons. Various government agencies have created several euphemistic synonyms for people with certain physical and mental disabilities. Much is heard about characters in works of literature, as well as in films and TV shows, being unfairly stereotyped because of the manner in which their handicaps are portrayed. Commercial textbook publishers must pay increased attention to the nature and treatment of handicapped characters in literary selections they place in revised anthologies.

One battle that is still being fought by politically correct advocates concerns English linguistics. Language and composition books have come under attack in this decade, not for the linguistic or rhetorical processes they feature, but for the content they have presented, at least until recently. The "he/she" issue is only one of these. The ongoing argument over "The Students' Right to Their Own Language" (NCTE Resolution, 1974) represents a more contentious issue. Those who favor a relativist position in the teaching of diction and usage frequently bear the politically correct emblem. They bitterly reject the notion of standard English being used as the norm and such dialects as black English being considered as lower level, less desirable linguistic styles. They also examine the racial, ethnic, and social class overtones in textbook examples used to illustrate parts of speech, kinds of syntactic structures, and features of mechanics in writing. They are especially concerned about the stereotypic examples used in the teaching of general (Hayakawan) semantics. As in so many areas of concern, the activists' attacks on these language and composition texts are consistently unyielding.

Looking toward the future, I can see a problem that will not diminish quickly but will increase both in scope and intensity. The quest for a language, literature, history, and politics that will satisfy these crusaders may well be an impossible one, given their uncompromising stance.

References

Hirsch, E.D., Jr. (1987). *Cultural literacy: What every American needs to know.* New York: Doubleday.

Hirsch, E.D., Jr. (1988). *The dictionary of cultural literacy: What every American needs to know.* New York: Doubleday.

Simmons, J.S. (1981). Proactive censorship: The new wave. *English Journal, 70*(8), 19.

Chapter 7

A Book Is Not a House: The Human Side of Censorship

Robert Cormier

Whenever the subject of censorship comes up, I don't think first of headlines or heated debates or letters to the editor or angry voices. I think instead of a girl in a school on Cape Cod in Massachusetts. She sat every day in the school library while the other members of her class were discussing *The Chocolate War*. Her parents had protested the use of the novel in the classroom, and a hearing had been scheduled. Meanwhile, the novel continued to be studied by the students, pending an official hearing. (In some schools, a book is automatically removed from the classroom prior to a hearing.) I think about that girl. Sitting in the library alone while her classmates were back in the classroom. Was she lonely, embarrassed? Did she feel isolated, ostracized? Did some of her classmates pass remarks about her? I don't know if any of this happened, although I suspect it did. I have this suspicion because a classmate of hers wrote to me about her predicament, and his letter showed sympathy and concern. It struck me then as it strikes me now that in a tender time of blossoming adolescence, when a teenager wants to belong, to be part of the crowd, part of *something*, this girl sat alone in the library, sentenced there by her parents. I wonder which was more harm-

From *Author's insights: Turning teenagers into readers and writers*, edited by Donald R. Gallo (Boynton/Cook Publishers Inc., Portsmouth, NH, 1992). Reprinted by permission of Robert Cormier.

ful—her isolation or reading the novel. Which brings us to the ironic P.S. in her classmate's letter to me: the girl had read *The Chocolate War* a year before the controversy and "liked it."

I also think of another girl, a senior in high school in Arizona who sent me a letter. This is part of what she wrote:

> A couple of weeks ago I was in my school's library and I was going to check out and reread *The Chocolate War* so my mind would be refreshed to read the sequel. I couldn't find it, even though the library holds some of your other books that I have read. I ended up checking it out at the public library.
>
> The next day I asked my English teacher why your book wouldn't be in the library because we had just been talking about book banning in one of my other classes. My teacher said she thought our superintendent had something against your book.
>
> My friend Jenni and myself asked the school librarian what books were banned from our library and yours was the only one. This was not fair at all so we went and talked to our principal who has since read it and TODAY said he is going to put it back on the shelf.
>
> No matter what others may say, keep writing because I love your books.

I think of those students, and I also think of teachers. I think of a teacher I met at an educational conference in New England. She told me that her great ambition was to teach *The Chocolate War*. She said she keeps ordering the book from her department head but the book never arrives. She suspects that her department head does not approve of the novel. He says nothing and she says nothing. She must say nothing because she is a single parent with two small children. She doesn't have tenure. "I would love to challenge him but I can't afford to," she told me.

I also think of a band of teachers in a northern Florida town who were at the center of a censorship controversy over *The Chocolate War* and *I Am the Cheese* and other books. One of the embattled teachers went to her mailbox after her English classes one day and found the following message, composed of words cut out of magazines:

> Woe to those who call evil good and good evil
> who put darkness for light

and light for darkness who put
bitter for sweet for they have
revoked the law of the lord
for this you all shall die
one by one.

The note then named that teacher, two others, and a television reporter who had written about the banning efforts in that southern town. Later, someone set a fire at the door of the reporter's home. The teachers received other anonymous letters and telephone calls using such words as *atheist* and *lesbian* and *daughter of Satan*. This was in the United States of America, in the twilight years of the 20th century.

Thomas P. "Tip" O'Neill, Jr., former Speaker of the U.S. House of Representatives, once said, "All politics is local." Censorship also is local, which means that it is personal, affecting individuals before it is taken up as a cause by groups and organizations and becomes the subject of headlines and talk shows and newscasts.

The human aspects are heart wrenching because they affect people who are particularly vulnerable:

- parents—like those on Cape Cod—agonizing over their children who face an increasingly hostile and threatening world, parents who sincerely believe that they are protecting their children when they keep them from reading certain books.

- young people besieged almost daily by invitations that are beguiling and intimidating and possibly destructive, all at the same time.

- teachers who attempt to lead their students through the cluttered hallways of knowledge and are often strait-jacketed by people who have never entered a classroom and faced 20 or 30 restless, inquiring, and sometimes bored young minds.

- the writer who seeks to capture lightning on paper, clustering words and phrases and figures of speech to bring character and incident to vivid life.

On the bulletin board above my desk is a paragraph taken from an essay by novelist Robert Daley in the August 18, 1990, issue of the *New York Times Book Review:*

> The job of a novel at its highest level is to illuminate the human condition. Entertainment is fine and the transference of ideas is nice, too, but the novel, like all art, has as its supreme goal to engage the beholder's emotions, to make him or her laugh and cry and suffer and triumph and—one thing more—understand.

Beautiful, breathtaking words because they describe exactly the kind of novel I try to write in my days and evenings at the typewriter. Whether I succeed or fail is for the beholders to decide, but my struggle is daily and honest, as well as a continuing revelation.

Writing a novel is a subjective occupation, in contrast to, say, building a house, which is completely objective. The builder follows an architect's blueprint, erects walls, installs a ceiling and floor, cabinets and bookshelves. At the end of the day's work, the builder looks at what has been accomplished and pronounces it a room. At the end of the day, the writer isn't sure about what has been accomplished. Words on paper, yes, but not in response to a blueprint. All the choices that were made. What to put in and what to leave out. This adjective or that. Or no adjective at all. Did this metaphor go askew, calling attention to itself? And the characters: did they come alive? Even when the writer is satisfied with the work and pronounces it, somewhat tentatively, a chapter, there is always the judgment of the reader, the beholder waiting.

This is what writing is all about—the sweaty work of creation, the frustrating and sometimes painful putting down of words on paper to move and excite the reader. And into all of this stomps censorship, flexing its muscles. Censorship tells us what to write and how to write it. Or what not to write. Does not trust the motives of the writer. Does not acknowledge the toil that goes into the writing of a book. Blunts the sharp thrust of creativity and, in fact, is afraid of it. Wants everything simple. Wants everyone in a book to live happily ever after.

Censorship goes beyond the writer, of course, to the reader, particularly children. Doesn't want children to read a paragraph that may make them pause and think. Doesn't want children to be challenged. Censorship sees danger everywhere:

- *Goldilocks* was banned because Goldilocks was not punished for breaking into the house of the three bears.
- Anne Frank's *Diary of a Young Girl* was removed from schools because a passage in the book suggested that all religions are equal.
- *The Chocolate War* is banned because of teenage attitudes and because the good guy loses in the end.

Censors wish to hand out blueprints for the writer to follow, blueprints that include designs that are safe and secure, that contain no concealed passages, no corners around which surprises or challenges wait. A house, in which every room is furnished with the bare necessities, with no shadows, no closets, no hidden corners. And no light. But a book is not a house.

> **"Censors wish to hand out blueprints for the writer to follow that include designs that are safe and secure, that contain no concealed passages, no corners around which surprises or challenges wait."**

My writing has always been a learning experience, and each time that I sit down at the typewriter I learn something about my craft and also about myself. I have learned, astonishingly, that not all censorship is bad and that, in fact, censorship for the writer begins at home. At the typewriter or the word processor.

This is what angers me most about censorship, the fact that I have already been censored—and willingly—before my manuscripts leave my house. I am that censor. And I've learned my lessons well.

Ironically, I learned about self-censorship long before any of my novels became targets for the book banners. My education occurred in the final stages of writing the novel that was to become *The Chocolate War.* The novel, which was published in the spring of 1974, was written in 1971 and 1972, long before censorship of young adult books became virtually an everyday affair.

What happened is this: the events in the novel were nearing a climax and I felt it necessary to include a scene to explain how the villain, Archie Costello, comes upon the idea for a unique but very cruel raffle of those chocolates that are the heart of the novel.

The scene I wrote shows Archie alone in this bedroom, masturbating. He is also disturbed and frustrated about what has been happening at Trinity High School and knows he must bring about a climax to the situation. The scene provides two climaxes—the consummation of that solitary act and the birth of the chocolate raffle. The language was not graphic. There were no four-letter words. But there would also be no doubt in the reader's mind about what Archie Costello was doing. Reading and rereading that chapter, pencil poised to cut or slash, I was satisfied that the scene was cleverly written, showed the connection between sex and power, and, hopefully, captured that forlorn and sometimes desperate act.

My high school son, Peter, had been my guide throughout the writing of the novel, advising me about current adolescent language, customs, styles. Writing the novel had been an exhilarating experience for me. I wrote with all the craft I could summon. More than craft, passion. I was emotionally involved with the characters and events, although I wondered, as I wrote, who would ever read this strange novel about high school students involved in a candy sale. I did not know at that time about the young adult audience, did not know that such a market existed. All I knew was that the novel rang true to me.

At one point, before I submitted the novel for publication, my daughter, Chris, then 15, asked to read it. Not an unusual request, because my wife and my children who were old enough always read my short stories and novels in manuscript form. But this time I hesitated. And knew why I hesitated: the chapter showing Archie alone in his room. I did not want her to read this chapter. A solution presented itself. I simply removed that chapter from the manuscript, warned her that she might find a gap in the action late in the novel but not to worry about it, and handed her the manuscript. She read the novel, gave it her enthusiastic approval, and said, incidentally, that she had not noticed any gap.

Off the manuscript went—that troubling chapter restored—to my agent and subsequently to four publishers, who did not care to publish the book. Not unless the "downbeat" or unhappy ending was changed. I refused to change the ending, not so much from noble impulses, but because I simply did not want to rewrite the book. I felt that to have a happy ending the entire novel would have to be rewritten and its flow of character and events altered to make that happy ending logical.

Eventually, the novel was accepted by Fabio Coen at Pantheon Books. He did not protest the unhappy ending, thought it logical and inevitable, given the circumstances of the novel. In a friendly conference in his office, he made a few editing suggestions—so few that they were scribbled on a scrap of paper. Finally, however, he paused, obviously troubled. He said that he had one major reservation about the novel, a certain chapter that was well written and clever—too clever, perhaps—and also gratuitous and out of character with the rest of the book. My mind made a sudden leap—did he mean that chapter in which Archie masturbated? Exactly, he said, suggesting that I reread the chapter once more in the context of the entire novel. He said he would ultimately abide by my decision.

I didn't need to read the chapter again—although I did, to fulfill my obligation. I knew instantly what I had done: I had been willing to inflict that chapter on other people's 15-year-old daughters but unwilling to inflict it on my own daughter. I removed the chapter.

That is how I learned the lesson of self-censorship. That censorship begins at home. That a writer works in isolation but is not alone. That cleverness for its own sake is hollow and meaningless. That writing is a two-way partnership between writer and reader.

All of this smacks of compromise and the danger of being too careful. But it is a compromise that challenges me to my best efforts, that keeps me on my literary toes, that makes me pause with my fingers on the typewriter keys in order to select the perfect word, the perfect simile or metaphor, the perfect motion in a story. Perfection is seldom achieved, but striving for it is, I think, a noble occupation.

The story never ends. And the battle is never over. Fifteen years after *The Chocolate War* was written, I sat at the typewriter as usual. Another novel. Another cast of characters. I had embarked on a novel that would eventually be published with the title *Fade*. Some things never change and among these things are the daily demands of creating characters on the page and setting them in motion.

In this particular novel, a sensitive teenage boy whose name is Paul is the recipient of the gift—or is it a curse?—of becoming invisible. Which, of course, is impossible. Or is it? This kind of enigma intrigues me and made the novel fascinating but difficult to write.

For the purpose of this article, let's suspend disbelief and accept invisibility as entirely possible so that we can focus on one demanding aspect of the novel. The aspect is this: it is necessary for Paul to be shocked by what he sees when he's invisible. Paul witnesses two unsavory events as he lurks unseen by others: one involves a sordid act between a middle-aged man and a teenage girl. The other involves an act of incest between two young people Paul admires.

Paul must be shocked by what he witnesses, so shocked that he begins to question whether invisibility is indeed the marvelous gift he had envisioned or a terrible burden that he must assume. The scenes must also shock the reader because the reader must share Paul's horror, must feel the revulsion Paul feels.

I wrote the scenes carefully with all the craft I could supply, rewriting as usual, trying to strike the right notes, to convey what was going on in order to make it all seem real. There was also the need to stop short of titillating the reader or sensationalizing the situations.

After the chapters were finished I was left with the eternal questions: Do they work? Would they be convincing to the reader? Two people whose opinions I value highly read the novel before it was submitted for publication. Both were enthusiastic about it, indicating that the novel had accomplished what I had set out to accomplish. But these two readers also were upset by those two vital scenes. They wondered whether the scenes were written too graphically. "Is it necessary to go into all those details?" one of them asked.

Here again, the writer faces the agony of choice and selection, a question of degree, the delicate balance that must be struck between verisimilitude and exploitation. Was I exploiting the situations, so set on shocking Paul that I had gone overboard? Where do you draw the line?

Rewriting was clearly in order and that is exactly what I did. The younger of the two readers was especially disturbed by the description of incest as witnessed by Paul. I rewrote the scene so that Paul turns away—he can't close his eyes to cut off his view because his eyelids, too, are invisible—and *hears* what is going on rather than sees what is going on. I felt this made the scene less offensive.

In the scene involving the man and the girl, I emphasized the squalidness of the situation, kept the act itself to a minimum. Yet, the act had to be graphically portrayed to justify its purpose in the novel.

The younger reader agreed that I modified the description of the incest but was still bothered by it. Yet, I knew that if she weren't bothered by it, then the scene probably wasn't working. The older reader accepted the scenes as rewritten but without enthusiasm. "I know they're necessary," she said, "but I wish they weren't."

There followed some days of agonizing over the chapters. Some more rewriting and then reaching the point where I felt I could do no more without losing all perspective and compromising myself.

Eliminating that chapter from *The Chocolate War* was, in retrospect, an easy solution. But those scenes in *Fade* remain troublesome for me even to this day. The choices that are really agonizing are those involving *degrees*—how much and how little? And there are no clear-cut guidelines. I have, finally, to be guided by my own instincts.

I have gone into detail about those writing problems to point out that the words that go into books are not chosen gratuitously or casually, that a writer does not press a button and have the words magically appear, that writing is a demanding, exacting occupation. Ah, but when the words sing and dance on the page, when characters leap to life and behave or misbehave, when people read your books and shake their heads and say, yes, this is how life is and how it must be—that is beautiful.

Those parents on Cape Cod continue to haunt me. I am a parent as well as a writer, and I sympathize with them. They acted in what they felt was the best interest of their daughter. They tried to protect her from the world. They had a right to do this, a responsibility to do it, in fact. Who can quarrel with parents who try to shelter their children from what they perceive as bad influences, whether it's a book or friends or strangers on the street?

My wife and I did the same as we ushered our three daughters and son through the frenzied days of childhood and the lacerating time of adolescence, setting up our family rules, our own curfews, our own rules of behavior.

But there's a place where we sharply differed from the Cape Cod family. Those parents did more than send their daughter away from the classroom and into the library. They also became part of a movement to censor *The Chocolate War*. They not only did not want their daughter to read the novel: they didn't want anyone else's daughter to read the book, either. This is censorship in its most basic, purest form. And this is why censorship is so difficult to fight. It's the act of sincere, sometimes desperate people who are frightened by the world they live in and in which they are bringing up their children. They are trying to do the impossible, to shield their children from this world, to control what they see and do, what they learn. At a moment when their children are reaching out beyond the boundaries of home and family, they are raising barriers to that reaching out. Instead of preparing them to meet that world, they want them to avert their eyes and remain in impossible exclusion. Beyond that, they insist that this same kind of sheltering be extended to the people next door or down the street or in the next town.

Various organizations—religious and social—are quick to support these parents,

> **"Censorship is so difficult to fight: it's the act of sincere, sometimes desperate people who are frightened by the world they live in and in which they are bringing up their children."**

and that's when headlines scream across the front pages, voices are raised in anger, picketing begins, and the threat of violence, or even violence itself, erupts.

The supporters of books also have their organizations. Teachers and librarians can turn to organizations within the American Library Association, the National Coalition Against Censorship, the Freedom to Read Foundation, and authors and publishers themselves for help in their battles against the removal of books from libraries and classrooms.

Every writer I know whose books are challenged enters that battle, flies across the country, makes the speeches, debates opponents, offers encouragement to the educators who find themselves targets of the book banners.

I believe, however, that the greatest thing writers can do is simply to keep writing. Writing honestly with all the craft that can be summoned. Writing to illuminate as well as entertain. Writing to challenge the intellect and engage the heart. To make the reader, in Robert Daley's words, laugh and cry and suffer and triumph and understand.

This is what I try to do each day when I sit at the typewriter. This is my best answer to those who would ban my books.

Section Two

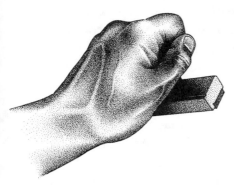

Complaints and Challenges in the Classroom

To underscore the breadth of the issue, the essayists in Section Two address censorship occurrences at both the elementary and secondary levels and in representative content areas. Although challenges to courses such as music, arts, and health and safety are not discussed in this section, censorship poses an equally dangerous threat to teaching and learning in these areas of the curriculum as well.

Shafer reviews various definitions of literacy and methods for literacy instruction that researchers have proposed in the past 10 to 15 years. He then illustrates some objections to these proposals. In her essay, McClain chronicles one of the most publicized censorship cases in recent years involving the Impressions elementary language arts series. Hydrick recounts several poignant incidents of censorship and potential censorship—inside and outside the classroom—she has witnessed as an elementary school teacher. Tomlinson and Tunnell document the flurry of complaints about literature selections often used in the early grades. Gallo, another tireless campaigner for teachers' and students' rights, discusses censors' concerns about realistic young adult novels. He also explains the alarming incidence of self-censorship.

Nelson and Allen both discuss the effect that censorship attacks have on the field of social studies. Nelson considers the importance of teaching critical thinking skills in social studies courses and reviews the frequent challenges that social science teachers face. Allen reveals the biases often found in elementary and secondary school history texts. He also describes the manner in which teachers reflect their biases in using such materials in the classroom. And to complete this section, Scharmann chronicles the ongoing battle between creationists and evolutionists—from the publication of Darwin's work to the legislation passed in the United States during the 1980s. All science teachers, administrators, and school board members should consider his recommendations for dealing with this controversial issue.

Chapter 8

Censors and the New Proposals for Literacy

Robert E. Shafer

Educational researchers have proposed a variety of new methods for literacy instruction as well as new definitions of literacy in recent decades. For example, Chisman (1990) has noted that a five-part definition of adult literacy—reading, writing, and verbal communication abilities as well as mathematics and problem-solving skills—is "accepted by most of the recent scholarly literature" and has "increasingly winning acceptance by policy makers and literacy providers as well" (p. 2). Chisman continues to note that this five-part construct is often referred to as "basic skills," a term that is used interchangeably with both "literacy" and "functional literacy." Pattison (1982) proposes that "literacy is a combination of variables—individual and cultural awareness of language and the interplay of this awareness with the means of expression" (p. 7). And Tuman (1987) views literacy in a psychological sense:

> Literacy is the ability to read and write as defined in terms of the ability to understand and create symbolic verbal meanings stored in some permanent form.... Literacy, then, is nothing less than our ability to deal with discourse that projects a world—to deal in other words with the world of texts (pp. 28–30).

Giroux (1987), writing from a Freirean perspective, conceives literacy as "critical literacy" tied to and grounded in "an ethical and political project that dignified and extended the possibilities for human life and freedom" (p. 2). He sees literacy as a social movement—"part of a larger struggle over the orders of knowledge, values, and social practices that must necessarily prevail if the fight for establishing democratic institutions and a democratic society were to succeed" (p. 2). Further, Giroux sees this struggle as ongoing in the United States:

> The language of literacy is almost exclusively linked to popular forms of liberal and right-wing discourse that reduce it to either a functional perspective tied to narrowly conceived economic interests or to an ideology designed to initiate the poor, the underprivileged, and minorities into the logic of a unitary, dominant cultural tradition. In the first instance, the crisis in literacy is predicated on the need to train more workers for occupational jobs that demand "functional" reading and writing skills. The conservative political interests that structure this position are evident in the influence of corporate and other groups on schools to develop curricula more closely tuned to the job market, curricula that will take on a decidedly vocational orientation and in so doing reduce the need for corporations to provide on-the-job training. In the second instance, literacy becomes the ideological vehicle through which to legitimate schooling as a site for character development; in this case, literacy is associated with the transmission and mastery of a unitary Western tradition based on the virtues of hard work, industry, respect for family, institutional authority, and an unquestioning respect for the nation. In short, literacy becomes a pedagogy of chauvinism dressed up in the lingo of the Great Books (pp. 2–3).

Giroux's "second instance" undoubtedly brings to mind the work of Hirsch (1987) and his concern for "cultural literacy" or "core knowledge." Hirsch's *Cultural Literacy: What Every American Needs to Know,* as Simmons discussed in Chapter 6, proposes that there is a core of knowledge in history, science, literature, and the arts that every American needs to know, which should be taught specifically in public schools.

As another example of the new definitions of literacy, the concept of media literacy—meaning the development of critical abilities to evaluate the output of electronic media—was advanced by McLuhan in his early book *Understanding Media* (1962). Strassman (1983) has also expanded traditional definitions of literacy to include the "interactive computer medium" for communication; and Saloman (1983) has discussed media literacy with particular reference to television. This type of literacy will undoubtedly continue to be an important aspect of many school programs.

As definitions of literacy have changed to accommodate new technologies and shifting sociopolitical views, so too have the implications of recent research into reading and writing processes changed literacy instruction and learning. Bloome (1987) has noted that this research resulted from moving the study of literacy from the laboratory to the real world and using a variety of new methods (for instance, ethnomethodology) to study it "from the perspective of a broad range of disciplines such as anthropology, sociolinguistics, cognitive psychology, administration and policy studies, English and literary criticism, linguistics, educational sociology, special education, and developmental psychology" (p. xv). An early example, and perhaps the most strikingly original one, is Emig's (1971) study of the composing processes of 12th graders. She used case-study techniques, in particular one that she called "composing aloud," to examine how good writers compose in the "extensive and reflexive modes." Emig discovered that when students write for their own purposes, they spend a great deal of time prewriting, planning, and revising; she called this "reflexive writing" (p. 91). In the school-sponsored writing Emig observed, very little time was allowed for these activities. She labled school-sponsored writing "extensive" writing, noting that the writer was usually detached from his or her subject and that "adult others, notably teachers, are the chief audience for extensive writing" (p. 91). Emig's findings clearly showed that many teachers did not understand that writing is a process, requiring time for prewriting, planning, and revision and that attention to that process will result in both better writers and better products. During the 1970s and '80s the teaching of writing changed as many teachers began to concentrate on allowing time for the "writing process" in their classrooms. This movement was both facilitated and enhanced by the Bay Area Writing Project, now known as the National Writing Project in the United States.

As the writing process was being explored, researchers were also studying reading and the connections between reading and writing. They built on the pioneering work of Louise Rosenblatt (1938/1983, 1978) and her development of a transactional theory of reader response (explained by Simmons in Chapter 1) and began to design an intriguing model of the reading process. They suggested that print provides only the potential for meaning, but that it is the reader who always creates meaning from the text. Moving further along the same theoretical path, Brent (1992) has proposed that the reader's construction or creation of meaning is an essential aspect of the writer's process of invention.

These developments—concerned with cognitive and affective aspects of literacy learning as well as its social and political meaning and status within society—could not help but bring forth varied responses from many communities. Teachers, curriculum workers, school administrators, and parents were discouraged by the failure of early behavioristic accountability models in reading as well as the lack of attention to writing. Many welcomed the work of researchers such as Emig and the reader response theorists; teachers began to experiment with process writing combined with the use of literature in place of basal reading programs in their classrooms. Shafer, Staab, and Smith (1983) described such an experiment in a Phoenix, Arizona, elementary school in the early 1980s. Teachers began to meet voluntarily after school and on Saturdays to discuss these innovations; local and regional teacher networks were gradually formed. In the later 1980s, "whole language teachers," as they called themselves, flooded the convention programs of the International Reading Association and the National Council of Teachers of English with meetings about whole language teaching. There is still disagreement on a precise definition of whole language: for example, Froese (1991) describes it as "a child-centered, literature-based approach to language teaching that immerses students in real communication situations whenever possible" (p. vii). On the other hand, Edelsky, Altwerger, and Flores (1991) characterize whole language as the following:

> A unity of framework, theoretical base, and congruent practice...a belief that reading and writing are learned through really reading and writing (not through doing reading and writing exercises) using genuine texts—children's literature, song lyrics, dictionaries, and so on (pp. 6–7).

Objections to the New Proposals

During the 1980s, whole language became a grass roots movement throughout the United States, Canada, and many other countries, where it affects elementary language arts and reading programs in particular. Because many or most whole language teachers began to work with diverse literary texts, it was inevitable that those groups and individuals within the community who had been objecting to the use of certain books, texts, and films in schools would now have an even greater variety of materials and practices to target. In particular, objections to the new curriculum developments are focused on the uses of personal or journal writing in classrooms as a part of prewriting activities and on various works of children's literature in thematic units or in whole language programs; some even object to the term "whole language" itself. Brinkley (1991) has done research on the religious right's objections to whole language programs that include protests of the New Age religion, as discussed in Marzano's Chapter 4. (See also McClain's following chapter for details of challenges to the Impressions series whole language reading program.) Brinkley also elaborates on the particular objections that ultrafundamentalist Christians have to terms including "global holism," "multiculturalism," and the "empowerment" of students as writers. She cites a variety of specific examples such as the concept of a student-centered program, which may appear to fundamentalist parents as "self-centeredness." For instance, the assignment, "Write about a time when your parents embarrassed you," would most certainly be protested by these parents.

Brinkley also notes criticisms of the new definitions of reading similar to those Simmons and Whitson outlined earlier in this volume:

> If, as whole language theorists believe, meaning is constructed by an active reader, then meaning is a relative thing and is not entirely contained in the text, for every reader constructs at least a slightly different meaning. This logic is important to understanding the fundamentalists' perspective because of the enormous significance placed on comprehending biblical texts. For those who believe in a literal reading of the Bible, to suggest that meaning does not exist in a text reduces the impact of the Bible as the

"Word of God." To suggest that readers can construct their own meaning of the Word of God allows for a variety of interpretations that fundamentalists reject (p. 14).

Other objections are directed at the idea of conceptualizing reading and writing as meaning-making processes. With regard to writing, Phyllis Schlafly told Tom Brokaw in a January 11, 1989, interview on NBC's Evening News program that a major goal of the Eagle Forum is to force the removal of all journal writing from U.S. schools. They may be achieving this goal: Vaughn Delp, a teacher with many years' experience in the Humbolt School District near Prescott, Arizona, used journals, narrative autobiographical writing, and other writing process techniques in her high school classroom. After two members of the radical right were elected to her district school board, Delp began to receive anonymous telephone calls at home in which the callers criticized her practices and stated that they were praying for her. This harrassment continued after Delp requested students to write a response to Edwin Arlington Robinson's poem "Richard Cory." She utimately resigned (V. Delp, personal communication, May 21, 1994).

Writing about personal experiences and personal responses to a work of literature are practices frequently targeted by right-wing groups as "invasions of privacy." Moffett (1992) calls these "liberal-sounding objections" (p. 10). He further notes the comment of writer John Barth in his novel *Giles Goat Boy*: "Self-knowledge is bad news" (p. 10).

In another example, in California, various lawsuits and objections from conservative groups such as the U.S. Justice Foundation and the Rutherford Institute threaten the California Learning Assessment System, a statewide test of reading, writing, and mathematics scheduled to be given during the summer of 1994. Objections are not only about excerpts of works by writers Alice Walker and Annie Dillard, who are criticized for presenting "racial stereotypes," but also because the test does not specifically assess grammar, punctuation, and capitalization. Critics also object to the fact that the test asked students to write about their opinions and feelings and therefore ostensibly invades their privacy (Diegmueller, 1994, p. 1).

Censorship can also be exerted by government institutions. Goodman (1992) describes a situation in which the U.S. Congress ordered the Department of Education to do a study that would enable phonics to receive certification as the official government reading method. The Department of Education, which had funded the Center for the Study of Reading then at the University of Illinois, passed the charge to CSR to develop materials supporting this policy or be threatened with a funding cut if they declined. Officials of CSR found Marilyn Adams (1990), who wrote the book *Beginning to Read* to satisfy the charge. CSR then assigned Jean Osborn and her colleagues to write a digest of the book, which was ultimately sent to school superintendents throughout the United States.

Moffett (1994) contends that the traditional curriculum is very much the way it is for the purpose of controlling content. He specifically notes that "particles" with reference to phonics and grammar are "perfect for this because they avoid real subject matter—and indeed most meaning at all.... Censors actually prefer phonics for teaching literacy because letters and syllables have the least meaning and therefore render texts innocuous" (p. 97).

Reflections

So we see that there are numerous differing views between and among various groups regarding newer developments in the English language arts curriculum. Current movements to develop standards of achievement in English may only heighten these differences. It is, indeed, possible to be disillusioned about future processes for the teaching and learning of literacy if we anticipate even more complaints and challenges than we have already had. In the words of Giroux, cited earlier, we may well consider that U.S. education is in the grip of social, economic, and political forces that do not really want children to be educated in the critical literacy sense at

> "It is, indeed, possible to be disillusioned about future processes for the teaching and learning of literacy if we anticipate even more complaints and challenges than we have already had."

all. Moffett (1988) seems to echo the same thoughts when he proposes,

> A majority of the public wants schools to control the content of reading and writing. But so long as students do not find and choose the content of reading and writing for themselves, they remain essentially unengaged with school work and never learn to make the decisions that lie at the heart of composing and comprehending. Furthermore, both laity and educators fear the liberation of thought and behavior that students would achieve if talking, reading, and writing were taught most effectively—that is, if these powerful tools were freely given to youngsters for their personal investigation. Parents and teachers are unconsciously hedging and stalling on implementing a successful language arts curriculum (p. 200).

If we want to educate our students effectively, we cannot stall on implementing better language arts curricula. We must continue to research and teach with new methods of literacy instruction. This means that we also must work with parents and community members to help them understand the school's role in literacy improvement. Moffett also stresses, "A solution to this problem calls for a new covenant between school and home. Educators will have to take the initiative and enlist the laity in the teaching of those very processes of inquiry that they distrust" (p. 204). If this can be done, effective schools for the future will be ensured.

References

Adams, M.J. (1990). *Beginning to read: Thinking and learning about print*. Cambridge, MA: MIT Press.

Bloome, D. (Ed.). (1987). *Literacy and schooling*. Norwood, NJ: Ablex.

Brent, D. (1978). *Reading as rhetorical invention*. Urbana, IL: National Council of Teachers of English.

Brinkley, E. (1991). *Intellectual freedom and the whole language movement*. Unpublished research report, Western Michigan University, Kalamazoo, MI.

Chisman, F.P., & Associates. (1990). *Leadership for literacy*. San Francisco, CA: Jossey-Bass.

Diegmueller, K. (1994, May). Model exam in California is target of new attacks. *Education Week*, p. 1.

Edelsky, C., Altwerger, B., & Flores, B. (1991). *Whole language: What's the difference?* Portsmouth, NH: Heinemann.

Emig, J. (1971). *The composing processes of twelfth graders.* Urbana, IL: National Council of Teachers of English.

Froese, V. (Ed.). (1991). *Whole-language: Practice and theory.* Boston, MA: Allyn & Bacon.

Giroux, H.A. (1987). Literacy and the pedagogy of political empowerment. In P. Freire & D. Macedo (Eds.), *Literacy: Reading the word and the world* (pp. 1–27). South Hadley, MA: Bergin and Garvey.

Goodman, K.S. (1992). Why whole language is today's agenda in education. *Language Arts, 69,* pp. 354–363.

Hirsch, E.D., Jr. (1987). *Cultural literacy: What every American needs to know.* Boston, MA: Houghton Mifflin.

McLuhan, M. (1962). *Understanding media.* New York: McGraw-Hill.

Moffett, J. (1988). *Coming on center* (2nd ed.). Portsmouth, NH: Heinemann.

Moffett, J. (1992). *Harmonic learning.* Portsmouth, NH: Boynton/Cook.

Moffett, J. (1994). *The universal schoolhouse.* San Francisco, CA: Jossey-Bass.

Pattison, R. (1982). *On literacy.* New York: Oxford University Press.

Rosenblatt, L.M. (1983). *Literature as exploration* (2nd ed.). New York: Modern Language Association of America. (Original work published 1938)

Rosenblatt, L.M. (1978). *The reader, the text, the poem: The transactional theory of the literary work.* Carbondale, IL: Southern Illinois University Press.

Saloman, G. (1983). Television literacy and television vs. literacy. In R.W. Bailcy & R.M. Fosheim (Eds.), *Literacy for life* (pp. 67–78). New York: Modern Language Association of America.

Shafer, R.E., Staab, C., & Smith, K. (1983). *Language functions and school success.* Glenview, IL: Scott Foresman.

Strassman, P.A. (1983). Information systems and literacy. In R.W. Bailey & R.M. Fosheim (Eds.), *Literacy for life* (pp. 115–121). New York: Modern Language Association of America.

Tuman, M.C. (1987). *Preface to literacy.* Tuscaloosa, AL: University of Alabama Press.

Chapter 9

The Impressions Series: Courtroom Threats to Schools

Ruth A. McClain

Many censorship groups in the United States threaten school districts with lawsuits and force the removal of targeted books from classrooms and libraries. Censors are well aware that most schools face budget crunches that reduce teaching staff and cut programs. Because of this, censorship attacks force school districts to choose between appeasing censors' demands or cutting programs to find funding that will enable the district to defend its curricular choices (People for the American Way, 1990a). Recent lawsuits targeting the use of the Impressions reading series in school districts throughout the United States illustrate how this tactic is being employed in a growing attempt at censorship.

In the early 1980s the Canadian-based Holt, Rinehart and Winston publishing company began developing a whole language reading series to emulate New Zealand's successful whole language programs. Impressions—an elementary literature-based reading series—was published in 1984 and promoted as a program to help students become proficient language users through "experience and experimentation" (Holt, Rinehart and Winston, 1990): students experience language by listening and reading, and they experiment with language by speaking and writing.

Impressions, which is still being used, is based on sound research and classroom experience. It includes writing by award-winning authors such as Martin Luther King, Jr., Lewis Carroll, Rudyard Kipling, and Laura Ingalls Wilder, many examples of multicultural literature, and stories and poems that children find interesting and enjoyable. Both teachers and students were enthusiastic about the series because, in contrast to traditional basals, it contains fantastic selections such as "The Girl Who Cried Flowers"—a story about a girl who becomes an olive tree with beautiful flowers when she dies.

Initial Attacks

With all of Impressions' good intentions, what went wrong? The controversy over the series first surfaced in 1987 in several small communities in Washington and Oregon. Religious activists and parent groups charged that the texts were nothing more than primers on witchcraft, Satanism, and the occult and clamored to have the books removed from classrooms. One parent even argued that the books served no purpose except to introduce children to witchcraft step by step. Some insisted that the series was too violent and depressing; others opposed the use of Canadian spellings and the inclusion of Canadian settings; and still others claimed that the series lacked phonics and encouraged antifamily values (Instructional Materials Review Committee, 1987).

To better understand the Impressions controversy, it is important to learn more about how the religious right perceives its role in setting educational policy. In most school districts, parents generally do not feel they need to get involved in evaluating textbooks or curricula because they trust educators' and administrators' judgment to choose appropriate materials for their children. But what happens when an element of distrust develops? What happens when parents—who assume the schools are still the way they used to be when they were students—deem the curriculum inappropriate? They get angry; they get mobilized. Enter members of conservative religious groups, who believe that they have both the right and the responsibility to dictate what will or will not be taught in the schools.

In *Curriculum Challenges from the Religious Right: The Impressions Reading Series* (1991), Adler points out that objections to curricula from the religious right can be organized into three broad categories (also discussed briefly in Section One of this volume):

1. "If it was good enough for me, it's good enough for my kids." Curriculum innovations are suspect from a conservative viewpoint. The religious right places emphasis on traditional classroom procedures—lecture, recitation, supervised study.

2. "Children don't need to solve moral problems—they are told how to do it in the Bible." Evaluation of literature and decision making are viewed by the religious right as undermining the authority of the family, the church, and the Bible.

3. "No expert from a Godless university is going to tell me what is good for my child." Curriculum changes generated by well-educated professionals are seen as an affront to a common-sense approach by fundamentalists (p. 15).

Since it was initially attacked in 1987, Impressions has been challenged repeatedly around the United States and at least 18 times in California alone. A People for the American Way report indicates that the complaints against Impressions have changed very little since the first attacks: "The most frequent charges are that the series promotes Satanism, witchcraft, and the occult; that it is morbid and violent; and that it undermines parental authority" (p. 8).

Some far-right groups, including the American Family Association, Christian Educators Association International, the Traditional Values Coalition, and Citizens for Excellence in Education, have mounted organized campaigns against the series. Robert Simonds of CEE declared "war" on Impressions and claimed he would "bring public education back under the control of the Christian community" (People for the American Way, 1990b, p. 2). The enemies, according to Simonds, are "atheist" groups such as the National Education Association, the American Civil Liberties Union, and People for the American Way.

The Allegations

The Willard, Ohio, school district adopted the Impressions series for use in September 1990. Almost immediately the district began receiving complaints from parents who alleged that stories and poems about witches and goblins in the Impressions series were frightening their elementary school children. They voiced objections that echoed those previously heard in other districts:

1. The series encouraged rebellion and a lack of respect for parents.
2. The stories dwelled too heavily on death and suicide.
3. The series promoted witchcraft through the teaching of chants and spells.
4. The series contained no "quality" literature.

Some parents then approached the Willard Board of Education and asked that their children be excused from the Impressions reading. They thought that students should have alternative reading material, but the board informed them that students had to return to classes and continue using the series until the controversy could be resolved by a committee of parents, citizens, and educators. But before a committee was formed, in November ten Willard parents, represented by Don Wildmon of the American Family Association, filed a US$1.2 million lawsuit in a federal court. The parents, who claimed that the Impressions program was teaching their children about witchcraft, named the Willard Board of Education and the district superintendent as defendants.

In January 1991 the Willard parents dropped the lawsuit for reasons unknown. While this appeared to be good news at the time, it was, in fact, only a ploy to give the board time to consider a compromise proposal. This compromise—presented by a parents' group known as Citizens for a Better Curriculum—would provide alternative classes for those students whose parents did not want them to participate in classes using Impressions. If the board refused the compromise, then the committee threatened it would seek repeal of the tax levy approved by Willard voters in the 1990 fall election.

The controversy raged. The board president, who had sided with the parents' group, criticized the Willard Education Association for its support of what he deemed a controversial textbook series; he was quoted by the *Sandusky* (Ohio) *Register*

(Turnbell, 1991) as saying that teachers had made a mistake when they questioned parents' right to object to what their children were reading in school.

Willard teachers were asked by the administration because of the public concern to review the controversial series, note student reactions and parental concerns, and report their findings to the board. The WEA was greatly concerned not only by the misinformation being disseminated about the Impressions series but also by the misinterpretation of terms used regarding the censorship issue. For example, Citizens for a Better Curriculum referred to the textbooks themselves as "the curriculum" when, in fact, textbooks make up only one part of any school curriculum.

The Willard 1990–91 school year ended, and the issue of the repeal of the previously approved tax levy was to be placed on the November 1991 ballot because the board refused the compromise. The *Willard Times-Junction* (1991) reported that this "was a decision based on the political climate to see if [it] would bring about the changes these religious people wanted" (p. 6A).

In the meantime the district superintendent resigned after he received personal threats because of his support for the series, and the Willard teachers formed a coalition of their own called Coalition for Freedom to Learn. The dissenting Willard school board president, who had joined forces with the parents against the series, challenged the incoming superintendent to a debate about the validity of using the series: the challenge was declined. Instead, the superintendent made his office available to accommodate parents seeking information about the series. In addition, he made a great effort to speak to all civic groups in the community and educate them on censorship issues.

Ultimately, the board voted 4–1 to retain Impressions. The Citizens for a Better Curriculum did not accept the majority view, however, and continued to threaten school personnel and board members. The community became further divided when people on opposite sides of the controversy ceased speaking to one another. In the meantime the Coalition for Freedom to Learn and community members campaigned to defeat the tax levy repeal in the upcoming election. Their efforts proved successful when voters elected against the repeal.

Thanks to a united effort, the Willard School District survived the controversy, but complaints about the series continued to surface in other school districts, according to People for the American Way. In Woodland, California, for example, the allegation was made that an illustration of two women and a child dancing in the short story "Hooray for Three" promoted homosexuality. Still another attack involved a story in which a witch discovers a "hairy toe" in her pot of stew and devours it, allegedly suggesting cannibalism. And, as in Willard, there were numerous complaints that the series failed to teach phonics.

The Facts

The Impressions series is educationally sound. Kenneth S. Goodman, one of the foremost authorities on reading instruction, advocates the whole language approach to teaching reading. Goodman (1986) states that this approach requires that students read good literature and that phonics be taught only in the context of such reading. He and other specialists contend that the controlled vocabulary and short, choppy sentences found in traditional basals interfere with learning to read and deprive students of the enjoyment that can result from reading real literature. The Impressions series does integrate reading, writing, speaking, and listening, and phonics is taught, not as a separate activity, but with these language skills. Impressions offers many poems and stories that contain quality writing with interesting sound patterns, and students genuinely enjoy reading them.

Goodman also stresses that an effective whole language program must extend students' imagination and emotional responsiveness. Impressions has proven its educational soundness on this front as well. Adler (1991) explains,

> One of the salient features of the Impressions series is the large number of stories from the fantasy genre.... According to J.L. Singer in *The Child's World of Make Believe*, "Fantasy is clearly important for children, especially when dealing with life's difficulties, which are many if you happen to be a child in 20th-century America" (p. 5).

While Impressions does contain stories that deal with witches and ghosts, those stories were meant to be used in conjunction

---

with the secular Halloween celebration. They neither affirm nor deny any religious ideology—they only capture students' interest and stimulate their imaginations.

In addition, many of the objections to Impressions regarding witchcraft are based on simplistic and unfounded interpretations of selections and illustrations. For example, in Yucaipa, California, some parents complained that they could see the face of a devil in one of the series' illustrations. A school official examined this illustration but admitted he was unable to see anything resembling a devil. According to People for the American Way, he was then instructed by the parents to photocopy the illustration, turn it upside down, and hold it up to a mirror: the official was still unable to see a devil.

Another objection to Impressions is that it focuses too much on death. The religious right argues that when children are confronted with such material, they are emotionally upset and have nightmares. But elementary school children are often interested in reading about themes concerning death, especially in fantasy and supernatural stories (see Tomlinson's and Tunnell's Chapter 11). This interest is both natural and healthy, and dealing with childhood fears in fiction can facilitate dealing with real fears when they are encountered. Esmonde (1987) states, "The best fantasy literature, so often reviled as escapist, deals with the subject of death honestly, neither disguising the pain of the survivors nor avoiding the question of an afterlife" (p. 6).

To say that the entire Impressions series is dominated by morbidity is to practice selective reading. Many of the individual stories and poems singled out as promoting negativism are among those most often recommended for children's reading: stories such as "I'm Skeleton," "Witch Goes Shopping," and "Mummies Made in Egypt" are age appropriate and suitable to the emotional and psychological development of elementary school children. (See also Tomlinson's and Tunnell's discussion of young readers' preference and interest studies.)

Many of the objections also focused on the teacher resource books, which were placed in the superintendent's office for public scrutiny after the initial complaints. Students, however, do not use the resource book, and it is even optional for the teacher.

While much of the controversy has focused on the objections and objectors, one element has been too long overlooked—the students, teachers, and parents who have been and still are ardent supporters of the series. According to People for the American Way educators who use Impressions report increased interest and enthusiasm in reading among students; school librarians report that students regularly seek out favorite authors after having been introduced to them through Impressions; supporters praise the series for engaging students' minds with quality literature rather than "dumbing-down" the texts. We should continue to fight for these books that help children to learn and to enjoy reading.

Reflections

The Impressions controversy has been and continues to be a political and ideological crusade—a struggle for power. Opponents of the series want us to believe that educators we once considered reasonable are now part of some diabolical plot to undermine the morality of today's students. There are those whose perspective is so narrow that they fear uncontrolled ideas and divergent points of view. Free inquiry and exploration should be the watchwords of education.

I sit here with a stack of Impressions materials on my table, noting what the censors deem scary and objectionable. Yes, there are illustrations and stories about ghosts and death, but these wonderful stories and poems capture the magic of the imagination and help promote reading.

References

Adler, L. (1991). *Curriculum challenges from the religious right: The Impressions reading series.* Chicago, IL: American Educational Research Association.

Esmonde, M.P. (1987). *Beyond the circles of the world: Death and the hereafter in children's literature.* Lanham, ME: University Press of America.

Goodman, K.S. (1986). *What's whole in whole language?* Portsmouth, NH: Heinemann.

Holt, Rinehart and Winston. (1990). *Knock at the door.* (Teacher's Resource Book, Impressions Series). Toronto, ON: Author.

Instructional Materials Review Committee, Anacortes School District 103. (1987). Unpublished final report, Anacortes, WA.

People for the American Way. (1990a). *Attacks on the freedom to learn.* Washington, DC: Author.

People for the American Way. (1990b). *Religious right's attack on the Impressions Reading Series.* Washington, DC: Author.

Turnbell, M. (1991, January 9). Ex-Willard school chief says book stance fuels 'boycotts.' *Sandusky Register,* p. 3.

Willard (Ohio) *Times-Junction.* (1991, October 31). On Levy Repeal— No!, p. 6A.

Chapter 10

The Elementary School: Censorship Within and Without

C. Jane Hydrick

Censorship is alive and well in the elementary classroom. But aside from the sensation caused by an occasional assault such as the one launched against the Impressions series chronicled by McClain in the previous chapter, news stories about such censorship are scattered and not particularly detailed. It is the literature used at the secondary level, as Gallo notes in Chapter 12, that is most often challenged; but literature published for younger readers is potentially just as offensive as some of the books censored at the secondary level. However, this literature is not a significant part of the elementary curriculum, in contrast to the major role that controversial books play in secondary schools. In addition, most of the often-censored themes explicit in secondary level books, such as homosexuality, drugs, or divorce, are not discussed at the elementary level—at least, not to the extent they are in the high school classroom.

Many elementary classroom teachers are realizing that their own classroom climates might perpetuate the censorship of ideas and responses. It is not the published materials that they use so much as it is how they orchestrate the discussions, activities, and climate of intellectual freedom in their classes that determines whether censorship pervades (also noted by Small in Chapter 18).

In *Celebrating Censored Books!*, Karolides and Burress (1985) include a list of the 30 books most frequently challenged between 1965 and 1982. Only two titles, *The Adventures of Huckleberry Finn* and *The Diary of a Young Girl*, might be used regularly at the elementary level. The censorship problem in elementary classrooms lies not so much in publications that are challenged outside the classroom as in publications that never make it into the classroom for fear that they could be challenged. Books can be censored simply by being kept out of the classroom or by being altered by teachers and administrators practicing the self-censorship frequently discussed in this work. For example, I once walked into a third grade room after school hours and found the teacher drawing on a page of a book about Benjamin Franklin—a book that I knew she planned on using in a literature-study group the next week. The teacher is an extraordinary artist, so I thought perhaps she was embellishing one of the illustrations in the book. When I asked her what she was doing, her reply surprised me. One of the illustrations portrayed Benjamin Franklin as a young boy swimming naked in a river. The teacher was drawing swimming shorts on little Ben in each of the 35 student copies because she did not want to risk any repercussions from parents.

Faced with Controversial Books: Teachers' Self-Censorship and Students' Maturity

Take a slug
Squeeze its liver
Watch it wiggle
Feel it quiver

A few years ago I defended the right of my students to read the source of these words: a book that I despised but my own first grade daughter regarded as one of her favorites. One day the newspaper had published a story about local mothers who had organized an action group to have the book *Slugs* by David Greenberg removed from the city library's shelves. I agreed with the mothers' group that the book "contained disgusting rhymes and grotesque pictures" (*Mesa* (Ariz.) *Tribune*, pp. A1, A9). I also had to agree, however, with teachers and librarians in Vancouver, Washington, who had defended *Slugs* on the principle that children liked it, when a parents' group unsuccessfully attempted to have the book banned in 14 elementary schools in the Vancouver area. According to the article, *Slugs* had been hounded since its 1983 publication by unflattering reviews and by disgusted parents, teachers, and librarians.

Armed with my daughter's autographed copy of *Slugs* and the newspaper article, I decided to discuss the issue with my third graders. I was surprised when my colleagues refused to do the same or even share the book with their own classes. Had I brought *Slugs* to read to my class before the condemning newspaper article was published, other teachers might have shared it as a readaloud. But the article gave the book a certain degree of notoriety, and the teachers felt they might have to defend its selection to parents—a selection they felt more comfortable not making. This was particularly true when there were shelves of more neutral, inoffensive literature from which to choose.

When I read *Slugs* aloud to my own third grade class, the reactions were mixed, as I had anticipated: some loved it, others hated it. The children's reaction to the newspaper article reflected their feelings about the book. Those who had loved the book were incensed that it might be pulled from the shelves; those who hated the book supported the efforts to censor it. The ensuing class discussion was lively. I suggested to the students that we follow the example of the parents' group in the article and make a list of books that we would like removed from our own school library shelves. There was not one book that the whole class could agree on. Some students were polarized according to sex, others according to interest, and some because of their preferences of illustration, format, or genre. After almost an hour of debate in an attempt to reach consensus, the class reluctantly agreed that book availability had to accommodate many different tastes and needs. I reread the newspaper article to my students, and they then realized that the issue was not whether *Slugs* was a good book, but whether it ought to be available for someone who might want to read it.

Three years later, another censorship issue sparked another lively debate in my classroom, this time with fourth and fifth graders. An article in the *Arizona Republic* (1992) related an incident in Nashua, New Hampshire. A mother was putting a *Where's Waldo?* puzzle together with her five-year-old daughter and ten-year-old son when she noticed that there was a bare-breasted woman in the beach scene. Outraged, she complained to the store where she purchased the puzzle and managed to have remaining copies pulled from the shelves. The operations manager at the store was quoted as saying, "It's very small, but the woman was definitely sunbathing topless. We responded seriously to the complaint" (p. A20). The Waldo books and puzzles are favorites in my classroom, so the fourth and fifth graders conducted a firsthand inspection of the puzzle and concluded that, although the woman was indeed bare-breasted, (1) she was "a cartoon, not a real person like some of them in the *National Geographic* magazines, and we have them in the classroom, so it's even more okay for a cartoon"; and (2) "it's a puzzle and we can put it together if we want to but we don't have to so if somebody doesn't want to see her, they don't have to."

National Geographic magazines have been a rich, albeit slightly controversial, source of information and entertainment for our classroom. When the school librarian heard that we were the only classroom that would use them, we inherited several shelves' worth. The children use them for independent reading and as resources for reports. There is still an occasional giggle when they find an article with photographs of an indigenous tribe wearing less than North American society demands, but it is either ignored or met with a comment such as, "They must have found June 1979."

When parents or teachers object to a passage or illustration in a book because it is offensive and might affect impressionable children, they would do well to consider these following examples. Maurice Sendak's *In the Night Kitchen* is removed from shelves in some primary classrooms because an illustration portrays a character falling with bottom naked into a bowl of dough. When children comment on that particular section, they often seem more offended by the notion of naked body parts nestling in the dough than they are by the illustration. The whole book is a delightful excursion into utter fantasy and is usually well received by young readers.

Witches by Roald Dahl is a favorite of young readers, but it has been censored by teachers (not read aloud, not included in classroom libraries, not used for literature-study groups) because

Hydrick

of anticipated problems with parents. (See also Chapter 11 by Tomlinson and Tunnell.) One third grade teacher in my school stopped reading *Witches* to her students after receiving a note from a parent who did not want her child "frightened." All the students—including the child whose parent wrote the note—were upset when the teacher stopped the readaloud and did not understand when she told them that she could not continue because the book was not on the "approved list."

For the past three years, I have led my classes in a year-long author study of Dahl. We select one book as a readaloud, and the other Dahl books are read by individual children or in small literature-study groups. As part of the author study, we pull out phrases and situations Dahl uses that typify his works. The children keep extensive literature logs in which they respond to Dahl's books and make connections with their own experiences, other texts, and concepts. The controversial nature of Dahl's books elicits—for the first time in some fourth and fifth graders—the willingness and ability to take the risk of critiquing the author's perspective and craft and even challenging him.

In a student-initiated letter to the school librarian requesting that more of Dahl's books be purchased, the children included many of the comments they had written in their literature logs.

> He brought the fun of reading into my life and probably many more. Roald Dahl gets many good comments about his writing. I give him four stars.

> He uses words that I have never heard of. I started a list of words and phrases that he used alot. The list is already seven pages long and getting longer!!!!!!! and now when some of us read together we read my list and we laugh until we cry.

> Once you start reading a book by Roald Dahl you can't put it down. He writes in a weird way, but it's also wonderful at the same time.

> There's lots of Dahl's writing that I don't like but I still think he's a great writer. He's the most hilarious author I have read in a long time. His book *The BFG* is wonderful in a silly little way. *The BFG*'s absurd style of language like the words "whizzpop" and "search every crook and nanny" are very imaginative. He knows what we kids like to read.

He is a fabulous author, and children of all ages love his books, whether they read them by themselves, or whether someone else reads to them.

When I started to read the books written by Roald Dahl it made me want to read all over again. Now I'm reading books almost every day, not only Roald Dahl books but all sorts of books.

Good Choices Lead to Good Learning

It is easier for classroom teachers to defend and include some titles than others in their classroom activities and curriculum. For example, teachers find support for their book selections in published lists and honored books as the authors mention in Chapters 11 and 12. Choices for readalouds and literature study are often made from book lists approved by district committees, education associations, and subject-matter organizations, and from the Caldecott and Newbery Award books because they have been deemed acceptable for classroom use. Teachers can include potentially controversial books such as *Bridge to Terabithia* or *The Great Gilly Hopkins* by Katherine Paterson, *A Wrinkle in Time* by Madeleine L'Engle, and *Maniac Magee* by Jerry Spinelli in their curriculum, knowing that their selections are supported by "authorities."

But teachers still need to handle controversial books with care in the elementary classroom and be prepared for adverse reactions. When several fifth graders were engaged in a group reading of *Julie of the Wolves* by Jean Craighead George, they came to a passage where Julie is attacked by her husband, Daniel:

"Daniel, what's wrong?"
"They're laughing at me. That's what's wrong. They say, 'Ha, ha. Dumb Daniel. He's got a wife and he can't mate her. Ha.'"
He pulled her to her feet and pressed his lips against her mouth. She pulled away.
"We don't have to," she cried.
"They're laughin'," he repeated, and tore her dress from her shoulder. She clutched it and pulled away. Daniel grew angry. He tripped her and followed her to the floor. His lips curled back and his tongue touched her mouth. Crushing her with his body, he twisted her down onto the floor. He was as frightened as she.

The reading group was quiet and embarrassed. Several of the children's faces colored, and they glanced nervously at one another. A few whispered, "Yuck!" or "God!," but most of them were silent. The teacher, who hadn't read the book, expressed in a grade level meeting in our school that she had thought at the time, "Great—they'll run home with this, and I'll be drummed out of the district!" She began a discussion by saying, "I feel really embarrassed right now because of what we read, but I'm outraged that this happened to Julie. What do you all feel?" The children were a little slower to enter this discussion than they usually were, but once they began, the discussion was intense, and every child participated. They were initially upset that their heroine should have this happen to her, but realized it had to be something "this horrible, this absolutely the worst possible" to force Julie to change her life.

The passage continued, "Julie rolled to her stomach and vomited. Slowly she got to her feet. 'When fear seizes,' she whispered, 'change what you are doing. You are doing something wrong.'" The issue under discussion was no longer the almost rape: it was the role that the incident played in Julie's decision to change her life and the literature-study group's feeling that the experience helped Julie. The group agreed that the author had selected well. Not only were the readers' feelings of defense and support for Julie intensified, but Julie's journey toward self-identity was well served by this incident.

In a discussion of *The Great Gilly Hopkins* by Katherine Paterson, some fourth graders stated that they were offended by the language that Gilly used. Others agreed that it was probably not language that any of them would feel comfortable using, but in the book Gilly's "bad language" was an important part of the story. The children decided that if Paterson had made Gilly's language more like their own, it would be artificial. Gilly Hopkins is a lonely, bitter foster child who wants to be Galadriel—the cool, loved daughter of a Hollywood star. Paterson portrays Gilly as slowly becoming more like Galadriel with the love she finds in her foster home. It is the unfolding of that love and Gilly's response that endears the book and its characters to young readers. So the fourth graders' discussion of Paterson's book that began with an initial reaction of offense at a character's language turned into an opportunity for the readers to critique the author's craft of character portrayal and development.

In another illustration of how well children are able to understand and maturely deal with controversial issues (with an elementary teacher's guidance), my daughter's second grade class researched and wrote a book on the human body. The introduction, entitled "About this Study," tells the background of how the book came to be:

> This study of the human body evolved from the questions and issues which have arisen in our class throughout the school year. When Magic Johnson made his announcement about being infected with the HIV virus, many questions needed answers. Later, during our study of *The Secret Garden* there was a discussion of one of the characters and whether or not he had a dad. One of the students said, "Everyone has a dad!" Another child replied, "Unless his mom went to a sperm bank!" This set off additional conversation, and we all decided we needed to know more (from *The Human Body*, published by the second grade class at Awakening Seed School, 1992).

The introduction concludes with this:

> Two of the children described the experience so well: "We thought we were just going to learn about sperms and eggs. We didn't know there was going to be all of THIS!"

The book contains their research as well as personal commentary. The learning experience of creating the book would not have been possible if the teacher had censored the topic, the discussion, or the research. The section on the reproductive system, for example, concludes with this:

> When we first learned about all of this we were giggling and we thought it was disgusting. But now we realize how important it is. It is important because if we didn't have the reproductive system we would never be alive.

Censorship Outside the Elementary Classroom

I have presented instances in which elementary teachers have exercised censorship of classroom materials in anticipation of parent or administrative disapproval and described several examples of how elementary students are capable of dealing with controversial subject matter in a sensible and fair manner. Censorship of elementary material also occurs outside the school and is reported in newspapers much more frequently than is censorship that happens inside the elementary classroom. In December 1992 the superintendent of a small school district in Arizona made a unilateral decision to ban the "bookmobile" from its service to an elementary school. In a letter to the county library officer (P. Lewiston, personal communication, December 8, 1992) the superintendent wrote about his own son, a fifth grader:

> He brought a paperback novel to his mother and suggested that he thought the book was possibly something he should not be reading, and that he recognized seeing the "F" word while reading it. A cursory gleaning of the content not only revealed prevalent use of the "F" word and other patently offensive language, but at least four separate acts of intercourse and oral copulation found throughout the length of the book, described in their full graphic and specific terms, complete with the attendant erotic physiological responses ("moans and groans") of the participants. Such material is no less than full blown pornography.

Later in the letter, the superintendent wrote in more general terms:

> Public education today needs all the support it can get. Public services such as the library can and should be an integral partner in providing for our community's educational needs. However, societal considerations too have to be taken into account. The state of our moral constitution as a society is in obvious disarray.... A degree of rational judgment and control must be applied somewhere, at some point, and it is falling more and more to the few enclaves of consistent traditions of morals and values left in our society, among them the school and public library.

The superintendent and county library officer agreed that for more than 25 years the bookmobile had provided a unique service to the entire county and had served as a primary resource for a wide range of materials to the schools. In the library officer's response to the superintendent (D.A. Gaab, personal communication, December 28, 1993), however, she noted,

Public libraries do not act in loco parentis, as schools do. In a society like ours, in which there is great diversity of opinion and values from family to family on all types of controversial issues, the public library cannot impose any one standard or value for all children. When a parent signs a child's library registration card, he/she agrees to be responsible for his/her own child's use of library services and materials.

Two weeks later, in an open letter to the district parents, the superintendent gave further cause for his banning of the bookmobile:

I will not put myself in a position of responsibility where there is any possibility of any child obtaining sexually explicit or dangerously deviant material.... My action was swift, due to my resolve to ensure that no other child would possibly obtain such material at the next bookmobile visit, only two school days away... (P. Lewiston, personal communication, January 15, 1993).

At the same time, an editorial in a local newspaper exclaimed, "This is not meant to encourage censorship. It is not an effort to ban books. This editorial is aimed at promoting common sense...simple values" (*Arizona Range News,* 1993, p. 1). The common sense the writer proposed was that the bookmobile "take a good hard look at what it stocks and immediately implement a system to monitor its books. Remember, our tax dollars are buying these books and supporting the bookmobile." The editorial ended with this suggestion: "If it takes banning books to put some values back into society, then we might need to think about banning books."

The same week, in another newspaper a columnist offered support for the bookmobile:

Parents, not librarians or school superintendents, should decide what their children read at home. It's their responsibility, legally and morally, to do so. And if parents do take personal responsibility for their children's reading, listening, and viewing habits, and in doing so, provide loving, wise supervision and guidance—those kids will grow and learn in a positive way, despite all the negative influences surrounding them. If parents don't do so, their children will learn all the wrong lessons, regardless of what's on the bookmobile's shelves. Book banning or bookmobile boycotting won't solve the problems of the world. Nor will it protect children from corrupting influences. But it might stunt young minds in need of intellectual nourishment (Anderson, 1993, p. 4).

When the district's school board convened to make a decision to support or oppose the superintendent's banning of the bookmobile, one group of parents submitted a petition with over 200 signatures in support of keeping the bookmobile service. Another editorial from a larger city's newspaper stated,

> Banning the bookmobile is no way to help children make that distinction (between good and bad literature). It sends them only one message: that a ban on all reading material is the appropriate way to protect them from the "bad" literature. And that message is far more dangerous than a book with a few erotic passages (*Arizona Daily Star*, 1993, p. 2).

Others came forward to plead for the unique services the bookmobile provided as a source for fiction and nonfiction material to the school.

After listening to both sides of the issue, the board voted 4–1 to uphold the superintendent's ban, with one board member saying the bookmobile should not be allowed to visit the school until the county could ensure that some books wouldn't "fall into the wrong hands" (*Arizona Daily Star*, 1993, p. B1). A teacher defended the superintendent's action claiming, "The teachers can be liable if inappropriate literature gets into the hands of the students" (p. B1). A father of two school-age daughters said the superintendent "has the right to protect our children...children's minds have got to be protected" (p. B1). At the time this chapter was written, the ban was still in effect.

Elementary Classrooms in the Future

It is disturbing to realize that books are kept out of classrooms by forces outside of the classroom as well as by teachers who sometimes alter texts and illustrations in anticipation of problems with parents or supervisors. Perhaps even more disturbing, though, is the realization that some classroom teachers are not aware that they manipulate classroom climates and hinder children's learning as a result. The classroom climate can foster diversity, creativity, and ingenuity of thought and endeavor or it can limit learning experiences.

For many years, most elementary classrooms were dominated by the curriculum contained in a basal reading series and other prescribed texts. The teacher's manual consisted of scripted lessons in which children were asked to respond to questions regarding the reading. In recent years, however, movements such as whole language have contributed to the replacement of the set-meaning text notion with the idea that each of us responds to any text in a unique way. Ten years ago, a teacher reading *Charlotte's Web* aloud to a class might have been horrified to discover a child who did not love Charlotte, and perhaps would have encouraged that child to "come around." In today's classroom, whether *Charlotte's Web* is used in a literature-study group, as a readaloud, or as an individual reading selection, the teacher well versed in reader response theory will support any child's personal response to the story and encourage students to articulate their feelings and interpretations, however they may or may not agree with traditional responses.

There appears to be more latitude in today's classrooms for a diversity of responses in every subject area—from math to science to social studies to language arts. The black and white world of indisputable fact is yielding slowly to a world of negotiated meaning and relativity. In this new world there is no room for censorship.

References

Anderson, M. (1993, January 22). Columnist's support. *The Daily Dispatch*, p. 4.

Arizona Daily Star. (1993, February 5). Board votes, p. B1.

Arizona Daily Star. (1993, February 5). Editorial, p. 2.

Arizona Range News. (1993, February 11). Editorial, p. 1.

Arizona Republic. (1992, October, 19). "Where's Waldo?" In the dog-house, p. A20.

Karolides, N.J., & Burress, L. (Eds.). (1985). *Celebrating censored books!* Urbana, IL: National Council of Teachers of English.

Mesa (Ariz.) *Tribune.* (1989, September, 27). Bugged by slugs, pp. A1, A9.

Chapter 11

Children's Supernatural Stories: Popular but Persecuted

Carl M. Tomlinson
Michael O. Tunnell

Supernatural tales have always drawn children to the printed page. "Supernatural" is defined in *The Random House Dictionary of the English Language* as "of or pertaining to, or attributed to ghosts, goblins, or other unearthly beings; eerie; occult." The same source defines "occult" as being "beyond the range of ordinary knowledge or understanding; mysterious." A supernatural tale, then, is one in which unearthly beings or mysterious events figure prominently, as in ghost stories, mysteries, fantasy, and stories of horror and sorcery. Teachers and librarians have long been aware of children's fascination with these stories; researchers, too, have noted their significance and ability—like that of all high-interest genres—to encourage the self-initiated reading practice that creates literate people (Fielding, Wilson, & Anderson, 1984).

While children have been drawn to supernatural tales, some adults have decried them, as happened with the Impressions series described in Chapter 9. It is a fascinating dichotomy, this perennial popularity and persecution of children's stories that deal with supernatural themes. But spooky tales seem to have become more objectionable than usual within the last decade. Alexander (1992), for instance, reports that witchcraft is one of the subjects most frequently cited as offensive by censors in California, and Doyle (1991) reports that 22 percent of books challenged or banned in the United States from May 1990 to May 1991 involved supernatural topics. Could it be that these stories are being challenged more often because they are more popular with children than ever?

Popularity of Supernatural Stories with Children

The formulaic nature of supernatural tales, as described by Danielson (1983), may be one reason children like them. They provide a predictable, familiar reading or listening experience. Young readers know how these stories work, and they not only expect but greatly enjoy the surprising or shocking turns of event.

Young readers' taste for supernatural tales becomes apparent when reading preference and interest studies are examined: a review of the most important of these studies of the last 50 years reveals that the supernatural story has long been one of the top three or four choices and often the top choice. As Table 1 shows, children—regardless of their sex, ethnicity, or IQ—have consistently chosen mystery, ghost, fantasy, and horror stories as their preferred reading.

Another indication of the popularity of supernatural tales with children is how often they are selected as the winners of children's book awards. Of particular interest are children's choice awards, which are given in various U.S. states and decided by popular ballot. In most of the 38 children's choice award programs in the United States, nominations are made by children who then must read a minimum number of books on the final list in order to be eligible to vote for their favorite. According to Jones's *Children's Literature Awards & Winners* (1988), of the 426 children's choice award books from 1977 to 1987, 40 titles were easily identifiable as supernatural tales—a significant figure when the variety of genres published is considered. Other sources reveal that such stories have recently won children's choice awards with even more frequency. For instance, the Rebecca Caudill Young Reader's Book Award, instituted in Illinois in 1988, had two ghost story winners in its first five award years. Even more impressive is the fact that Mary Downing Hahn's *Wait Till Helen Comes* and Betty Ren Wright's *The Dollhouse*

Table Incidence of Supernatural Stories as a Preferred Genre in Children's Reading Interest Studies

Researcher (year)	Subjects	Top Genre Choices
Thorndike (1941)	children ages 10–15	**mystery**, animal stories, mild adventure
Ashley (1970)	900 fourth to seventh graders	mysteries, adventure, comics, **ghost stories**
Barchas (1971)	children from four ethnic groups	**mystery**/adventure, animal stories, humor
Downen (1971)	third to fifth graders	Boys: **mystery**, sports, how-to books Girls: **mystery**, fairy tales, **modern fantasy**
McKay (1971)	gifted and average students	All IQs: adventure, animal stories, sports, **mystery** Higher IQs: biography, humor, **mystery**
Chui (1973)	fourth graders	Boys: sports, biography, **mystery** Girls: **mystery**, humor, adventure
Beta Upsilon Chapter, Pi Lambda Theta (1974)	children ages 9–10	Boys: science, sports, **mystery** Girls: **fantasy**, **mystery**, books about people
Conway (1975)	fourth to eighth graders	Boys: **mystery**, hobbies, sports; Girls: romance, feminine activities, **mystery**/detective
Gallo (1983)	elementary and secondary students (1646 males, 1752 females)	**mystery**, romance, **horror/supernatural**
Hawkins (1983)	gifted fourth to sixth graders	**mystery**, **fantasy**, adventure, humor
Haynes (1988)	fourth graders	Boys: adventure (**mystery**/suspense, sports, other worlds/**modern fantasy**)[a], space, adventure (animals, **mystery**, other worlds/**modern fantasy**) Girls: realistic (**mystery**, animal, sports), growing up, adventure (**mystery**, personified animals/**modern fantasy**, other worlds/**modern fantasy**)

Note: Stories of the supernatural were included in the mystery or fantasy category unless otherwise noted.
[a]Highly correlated items were grouped together through factor analysis to form categories.

Murders and *Christina's Ghost*—ghost stories all—together garnered 26 children's choice awards between 1988 and 1992.

Persecution of Supernatural Tales for Children

Censorship attempts on supernatural tales have increased significantly in the last decade. Many of these recent challenges echo those reviewed by the previous authors in this work: censors have claimed that Daniel Cohen's *Curses, Hexes, and Spells* is a virtual "how-to" manual on devil worship and that Zilpha Keatley Snyder's 1971 Newbery Honor Book *The Headless Cupid* could lead young readers to embrace Satanism (Doyle, 1991). Censors have also objected to the three guardian angels (Mrs. Who, Mrs. Which, and Mrs. Whatsit) in Madeleine L'Engle's Newbery Award–winning time-warp fantasy *A Wrinkle in Time* on the grounds that these characters promote belief in witchcraft, crystal balls, and demons (Doyle, 1991). And protesters allege that Eve Merriam's poetry in *Halloween ABC* encourages devil worshipping and that Patricia Clapp's work of historical fiction *Witches' Children: A Story of Salem* entices readers to dabble with the occult (Doyle, 1991).

During an interview with Mark West (1988), children's book editor Phyllis J. Fogelman remarked,

> In the 1970s and early 1980s most of the censorship letters received by publishers related to sexuality, but now censors are broadening their scope to include anything that seems even vaguely anti-Christian to them. For a number of fundamentalist groups, certain words are seen as red flags. If a book simply includes the words *devil* and *witch*, it's enough to cause these people to file a complaint (pp. 111–112).

It is disconcerting that censors have such little respect for children and find them so impressionable that they will inevitably act on what they read. The logical extension of this would suggest that children are not being taught at home to distinguish between right and wrong, fantasy and reality—something one would think fundamentalist Christian parents would be good at doing. Do these parents have so little confidence in their child rearing that they believe that their children cannot make sound moral decisions after reading "questionable" materials? Censors, who are convinced of the highly impressionable nature of children, seem to believe that reading about devils, witches, and ghosts not only makes young readers believers in these incarnations, but also influences them to inevitably become devil worshippers.

Opponents of the censors take quite a different view of these books and their effects on young readers. Selectors—those who believe in the right to object to a book but reject the notion of denying that book to everyone else (Jalongo & Creany, 1991)— find in the same books some positive values for children, some of the same values found in the Impressions reading series, as McClain noted earlier in Chapter 9, and in other controversial books, as Hydrick explains in Chapter 10. They find that such well-written, thoughtful books as L'Engle's and Clapp's not only foster children's imagination and creativity (Schlessinger & Vanderryst, 1989), but also help children confront their own capacity for wrongdoing (Raburn, 1985); they recognize that books such as Cohen's help children satisfy their curiosity about the unknown (Danielson, 1983). Finally, they realize that many ghost stories simply give children a satisfying thrill by allowing them to meet the challenge of fear without the risk of harm (Barish, 1991).

> **"Censorship, therefore, on a very direct, immediate level may possibly interfere with a child's attainment of reading fluency."**

Censorship's Effects on Children

In reading research this statement has become nearly axiomatic: children improve their reading ability by reading (Leinhardt, Zigmond, & Cooley, 1981). It follows that anything that impedes children's self-initiated reading practice does not, at the very least, promote reading fluency and, at most, may hinder it. Censorship of supernatural stories denies children a substantial body of literature of proven popularity—literature that many children would choose to read given the opportunity. Censorship, therefore, on a very direct, immediate level may possibly interfere with a child's attainment of reading fluency.

What of the long-term, indirect effects of censorship? Wray (1988) argues that *autonomy*—the ability to define purposes for oneself and to evaluate information—is essential to literacy; these same abilities are also fundamental to the development of critical thinking. Will children who never have the opportunity to judge for themselves whether a book has something worthwhile to offer be able, as adults, to select and evaluate literature for their own purposes? In Wray's words, "Autonomy cannot be developed in children by depriving them of it" (p. 40). Selectors know that children's vicarious experiences in confronting, engaging, and judging the forces of good and evil in many supernatural stories exercise their critical thinking skills—skills that later can be applied to real-life experiences. We must consider whether children who never are allowed to differentiate between real and unreal or good and bad will be able to recognize the moral issues presented by society. Further, if they recognize the issues, will they then have the inclination to consider all pertinent perspectives in order to make informed decisions? There are no definite answers to these questions, but the skill and conviction with which we exercise our autonomy are surely improved with practice.

We believe that when their books are censored, students lose. The examples of how attacks on supernatural stories can negatively affect children are indicative of the danger inherent in censorship of children's books in general. When censorship undercuts students' freedom to match their book choices with their interests and then to evaluate the wisdom of their choices, their opportunities to develop as readers and thinkers are diminished.

References

Alexander, F. (1992). The censorship challenge. In B.E. Cullinan (Ed.), *Invitation to read: More children's literature in the reading program* (pp. 166–176). Newark, DE: International Reading Association.

Ashley, L.F. (1970). Children's reading interests and individualized reading. *Elementary English, 47*(8), 1088–1096.

Barchas, S.E. (1971). *Expressed reading interests of children from differing ethnic groups.* Unpublished doctoral dissertation, University of Arizona, Tucson.

Barish, E. (1991, November 3). Scare tactics. *Chicago Tribune Magazine,* pp. 16, 20.

Beta Upsilon Chapter, Pi Lambda Theta. (1974). Children's reading interests classified by grade level. *The Reading Teacher, 27*(7), 694–700.

Chui, L. (1973). Reading preferences of fourth grade children related to sex and reading ability. *The Journal of Educational Research, 66,* 369–373.

Conway, E.H. (1975). *Reading interests of children in grades four through eight.* Unpublished doctoral dissertation, University of Alabama, Tuscaloosa.

Danielson, L. (1983). "The National Inquirer," Peter Straub, and Henry James all in the same classroom. *Illinois English Bulletin, 70*(2), 1–10.

Downen, T.W. (1971). *Personal reading interests as expressed by children in grades three, four, and five in selected Florida public schools.* Unpublished doctoral dissertation, Florida State University, Tallahassee.

Doyle, R.P. (1991). *Banned books week '91: Celebrating the freedom to read.* Chicago, IL: American Library Association.

Fielding, L.G., Wilson, P.T., & Anderson, R. (1984). A new focus on free reading: The role of trade books in reading instruction. In T.E. Raphael (Ed.), *The contexts of school based literacy* (pp. 149–160). New York: Random House.

Gallo, D.R. (1983). *Students' reading interests—A report of a Connecticut survey.* New Britain, CT: Central Connecticut State University. (ERIC Document Reproduction Service No. ED 232 143)

Hawkins, S. (1983). Reading interests of gifted children. *Reading Horizons, 24,* 18–22.

Haynes, C. (1988). *The explanatory power of content for identifying children's literature preferences.* Unpublished doctoral dissertation, Northern Illinois University, DeKalb.

Jalongo, M.R., & Creany, A.D. (1991). Censorship in children's literature: What every educator should know. *Childhood Education, 67*(3), 143–148.

Jones, D.B. (1988). *Children's literature awards & winners* (2nd ed.). Detroit, MI: Gale Research.

Leinhardt, G., Zigmond, N., & Cooley, W.W. (1981). Reading instruction and its effects. *American Educational Research Journal, 18,* 343–361.

McKay, M.A. (1971). *Reading interests of intermediate students.* Unpublished doctoral dissertation, University of Pittsburgh, Pennsylvania.

Raburn, J. (1985). Shuddering shades! A ghostly booklist. *Top of the News, 41*(3), 274–281.

Schlessinger, J.H., & Vanderryst, J.D. (1989). Supernatural themes in selected children's stories of Isaac Bashevis Singer. *Journal of Youth Services in Libraries, 2*(4), 331–338.

Thorndike, R.L. (1941). *A comparative study of children's reading interests.* New York: Bureau of Publications, Teacher's College, Columbia University.

West, M.I. (1988). *Trust your children: Voices against censorship.* New York: Neal-Schuman.

Wray, D. (1988). Censorship and literacy. *Reading, 22*(2), 137–142.

Chapter 12

Censorship of Young Adult Literature

Donald R. Gallo

The Adventures of Huckleberry Finn by Mark Twain
Antigone by Sophocles
Black Boy by Richard Wright
Brave New World by Aldous Huxley
Bridge to Terabithia by Katherine Paterson
The Catcher in the Rye by J.D. Salinger
Catch-22 by Joseph Heller
The Chocolate War by Robert Cormier
The Color Purple by Alice Walker
The Crucible by Arthur Miller
A Day No Pigs Would Die by Robert Newton Peck
The Diary of a Young Girl by Anne Frank
Fallen Angels by Walter Dean Myers
A Farewell to Arms by Ernest Hemingway
The Grapes of Wrath by John Steinbeck
A Light in the Attic by Shel Silverstein
The Merchant of Venice by William Shakespeare
1984 by George Orwell
One Day in the Life of Ivan Denisovich by Alexander
    Solzhenitzyn
The Outsiders by S.E. Hinton
The Pigman by Paul Zindel
Slaughterhouse-Five by Kurt Vonnegut, Jr.

To Kill a Mockingbird by Harper Lee
The Wizard of Oz by Frank Baum

Any well-read individual will recognize most of these titles as being among the most highly regarded literature from ancient to modern. All of these books are on required reading lists somewhere between grades 6 and 12 in many U.S. and Canadian schools, both private and public. Many of them have been revered for centuries (*Antigone*, for instance), others for only recent decades (*Brave New World* or *To Kill a Mockingbird*), and several for just the past few years (*Fallen Angels*). All of these books have been the focus of censorship attacks, with *Huckleberry Finn* topping the list. These are only a small number of titles and authors that have been challenged, with new titles being added to the list each year.

It means nothing to the attackers that these books have been viewed by scholars as outstanding contributions to the fields of world literature, British literature, American literature, or young adult literature. Several in the latter category have been honored by the Young Adult Services Division of the American Library Association (1988) as being among "The Best of the Best Books" published for teenagers during the past 25 years.

Common Rationales for Attacks on YA Books

Books for teenagers, more commonly known as young adult— or just YA—literature, are often more susceptible to censorship attempts than are classics. Parents—as well as teachers—are less likely to support a newer, unfamiliar book because they did not grow up with it. For example, creative English teachers in the early 1960s encountered great resistance to their teaching *The Catcher in the Rye* because parents and older colleagues had not read that novel. Many of today's English teachers, having grown up with (or after) Salinger, view *Catcher* as a modern classic and use it as required reading. In fact, its contents and language are tame in comparison to some books written for teenagers today. (Familiarity with and greater acceptance of *The Catcher in the Rye*, however, have not diminished attacks on it. As a result of its relatively frequent use as well as its controversial history,

Catcher continues to remain near the top of the list of the most frequently challenged books in the United States.)

Similarly, *The Outsiders*, *The Pigman*, *The Chocolate War*, and a few other YA novels that have been around for 20 years or more are now viewed as classics and are widely taught. But comparatively few teachers feel comfortable teaching newer YA novels such as Chris Crutcher's *Chinese Handcuffs*, Ouida Sebestyen's *The Girl in the Box*, or Bette Greene's *The Drowning of Stephan Jones*, regardless of their quality, because those books have not yet proven themselves over time. Many teachers still teach the "tried and true" because they are uncomfortable with uncertainty and they fear the unknown. Further restraints on what literature teachers can use in their classrooms are imposed by school administrators who have never heard of particular titles and by school board members whose own education did not include those books or authors.

Censors also target contemporary YA books because of their content. Unlike their predecessors from the 1940s and '50s—peopled by the squeaky-clean Nancy Drew or the politely polished Hardy boys, where good was clearly delineated from evil, which was always punished—the characters in the best of today's YA literature are realistically portrayed, deal with issues that are more gray than either black or white, face painful realities of contemporary society, such as divorce, abortion, alcoholism, homosexuality, child abuse, physical disabilities, death, corrupt officials, and AIDS, and represent a wider variety of ethnic groups. The reaction from protesters is to demand content that is consistent with their personal worldview, to the exclusion of all other viewpoints, as detailed in earlier chapters.

For example, during the 1992–93 school year Madeleine L'Engle's *A Wrinkle in Time* was attacked in one Texas community by people who believe it is "anti-Christian," while citizens in other Texas towns objected to *Lord of the Flies* and *Romeo and Juliet* because of their "sexual content" (Dart, 1993). In Windsor, Connecticut, *The Effect of Gamma Rays on Man-in-the-Moon Marigolds* by Paul Zindel was attacked because it contains profanity, alcohol abuse, and cigarette smoking (Suhor, 1993, p. 7). And in Des Moines, Iowa, a parent objected to the profanity and violence in both the film and the book *The Outsiders* by S.E. Hinton (Suhor, 1993, p. 6).

A 1990–1991 middle school controversy in Harwinton/ Burlington, Connecticut, is a case in point. A parent, frustrated with her inability to have Katherine Paterson's *Bridge to Terabithia* removed from her son's sixth grade reading list a year earlier, objected to eighth graders having to read books such as *A Day No Pigs Would Die, Summer of My German Soldier*, and *The Pigman*. She and her supporters alleged that these popular books were "undermining family values," making "subtle attacks on church or God," and focused on death. She added that other books "promote the occult and witchcraft," though she named none specifically (D. Beach, personal communication, November 2, 1990). During a radio talk show this parent stated her belief that controversial literature should not be used as classroom material; she also said that as a parent she wants her children to avoid situations and environments and books that contradict the values she wants them to learn during their impressionable years.

She not only has the right to make these statements, but as a parent she has a legal obligation to protect her children from harm. The problem is that she wanted to "protect" all other children in that school system by restricting what teachers could teach, and that is neither her right nor her obligation, as Cormier stressed in Chapter 7.

And, as all the authors in this anthology agree, if we do not provide our students with a variety of literature—however controversial—and teach them to read it and discuss it critically, we cannot hope that they will ever develop into sensitive, thoughtful, and reasonable adults. Author Richard Peck (1992)—himself the focus of parental censorship as well as public condemnation by the Eagle Forum's Phyllis Schlafly for his light-hearted *Blossom Culp* novels involving the supernatural—has created a banner we might all post over our classroom and library bookshelves: "Readers Have Nothing To Fear; Nonreaders, Everything" (p. 817).

There had not been until recently a body of literary criticism or analysis to help establish YA literature as worthwhile and legitimate. With the publication of *Presenting Robert Cormier* in 1985, Twayne Publishers instituted their Young Adult Author series of biography and criticism that now includes analyses of the works of many authors who write for young readers, including Sue Ellen Bridgers, Rosa Guy, S.E. Hinton, Norma Fox Mazer, Walter Dean Myers, Richard Peck, William Sleator, and Paul Zindel. Dell Publishing Company has also issued updated paperback versions of several books in this series so that information about these authors and their works is much more accessible to students and teachers.

But a body of literary criticism is, unfortunately, of little use to would-be censors. The angry parents in Connecticut were unfazed by a list of awards the books they were protesting had received. The parent who voiced her beliefs on the radio show stated that she didn't care what critics say and that she is the best critic of what is acceptable for her children to read. She demonstrated an attitude that is found in other censorship cases as well: she uniformly distrusted the teachers' judgments, questioned their morality, and ignored their expertise. This parent and other protesters acted as if the teachers had chosen the books arbitrarily, when, in fact, those educators had carefully selected the best books they could find that would both interest students and meet the learning goals of their curriculum.

Many would-be censors have objected to certain books without having read (or understood) the entire book—selected passages out of context are usually sufficient for them to defend their claims, as in the case described by Rosenblum in Chapter 5. Responding to notification that his short story "In the Heat," published in *Sixteen: Short Stories by Outstanding Writers for Young Adults* (1984), was attacked by a parent and her supporters, Robert Cormier wrote (see also Chapter 7 in this work),

> Although attempts at banning my work are not new to me, they are always upsetting. But especially upsetting is the attack on this short story. I'm astonished by this woman. If, after reading "In the Heat," a story that deals with the love between fathers and sons, the anguish that the death of loved ones brings, the ultimate comfort possible through family love—if, after all that, she can only find some words and phrases to fasten on, I can only wonder about her lack of sensitivity and compassion. And wonder what kind of mother she is to a vulnerable adolescent (R. Cormier, personal communication, January 8, 1991).

After the Attacks: Self-Censorship

In the Connecticut case, after several well-managed public hearings during which the books' detractors as well as their supporters spoke, the school board voted to retain the controversial books in the eighth grade curriculum. A key factor in these hearings were comments from former students about the effects that those books had had on them. Censors, however, do not usually listen to students, do not respect their opinions, do not even ask them what they think and feel (as Simmons observed in Chapter 1). However, in this case the decision makers did care and did listen, and then they voted to keep the books in their curriculum.

In spite of the positive outcome of this and other incidents, the fallout often has long-range negative effects. When teachers in other school systems see the trouble that colleagues get into elsewhere over teaching a book written by, say, Robert Cormier, they are more likely to avoid teaching anything by Cormier in order to prevent possible attacks on their curriculum. That word *possible* is the key. In fear of potential controversy, some teachers, library media specialists, and school administrators choose to self-censor certain books, thereby denying students access to those materials. They choose instead selections they expect will be safer. But English teachers as well as librarians and school boards delude themselves by assuming that they are safe with the "tried and true" choices: nothing is safe.

> **"In fear of potential controversy, some teachers, library media specialists, and school administrators choose to self-censor certain books, thereby denying students access to those materials."**

A few years ago I overheard two teachers from Texas telling a book salesperson that they would never order copies of my short story collection *Sixteen* for their junior high classes because one of the stories used the word "breast," and another used "damn." In another incident, a library media specialist in a Connecticut middle school told a college student interviewer that because there is a "small but vocal conservative element" in their town, she buys "less controversial" books for her school's library to avoid potential conflicts (Harvill, 1992).

In another Connecticut town, a junior high school English teacher attempted to teach Nat Hentoff's *The Day They Came to Arrest the Book*—a story about the controversy over the use of *The Adventures of Huckleberry Finn* in a fictional high school. The teacher had hoped to use this lively, informative, balanced account to help her students examine the issues in a true-to-life controversy. But before the class read very far into the book, a district administrator told the teacher she had to stop teaching it immediately—it was not on the approved list. Other books not on the "approved list" had been used by other teachers in that school system, but this one was singled out for an unusual kind of censorship—the censoring of a discussion of censorship. Because of budgetary cutbacks and recent teacher layoffs, the untenured teacher was in no position to challenge her superiors; so the issue went unreported and unrecorded, except for my being told about it by a concerned colleague.

A less obvious kind of self-censorship comes from major textbook publishers who wish to make their anthologies as appealing to as many people as possible (see also Allen's chapter in this section). Although this is understandable, in their fear of offending anyone, publishers often elect to exclude some selections that might otherwise be of value. For instance, Maureen Crane Wartski's "A Daughter of the Sea," a short story about racial prejudice against a Vietnamese girl, which appears in *Join In: Multiethnic Short Stories by Outstanding Writers for Young Adults* (1993), was recently being considered for inclusion in a major publishing company's literature series. But because some editors disapproved of the Vietnamese girl's being called a "gook" and "slope-head" by the class bully, the publisher decided against including the selection. Part of the point of Wartski's story is to show that the bully is prejudiced, but the editors rejected the story out of fear of offending Vietnamese students and their parents—in the same way that some black parents have been offended by the word *nigger* in *The Adventures of Huckleberry Finn* (as Simmons mentioned in Chapter 6). As a result of this kind of timidity on the part of textbook publishers, students read sanitized literature collections containing less substance and variety than they otherwise could have.

Future Challenges

There will be more and more attacks as we attempt to introduce new and exciting literature into our classrooms and libraries. We must be prepared for those attacks, and we must not censor ourselves by avoiding books that have been controversial. In addition, we must support one another within our departments and our school districts when *any* single book is attacked. There is a lot of sensitive, lively, thought-provoking literature being written for students today; they deserve to have access to those books and to have an open and supportive arena in which to discuss them.

References

Campbell, P.J. (1985). *Presenting Robert Cormier*. New York: Twayne.

Cormier, R. (1984). In the heat. In D. Gallo (Ed.), *Sixteen: Short stories by outstanding writers for young adults* (pp.154–162). New York: Delacorte.

Dart, B. (1993, September 2). Study ranks Texas third in school censorship efforts. *Austin American-Statesman*.

Harvill, K. (1992, November). Unpublished student report, Central Connecticut State University, Bridgeport, CT.

Peck, R. (1992, January 1). The great library-shelf witch hunt. *Booklist*, p. 817.

Suhor, C. (1993, February). Censorship update: NCTE protects the student's right to read. *The Council Chronicle*, pp. 6–7.

Wartski, M.C. (1993). A daughter of the sea. In D. Gallo (Ed.), *Join in: Multiethnic short stories by outstanding writers for young adults* (pp. 86–96). New York: Delacorte.

Young Adult Services Division. (1988). *Nothin' but the best: Best of the best books for young adults 1966–1986*. Chicago, IL: American Library Association.

Chapter 13

Social Studies and Critical Thinking Skills Versus Censorship

Jack L. Nelson

Because critical thinking is essential in a democracy, the central purpose for teaching social studies is to develop critical thinking skills in students, as Simmons and Whitson discussed in detail in Section One. But because censorship opposes the pursuit of these skills, social studies is the content area most often subjected to challenges. Thus the core of social studies is eroded by the existence and the threat of censorship.

As enlightened political philosophers and educators have argued, democracy depends on a knowledgeable populace, free to explore ideas. At the time of divine right of kings, democracy was considered a radical and dangerous governing system, but it has become the system of choice for most of the world's population. As de Tocqueville (1850/1969) noted in his examination of the United States, "The first duty imposed on those who now direct society is to educate democracy..." (p. 12). In dictatorships, where the government controls communication, politics, economics, and personal freedom, censorship is one of the means by which leaders maintain their position of power. Less obvious are the censorship and pressure to conform in more democratic systems, but such efforts to manipulate and control are still evident, and there is a tension that resists free expression of ideas, even in democracies.

The determining requirements for self-governance are freedom and knowledge; an ignorant or a restricted populace cannot sustain democracy. Dewey (1936) stated it succinctly: "Since freedom of mind and freedom of expression are the root of all freedom, to deny freedom in education is a crime against democracy" (p. 136). And Russell (1928) pointed out that without universal education, "democracy cannot exist except as an empty form" (p. 128). Education in a democracy requires access to and examination of knowledge, the freedom to explore ideas, and the development of skills in critical study.

Among the many social institutions, the most organized, popularly attended, and legitimate agency designed to express civic knowledge—the competence to be self-governing in democratic societies—is the school, as Simmons noted in Chapter 1. Schools have as one of their primary charges from society the responsibility to prepare young people for membership in society. They are expected to convey civic knowledge and values, correct presumed deficiencies that might result from other socialization agencies (for example, media, peers, family), develop critical thinking abilities, and provide ethical development related to active and positive membership in society (Nelson, Carlson, & Palonsky, 1993).

Critical Thinking and Social Studies

All school subjects share in this concern to teach critical thinking skills: math and the sciences advocate use of critical inquiry; the arts incorporate critical judgment with creative endeavor; and the more thoughtful approaches to vocational and physical education encourage critical thinking as necessary for personal improvement. Rote memorization, robot-like modeling behavior, and repetitive drill may often be used in introductory skill work in schools, but no school is satisfied to provide only this form of skill instruction. Development of critical thinking skills in students is the primary rationale for teaching the social studies, as mentioned earlier. Social studies exists as the educational link between the civil society and the stu-

"**Social studies exists as the educational link between the civil society and the student.**"

dent. It is intended to provide students with knowledge, values, and skills useful in their individual development as members of the society, with the improvement of society as a related purpose. There are several different descriptions of and terms used for critical thinking. Sternberg (1985) reported that thinking skills include problem solving, decision making, inferencing (deductive and inductive), divergent thinking, evaluative thinking, and philosophy and reasoning. These categories came from a compilation and dissemination of ideas from leading scholars on thinking processes. Each subskill requires access to information, consideration of alternative points, and a level of freedom to pursue the inquiry.

The best approach to developing critical thinking is the subject of some dispute in the field. One important issue involves whether critical thinking can properly be described as a process separate from its practice in examining a social issue. A general framework for explaining this skill is (1) identifying and defining an issue or problem; (2) stating a hypothesis or question; (3) gathering and evaluating information; (4) testing the hypothesis or considering a potential answer; and (5) drawing a tentative conclusion and making decisions (Nelson & Michaelis, 1980). But this is just a framework—not a step-by-step guide to practice critical thinking. Much of the early work on critical thinking attempted to describe it as though it were a separate process that included several distinct and teachable steps. But now there is an appropriate concern, as Parker (1991) indicates, about teaching thinking as a series of steps in mechanical form: the idea that reasoned and critical judgment is no more than a mechanical set of steps that can be mastered like the multiplication tables and applied at random as the need arises is inconsistent with the basic rationale for critical thought. A mechanical application of a sequence of steps is, in fact, antithetical to the idea of critical thinking, which is more holistic and complex, requiring sophisticated intellectual activities within the context of social or personal issues. It may be subject to analysis in terms of several steps, as the earlier framework suggests, but that does not mean that it is well learned by repeating those steps. Further, the mechanistic approach to critical thinking does not require the same level of access to information and freedom to explore that actual critical thinking demands.

Dewey (1933) recognized this problem in his initial formulation of the scientific method, a precursor of many models of critical thinking. Dewey noted that his description of steps in the process of scientific thought was only an analysis by hindsight of one way scientists develop ideas; but Dewey identified intuition and other possibilities as perfectly suitable ways for scientists to come to know things.

Contemporary views of good teaching methods in social studies incorporate critical thinking techniques into the substance of the course. Parker's (1991) analysis of research on critical thinking supports the idea that thinking not be taught as a separate set of steps, divorced from topics under study. This incorporation is easiest when social studies is recognized as the study of social problems or human issues, and its purpose is to examine an issue and apply thinking processes to make decisions about how to deal with it. Studying social studies through issues almost automatically involves critical thinking, because the content necessarily includes important questions with no obvious answers. Issues make it much more difficult to sterilize the content and make it neutral. Issues, also, are more likely to create concerns among teachers about controversy and potential censorship. Dealing with such topics as abortion, sex and sexual orientation, crime, AIDS, consumer protection, environmental protection, religion, privacy, and current political debates can make some teachers nervous but makes social studies much more exciting, meaningful, and realistic for students. Setting up classroom discussion around debates, role playing, simulations, conflicting essays, and other expressions of divergent views fits well with an issues approach and with the stimulation of critical thinking. Issues lend themselves to having students engage in interviews, surveys, interpreting data, critical reading, and posing ethical critera; each of these techniques includes critical thinking.

It is unfortunate for critical thinking advocates that most social studies curricula are dominated by the study of chronological history and separate social science disciplines, which can easily be taught as a series of finished events and social science vocabulary lessons. This can be, as some students know, a boring approach to social studies. High-quality social studies teaching in the standard disciplinary curriculum requires teachers to find ways to engage students in thinking processes by making history and the social sciences much more lively and relevant. This demands that history, sociology, political science, economics, geography, psychology, and anthropology be seen as unfinished and continuing areas of dispute that need student thinking throughout.

Having students take on the role of Native Americans at the time of Western European exploration of the New World can lead to serious questioning of textbook treatments of the period. Similarly, a debate over Columbus as hero or tyrant can be thought-provoking, but it can also upset some parents. If students conduct oral history interviews of local community members who have been on different sides in local political battles, it can lead to very appropriate questions for class examination but might cause disturbances in town. Student examination of historic efforts of the U.S. government and the local school board or town council to censor what people can read or hear can lead to important knowledge in a democracy, but it can also lead to calls to the principal.

Studying current social events by using economic, political, psychological, or sociological techniques can provide a more lively and vital course if students collect their own data and are given the opportunity to analyze it from divergent perspectives. A student-run survey of racist practices in local housing, the school, or the shopping district can be very interesting and educational, but it may raise some public questions. Student examination of sexism or social class discrimination in local businesses involves critical study, but it may become a lightning rod for attacks on the schools. Active student participation at local community meetings to practice what they are learning in political science classes gives students opportunity to apply critical thinking, but it may not be met with approval by all community leaders.

These are all good social studies teaching practices in their use of real human situations as the basis for practicing critical thinking and decision making. But they may cause some school administrators to caution teachers and some weak teachers to self-censor.

Censorship and Social Studies

Social studies has engendered much the same criticism as controversial literature, as discussed in previous chapters, mainly from conservatives in society and education who disapprove of its effort to integrate knowledge and teach critical thinking (Jenness, 1991; National Commission on Social Studies in the Schools, 1989; Ravitch & Finn, 1987). To iterate, this right-wing criticism holds that citizenship should be dependent on patriotic exercises, passive acceptance of traditional authority, and simple recitation of ethnocentric and nationalistic interpretations of historical information.

Jenkinson (1990), who authored Chapter 3 in this work and who has studied censorship issues in schools for about 20 years, has identified more than 200 targets of censorship; the first item on the list of 50 he included in 1990 was "critical thinking skills." Also included in Jenkinson's list were many of those topics mentioned in earlier chapters and others, such as news stories that cover human events like war, death, violence, and sex; values clarification or moral dilemmas; drug and alcohol abuse; and global studies.

Many of these issues are commonly discussed in social studies classes. It is apparent that because of its necessary link to historic, political, economic, and social issues, social studies is the most vulnerable of all subject fields taught in schools, as mentioned earlier (Nelson & Ochoa, 1990). Attacks from the right and left, liberal and conservative, radical and reactionary, traditional and progressive are commonplace. Social studies is overlaid with threats and actions of censorship that compromise the field's central purpose.

There are many examples of overt censorship, direct attempts to limit or restrict what teachers and students may study in social studies. Here are a few examples:

- While I was teaching in California, a local school board passed a motion that required any material that included Russia in it to be approved by the board. Rather than fight this absurd imposition in a courtroom, the social studies department responded by sending the board a list of all world maps and all textbooks that included Russia in the index and saying they could not teach until it was all cleared. The board rescinded the policy, but the threat to teachers remained.

- Man a Course of Study (MACOS) was a multidisciplinary project developed by widely respected Harvard University professors for use in upper elementary school classrooms in the United States to explore human cultures. MACOS was, in my view, the best of the elementary social studies projects in the 1960s. A controversy arose about the accurate depictions of some cultural behaviors, and many school districts restricted the use of MACOS. Despite its well-recognized quality, MACOS was virtually eliminated from school use by the mid-1970s. The National Science Foundation, which had financially supported the development of MACOS, was investigated by congressmen and decided to eliminate funding for social studies educational projects.

- Values education had emerged as an important topic for social studies teaching in the early 1970s in the United States. Most values education advocates wanted students to examine social values and engage in critical thinking. Values clarification, the most relativistic of nine major values education approaches, became known for some teacher techniques that right-wing critics claimed were invasions of family privacy. There were also claims of anti-Americanism made against values clarification. In response, school districts passed policies that prohibited or severely restricted values education and the use of values education materials. More than 20 years later, many schools still censor or restrict values education materials and teaching.

- I was recently called by the New Jersey American Civil Liberties Union about a potential censorship problem in the high school in Metuchen, a town noted for its high-quality schools and protection of academic freedom. Two honors students had decided that the school-sponsored newspaper was too bland and did not provide for student critical thinking on social issues. They obtained permission from some standard news magazines (such as *Time* and *Newsweek*) to reprint stories on social topics and started a privately operated student paper. The high school principal attempted to censor some material the students wanted to reprint, and they protested. Because the U.S. Supreme Court had decided in the Hazelwood case in Missouri that principals could censor school-sponsored papers, this principal apparently thought he had the authority to restrain the private paper. The board, after hearing most community members speak out against the censorship, did not pursue a censorship policy. In other districts, of if the students had not had the courage to protest, censorship would have been easy and hidden.

Whether a social studies teacher adopts a traditional view of the field (emphasizing history with "good" citizenship as a goal) or a more progressive view (stressing the study of social and personal issues and using multiple disciplines and ideas with the improvement of civilization as a goal) the subject material includes social dispute and divergent values. In the more traditional tract, the study of history is the study of conflicts over time. It is controversies and their resolution that inform historical scholarship, but that scholarship is subjective—that is, historians place different values on the same information. There is, then, controversy in the content of historical study as well as controversy in historiography. Nationalistic historical study—a common pattern in social studies courses in all nations—involves the attempted inculcation of patriotic versions of events and information and the censorship of historical material considered antipatriotic (Naylor, 1974; Nelson, 1978). Thus, the nature of even traditional social studies instruction is controversial. The more progressive forms of social studies are even more controversial because they teach value-laden historic and contemporary issues that arouse strongly held views of parents and others in the society.

In addition to direct complaints and attacks on social studies classes or material, there is another type of censorship evident in this field—covert or self-censorship, as Gallo described in the previous chapter. One example is the school principal who is contacted by a parent who protests a teacher's comments or use of certain material. The principal calls in the teacher and recommends against such behavior; the teacher acquiesces to avoid problems. Except for the complaining parent, the principal, and the teacher, no one else knows of the censoring. Another example is the school librarian who will not order a text for fear that it might offend some local group. Self-censorship may be a worse, and is a more extensive, obstacle to good social studies instruction and to the development of critical thinking than is overt censorship.

Self-censorship is usually hidden: the teacher merely decides not to deal with controversial material, and no one knows the better. There are some examples, however, of obvious teacher self-censorship. A teacher in a local school wanted her students to read *One Day in the Life of Ivan Denisovich* by Alexander Solzhenitzyn in her social studies class, but she was offended by the swear words in the novel. Using a pen, she marked out each swear word in each copy of her classroom set of books. A parent complained when she saw the book her child was reading for homework; she said that the teacher was censoring, and the board of education agreed. The teacher was required to replace the books with new, uncensored ones. My suspicion is that this board is unusual in its protection of student and teacher freedoms to examine controversy.

Most forms of self-censorship occur when a teacher knowingly avoids or sterilizes a controversy. Sometimes that avoidance is fully legitimate and well within the protections of teacher and student academic freedom. Other times the teacher restriction of what can be examined is clearly censorship without educational merit.

Over the past quarter century, I have interviewed teachers in schools in three U.S. states (New Jersey, Colorado, California) to discern their ideas about academic freedom and censorship. While nearly all teachers indicated that they think they have academic freedom in general, most avoided highly controversial topics. In response to questions on specific controversial topics in such areas as sex, religion, economics, politics, social class, and patriotism, the majority of teachers indicated that they would not treat such topics even though they agreed they were appropriate to social studies. This self-limitation of social studies topics is a form of self-censorship.

The teachers were asked why they would not discuss controversial topics that were obviously within social studies and relevant to the courses taught. They gave various reasons, which I categorized as personal, professional, and political. Personal reasons are exemplified by the response "I don't feel comfortable enough on that topic; it is too embarrassing to me." Professional reasons seem to be characterized by statements such as "The students I have now are too immature to deal with that topic." A political reason would be "The principal might call me in to warn me not to talk about that topic." Personal and professional reasons are clearly understandable and well within the good teacher's proper academic decision making. The political reasons, however, represent the chilling effect that actual and threatened public censorship of topics creates for social studies teachers. Political reasons are obviously not as educationally supportable as personal or professional reasons for restricting student inquiry. They also show the weakness of academic freedom as it is practiced in schools. It is unfortunate that over 75 percent of the teacher interviewed gave reasons that are in the political category.

It is in this difficult context of controversy and censorship that good social studies instruction attempts to provide critical thinking to students. Academic freedom for teachers and students is the one essential element in the schools of a free society. It is in the interests of society, schools, and students to foster and protect this freedom as a prerequisite for critical thinking.

References

de Tocqueville, A. (1969). *Democracy in America.* (J.P. Mayer, Trans.). New York: Doubleday. (Original work published 1850)

Dewey, J. (1933). *How we think.* Boston, MA: D.C. Heath.

Dewey, J. (1936). The social significance of academic freedom. *Social Frontier, 2,* 136.

Jenkinson, E.B. (1990). Child abuse in the hate factory. In A. Ochoa (Ed.), *Academic freedom to teach and to learn* (pp. 10–20). Washington, DC: National Education Association.

Jenness, D. (1991). *Making sense of social studies.* New York: Macmillan.

National Commission on Social Studies in the Schools. (1989). *Charting a course.* Washington, DC: Author.

Naylor, D. (1974). *An in-depth study of the perceptions of public school educators and other significant school-related groups concerning aspects of nationalistic education.* Unpublished doctoral dissertation, Rutgers University, New Brunswick, NJ.

Nelson, J. (1978). Nationalistic education and the free man. In R.P. Fairfield (Ed.), *Humanistic frontiers in American education* (pp. 139–147). Englewood Cliffs, NJ: Prentice Hall.

Nelson, J., Carlson, K., & Palonsky, S. (1993). *Critical issues in education* (2nd ed.). New York: McGraw-Hill.

Nelson, J., & Michaelis, J. (1980). *Secondary social studies.* Englewood Cliffs, NJ: Prentice Hall.

Nelson, J., & Ochoa, A. (1990). Academic freedom, censorship, and the social studies. *Social Education, 49,* 424–427.

Parker, W. (1991). Achieving thinking and decision-making objectives in social studies. In J.P. Shaver (Ed.), *Handbook of research on social studies teaching and learning* (pp. 345–356). New York: Macmillan.

Ravitch, D., & Finn, C. (1987). *What do our 17-year-olds know?* New York: HarperCollins.

Russell, B. (1928). *Skeptical essays.* London: Allen & Unwin.

Sternberg, R. (1985). *Beyond I.Q.: A triarchic theory of human intelligence.* New York: Cambridge University Press.

Chapter 14

History Textbooks, Critical Reading, and Censorship

Rodney F. Allen

Despite the democratic aims for education that Nelson detailed in the previous chapter, the dominant methods of instruction in history and the social studies are lecture, discussion, and recitation based on textbooks (Gross, 1988; Sewell, 1988) that contain prepared tests, worksheets, and guides to mastery. Ravitch and Finn (1987) describe the typical history classroom:

> Students listen to the teacher explain the day's lesson, use the textbook, and take tests. Occasionally they watch a movie. Sometimes they memorize information or read stories about events and people. They seldom work with other students, use original documents, write term papers, or discuss the significance of what they are studying (p. 194).

Teachers believe in the utility of textbooks and expect to "cover the content" during the school year. Students are expected to learn this information-oriented content—largely vocabulary and facts (Goodlad, 1984; Wineburg & Wilson, 1988). Research by Cornett (1987) and Hyland (1985) indicates that coverage of the history textbook is regarded as a teacher's primary obligation and that many teachers depend on the textbook for knowledge.

Textbook Criticism

While history teachers may find their textbooks useful, critical reviewers of those same books have complained about the texts' dull and lifeless prose, the superficial coverage of many topics, terms, and details without meaningful contexts, the lack of critical interpretation, the stress on the status quo, and the absence of conflict and controversy (Beck & McKeown, 1991). Critical reviews of civic and government textbooks by Carroll et al. (1987) and by Patrick and Hoge (1991) reinforce these conclusions.

The reason that the history textbook has consistently received poor reviews from scholars is twofold. First, because of the continuing controversy in historiography that Nelson noted, the content of textbooks is reduced to bland consensus views. And second, because of pressure from various parent and community groups, school district textbook-adoption committees are forced to purchase books that will not cause controversy—again, books that emphasize a consensus view. As a result, the most frequently adopted textbooks in U.S. school districts stress "safe" common beliefs and values (acceptable conventions) over controversy, conflict, and views that reflect diversity. Little attention is paid to rebels, dissenters, and naysayers, especially those who reject commonly held beliefs (Apple & Christian-Smith, 1991). Scant attention is paid to social class, the divisiveness of competing interests and loyalties, or the conflicting myths and symbols in our images of ourselves. Authors of history textbooks write about the ideal far less than the actual. Textbooks, thus, offer students what Apple (1993) calls "official knowledge" (similar to the "factual knowledge" that Simmons and Whitson referred to as what conservatives prefer their children learn).

Even when transcribing this "official knowledge," history textbook authors rarely define principal meanings and ambiguities of the key concepts and values in society (Apple, 1993). So much time and space are devoted to summarizing the "basic facts" of

> **"Stale, superficial, and platitudinous history books tend to support 'right-answer,' fact-mastery teaching and learning."**

history that little is left for meaning making, alternative interpretations, study of any issue or topic in depth, or lively discourse.

Therefore, stale, superficial, and platitudinous history books tend to support "right answer," fact-mastery teaching and learning. There is little textbook content or class time devoted to what Cherryholmes (1990) advocates for civic education: (1) the careful reading of texts to reflect on the stories and the meaning of those stories; and (2) the development of skills to critically read social and political texts for alternative meanings.

For example, consider the following excerpt:

> In 1812 a Russian visitor to the United States noted that almost everything in the nation appeared to be done by some sort of special machine....Some of these specialized tools were adapted from inventions of people in other countries, particularly the British.
>
> Americans also developed their own ideas. In 1785 Oliver Evans of Philadelphia designed a mechanical gristmill—a mill in which grain was ground into meal or flour.... Evans had developed an early way of using mechanical devices to do work formerly performed by people (Divine, et al., 1991, p. 315).

From this passage students proceed to read about interchangeable parts and the factory system, in which the academic focus is on the changing manufacturing scene early in the United States. No linkage is made with ideas of economic development in the students' own time or in the world community. No reflective questions are raised about innovation in societies or even about the demographics of early industrialization in the United States, the labor shortage that favored labor saving innovations and, alas, slavery.

The following textbook passages are directed to student mastery of the concepts of economic influences on farm life and the quality of life for women in the U.S. western plains in the 1800s:

> Between 1889 and 1893, some 11,000 Kansas farm families lost their homes. Their mortgages were foreclosed by the banks for failure to make their payments.... Thousands of farms lay abandoned for years, houses and barns decaying amid thistles and dust. The number of tenant farmer families—those who did not own the land they worked—doubled from 1 to 2 million between 1880 and 1900, most of the increase coming after 1890 (Conlin, 1991, p. 532).

Life on the plains was especially hard for women. They lived as colonial women had in the early days of the country. Because there were few stores on the plains, pioneer women made clothing, quilts, soap, candles, and other goods by hand. All the food needed through the long winter had to be cooked and preserved.

Families on the plains usually lived miles apart. As a result, families had to look after themselves. Women had many duties. They had to educate their children themselves.... Women helped with planting and harvesting and took care of sewing, cooking, washing and housekeeping (Davidson & Batchelor, 1991, p. 455).

These texts give the information. In contrast, the voice of Mrs. Susan Orcutt in the following letter to Kansas Governor Lewelling in 1894 conveys a pathos across time that the textbooks have not conveyed:

Dear Governor,
I take my Pen In hand to let you know that we are Starving to death. It is Pretty hard to do without any thing to Eat hear in this God for saken country[.] [W]e would of had Plenty to Eat if the hail hadent cut our rye down and ruincd our corn and Potatoes[.] I had the Prettiest Garden that you Even seen and the hail ruined It and I have nothing to look at[.] My Husband went a way to find work and came home last night and told me that we would have to Starve[.] He has bin in ten countys and did not Get no work[.] It is Pretty hard for a woman to do with out any thing to Eat when She doesent no what minute She will be confined to bed[.] If I was In Iowa I would be all right[.] I was born there and raised there[.] I havent had nothing to Eat to day and It is three o clock[.]
well I will close rite Soon
From Mrs. Susan Orcutt
(from the Kansas State Historical Society)

Mrs. Orcutt's text raises questions for students to read critically and to ponder. They can consider the problems of real income decline, drought, depression, and socioeconomic influences and ask, "Why does Mrs. Orcutt see Iowa as a place where she would be 'all right' in contrast to her plight in Kansas?" "What does here experience tell her about the comparative advantage of life in Iowa, where she implies that she had a community, a network of support?"

Self-Censorship in History Textbooks and Instruction

There is another factor that restricts the content of history textbooks and their use in the classroom: the self-censorship practiced by publishers and teachers, which Gallo and Nelson also pointed out. Publishers constantly assess current trends and public opinion when designing textbooks for schools. Their sales figures are also a constant source of feedback on current educational practice. This knowledge is used to keep authors and editors on the fairways of convention, away from the tall rough and sand-traps of controversy and alternative voices.

Teachers generally conform to the perceived norms of their community as well and design their lessons to avoid controversy. The socialization of new teachers even includes stories of parents' past complaints and school authorities' dictums (Nelson, 1991). Schools seem to have a "zone of tolerance" within which teachers of history and social studies are expected to instruct (Boyd, 1979), reminiscent of the "approved list" of literature for English teachers that Gallo and Hydrick referred to earlier in this work. While this zone may vary from school to school and region to region, teachers are expected to know the limits. Authorities who select history and social studies textbooks know the conventions and the limits as well. As Carlson (1987) argued, "Academic freedom dies from abandonment in local communities; it atrophies because teachers fail to exercise it for fear of being penalized" (p. 430).

Timid teachers and tepid texts should not be surprising. Both are caught in the turmoil over what history instruction should be. On the one hand, we have high ideals for teaching all social studies: we see it as reflective, even critical, inquiry on past and current issues. Others advocate that teachers should transmit culture, heroes, and great deeds and that students should passively accept this information. Both sides in this conflict agree that history instruction should impart some normative knowledge, but what are these norms, and who should determine them? In this context, history textbooks and courses of study become controversial and are targets for all parties who seek to influence or control what is taught and how history is learned (Cherryholmes, 1978, 1991).

Closed Areas: What We May Not Teach

In response to changing norms and conventions, authors of history and social studies curricula and textbooks frequently block off certain topics as "closed areas." Issues closed to critical reflection are those that confront conventional thinking, raise controversial issues, or offend powerful interests—commercial or political. In the United States, such censorship began early when in 1677, a synod of clergy in Boston, Massachusetts, listed 82 forbidden opinions that were to be rooted out of private and public discourse as unhealthy, unsafe, erroneous, and blasphemous (Fischer, 1989). Heresy was defined and heretics purged.

Following the U.S. Civil War in 1867, E.J. Hale and Son school publishers in New York advertised, "Books prepared for southern schools, by southern authors, and therefore free from matters offensive to southern people" (Nelson & Roberts, 1963, pp. 24–26). The pride in the United States that was spurred by World War I caused searches to eradicate what was unpatriotic and unpopular from history textbooks. Beginning in the 1920s Christian fundamentalists' aversion to evolution being taught in the curriculum began its influence on publishers and teachers (see Scharmann's following chapter). Beale's (1936) famous study in the 1930s showed teachers as largely fearful and reluctant to undertake the study of controversial topics. During World War II the zone of tolerance narrowed; following the war, in the atmosphere of anticommunist sentiment, many state governments issued mandates that required students to master fundamental truths about the evils of communism and the virtues of the free-enterprise system. In 1951 the National Education Association's Committee on Tenure and Academic Process warned teachers that sex, criticism of prominent people, criticism of church and state, race relations, and communism were dangerous territory, and labor relations were to be handled "with extreme tact."

In the mid-1950s, Hunt and Metcalf (1955) published their influential teaching methods book that urged secondary teachers to consider classroom teaching focused on social issues, both historic and current, to develop the social understanding that students need as citizens in democratic communities. Hunt and Metcalf specifically identified areas of American life that teachers were discouraged from discussing with their students. These "closed areas" focused on the problematic aspects of American culture, including "elements of personal and social conflict that are sometimes closed to rational examination." They also noted, "The closure may arise from community taboos or personal prejudice" (p. 24). Problematic areas of American culture included sex, courtship and marriage, race relations, religion and morality, social class, nationalism and patriotism, power and law, and economic system issues.

Each new era brought new orthodoxies and redefined heresies. Closing areas to reflective and critical thought has been enforced in schools through textbook-adoption or -selection procedures and through community pressure to muzzle thoughts or teaching activities that stray from orthodox sociopolitical belief (Apple, 1990, 1993; Apple & Christian-Smith, 1991). Publishers and teachers tiptoe around explosive topics, offer students tepid explanations, and gloss over closed areas that cannot be avoided altogether with "factual mush" (Delfattore, 1993).

> "**H**istory textbooks say more about how we were than how we are or came to be; they almost never stimulate reflection on what we might become."

Even when controversial issues have been included in history textbooks and instruction, they tend to be removed from our daily lives: they are safely in the past ("back then...") or far away geographically ("over there..."). Social education cannot come too close to personal experiences or to community realities. Remote and abstract is deemed better than here and now. Our history books say more about how we were than how we are or came to be; they almost never stimulate reflection on what we might become. If U.S. students study religion at all, it is the faith and community of Puritans or Bedouin, not religious traditions in Tallahassee, Florida, or Tacoma, Washington. Middle school students are more likely to learn "facts" about the religious traditions of the Buddhists in Japan than the Baptists of Dallas, Texas, or the Bahai of Detroit, Michigan.

The Geography in United States History video series produced by the Agency for Instructional Technology (1991) illustrates how society's and the schools' "zone of tolerance" affects the content of history textbooks. One 20-minute video program and accompanying lesson activities about Native American Indians focus on "The Clash of Cultures on the Great Plains, 1865–1890." Students view a magnificent color presentation on the Lakota people of the Sioux tribe and listen to the imitated voice of a Sioux leader, Red Cloud (1822–1909), to understand how the Lakota way of life changed as Europeans settled on the Great Plains. The program's instructional objectives emphasize the details of this cultural clash and the consequences it had for life on the Great Plains. But even this engaging program, which offers students more opportunity than do most history textbooks to examine and question past conflicts, still remains irrelevant to students' lives. Although the concepts of "subjugation" and "indigenous people" are covered in the video, when will publishers, authors, and teachers engage students in reflective inquiry on cultural clashes in their school, community, or region, using insights involving these concepts?

Another program in this AIT series is entitled "Americans Build the Panama Canal, 1901–1914." The video informs students about the project's conception—from Admiral Alfred Thayer Mahan's ideas on the importance of sea power to "U.S. development" to the U.S. government's perceived "need" for the Panama Canal as a link between the Atlantic and Pacific Oceans. President Theodore Roosevelt, who oversaw the project, is presented as insightful and determined. No mention is made of the concepts of "indigenous people" and "subjugation" (used in the earlier video program in this series); no mention is made of U.S. imperialism and empire. The voice heard in this program is Roosevelt's, and the text is Mahan's. The canal is portrayed as a grand trophy, earned through American know-how, diligence, and foresight. No alternative views are afforded to students; no questions are raised for critical reflection. Again, this instructional program is well within the zone of tolerance, but it is not linked to students' lives. For example, teachers could help students examine the theme of power and technology in the video series by asking them about the interstate highway that came through their neighborhood or the nuclear power plant in the nearby town. But, of course, in most communities teachers cross the zone of tolerance when they make such personal connections.

Inclusion: What Must Be Said

In the same manner that groups pressure publishers to exclude material, certain groups demand that other material is included in history textbooks, as Simmons explained in his Chapter 6 on political correctness. Inclusion in a textbook is perceived as a validation of one's group and its rightful place in American society. These demands for multiple voices make the textbook an increasingly massive tome, emphasizing detail and "coverage" over ideas and interpretation. The books must include every bit of information that a textbook evaluator, teacher, parent, or interest group may expect or demand to see.

Arguments favoring study of the Holocaust provide an example of how inclusion works. A survey for the American Jewish Committee reported that 22 percent of the adults polled said that it seemed possible that the Holocaust never happened; another 12 percent said they did not know if it was possible. The responses from younger people were distressingly similar (Roper Organization, 1993). More than 50 years after the Warsaw Ghetto Uprising and the liberation of Nazi death camps, there is growing ignorance about the Holocaust. Such surveys and the increasing interethnic tensions in Germany, the United States, and other countries heighten demands for increased multiethnic studies in history books. Each addition adds detail, but also reduces the space needed for in-depth study of themes and content.

For many years the Anti-Defamation League of B'nai B'rith has reviewed textbooks critically to eliminate stereotypes and promote the inclusion of lessons on toleration, discrimination, and ethnic cooperation (Anti-Defamation League, 1944; Perlmutter, 1992). Since 1965, the Council on Interracial Books for Children has examined storybooks and textbooks for negative portrayals of people of color; CIBC also addresses other forms of bias, including sexism and discrimination against the handicapped, elderly persons, and homosexuals (CIBC, 1980, 1982). In response, publishers have removed offensive material but then have closed off treatment of increasingly controversial topics. Ignoring sensitive topics seems to be much easier than expanding opportunities for the systematic study of intolerance, prejudice, and discrimination.

Demands for greater inclusion raise interesting questions for educators concerned about academic freedom, censorship, and history textbooks. Will the trend toward more inclusive curricula and texts with multiple voices and interpretations mean that, for example, Holocaust revisionists and deniers get a place to argue that the Holocaust never happened (Kakutani, 1993; Lipstadt, 1988)? Does the concern for adding content to history textbooks to enhance minority students' self-esteem mean that events will be reinterpreted or that new "questionable" information will be inserted (see, for example, Afrocentric claims from Asante, 1987, 1988; Semmes, 1992)? Or, will some groups still be ignored, as the Koreans are in Japanese textbooks (Halloran, 1993)?

Critical Reading and Today's Textbooks

Writing and publishing history textbooks will always be a political act in a democratic society. Establishing criteria for book selection and designing curricula using these textbooks are public policy matters and, as such, are part of that same political process. If we want books to include the open study of controversial issues and the careful documentation of diverse voices, then we must win them *first* in the political arena in order to have them in our classrooms.

In Chapter 1 of this volume, Simmons distinguished basic comprehension from critical reading. Current history textbooks are amenable to teaching strategies that only help students learn basic comprehension. These textbooks are poorly designed to support instruction and learning directed to critical reading. Teachers and students may find it possible with these texts to learn and apply discrete skills such as detecting bias, recognizing value orientations and ideologies, identifying unstated assumptions, and determining the relevance of information to a judgment or conclusion. However, it is far more problematic for students to grasp that history is written from one point of view, and that other voices offer alternative views. Those voices are not present in the textbook; it is a monologue. Students cannot easily integrate evidence to warrant conclusions, because they rarely read material that contains conflicts, controversial issues, and historical dilemmas; few problems are raised for students to solve (McKee, 1988). Important skills, such as evaluating a source of evidence, cannot be developed in the absence of real documents (Lipman, 1988; Yankelovich, 1991). Fear of censorship and the resulting self-censorship have created textbooks for history and other social studies courses that do not foster critical reading. The lack of engaging controversy, the stupor of excessive detail, and the absence of personal relevance for students result in a didacticism in the classroom—an anathema to motivation for critical reading in history courses.

Educators are left with one hope and one task. The hope may be found in the research that shows that those teachers best educated in the discipline of history do rise above the problems with textbooks (Wilson & Wineburg, 1988): they present multiple voices from other sources, offer interpretations, reflect with students on issues of cause and effect, link the past to the students' present, and use past conflicts to reveal the mysteries of limited government and democratic aspirations. The task is one of political education in communities. Educators must be active in the political arena and try to open "closed areas." We must work in communities to promote the open study of history. If we are successful, we will control our past and our future together.

References

Agency for Instructional Technology. (1991). *Geography in United States history: A video series with teachers' guide.* Bloomington, IN: Author.

Anti-Defamation League of B'nai B'rith. (1944). *The ADL Bulletin.* New York: Author.

Apple, M.W. (1990). *Ideology and curriculum* (2nd ed.). New York: Routledge.

Apple, M.W. (1993). *Official knowledge: Democratic education in a conservative age.* New York: Routledge.

Apple, M.W., & Christian-Smith, L.K. (1991). *The politics of the textbook.* New York: Routledge.

Asante, M.K. (1987). *The afrocentric idea.* Philadelphia, PA: Temple University Press.

Asante, M.K. (1988). *Afrocentricity.* Trenton, NJ: Africa World Books.

Beale, H.K. (1936). *Are American teachers free?* New York: Scribners.

Beck, I.C., & McKeown, M.G. (1991). Substantive and methodological considerations for productive textbook analysis. In J.P. Shaver (Ed.), *Handbook of research on social studies teaching and research* (pp. 496–512). New York: Macmillan.

Boyd, W.L. (1979). The politics of curriculum change and stability. *Educational Researcher, 8*(2), 12–18.

Carlson, K. (1987). Academic freedom in hard times. *Social Education, 51*(6), 429–430.

Carroll, J.D., et al. (1987). *We the people: A review of United States government and civics textbooks.* Washington, DC: People for the American Way.

Cherryholmes, C.H. (1978). Curriculum design as a political act. *Theory and Research in Social Education, 6*(4), 60–82.

Cherryholmes, C.H. (1990). *Political scientists on civic education: A non-existent discourse.* Elementary Subjects Center Series No. 15. East Lansing, MI: Michigan State University, Institute for Research on Teaching.

Cherryholmes, C.H. (1991). Critical research and social studies education. In J.P. Shaver (Ed.), *Handbook of research on social studies teaching and learning* (pp. 41–55). New York: Macmillan.

Conlin, J.R. (1991). *Our land, our time: A history of the United States.* Austin, TX: Holt, Rinehart and Winston.

Cornett, J.W. (1987). *Teacher personal practical theories and their influence upon teacher curricular and instructional actions: A case study of secondary social studies teachers.* Unpublished doctoral dissertation, Ohio State University, Columbus, OH.

Council on Interracial Books for Children. (1980). *Guidelines for selecting bias-free textbooks and storybooks.* New York: Author.

Council on Interracial Books for Children. (1982). *Stereotypes, distortions, and omissions in United States history textbooks.* New York: Author.

Davidson, J.W., & Batchelor, J.E. (1991). *The American nation.* Englewood Cliffs, NJ: Prentice-Hall.

Delfattore, J. (1993). *What Johnny shouldn't read: Textbook censorship in America.* New Haven, CT: Yale University Press.

Divine, R.A., Breen, T.H., Frederickson, G.M., & Williams, R.H. (1991). *America: The people and the dream.* Glenview, IL: Scott, Foresman.

Fischer, D.H. (1989). *Albion's seed: Four British folkways in America.* New York: Oxford University Press.

Goodlad, J.I. (1984). *A place called school.* New York: McGraw-Hill.

Gross, R.E. (1988). Forward to the trivia of 1890: The impending social studies program? *Phi Delta Kappan, 70*(1), 47–49.

Halloran, F.M. (1993, May). Conquering amnesia: Koreans nurse grievances from colonial rule, which Japanese prefer to forget. *Japan Update, 20,* 10–11.

Hunt, M.P., & Metcalf, L.E. (1955). *Teaching high school social studies: Problems in reflective thinking and social understanding.* New York: HarperCollins.

Hyland, J.T. (1985). *Teaching about the constitution: Relationships between teachers' subject matter knowledge, pedagogic beliefs, and instructional decision making regarding selection of content, materials and activities.* Unpublished doctoral dissertation, University of California, Los Angeles, CA.

Kakutani, M. (1993, April 30). Critic's notebook: When history is a casualty. *New York Times,* pp. C1, C31.

Lipman, M. (1988). Critical thinking—What can it be? *Educational Leadership, 46*(1), 38–43.

Lipstadt, D.E. (1993). *Denying the Holocaust: The growing assault on truth and memory.* New York: Free Press.

McKee, S.J. (1988). Impediments to implementing critical thinking. *Social Education, 52*(6), 444–446.

National Education Association, Committee on Tenure and Academic Process. (1951). *Freedom and the public school teacher.* Washington, DC: Author.

Nelson, J.L. (1991). Communities, local to national, as influences on social studies education. In J.P. Shaver (Ed.), *Handbook of research on social studies teaching and learning* (pp. 332–341). New York: Macmillan.

Nelson, J.L., & Roberts, G., Jr. (1963). *The censors and the schools.* Boston, MA: Little, Brown.

Orcutt, Susan. (1894, June 29). A letter to Kansas Governor Lewelling. Kansas State Historical Society, Topeka.

Patrick, J.J., & Hoge, J.D. (1991). Teaching government, civics, and law. In J.P. Shaver (Ed.), *Handbook of research on social studies teaching and learning* (pp. 427–436). New York: Macmillan.

Perlmutter, P. (1992). *Divided we fall: A history of ethnic, religious, and racial prejudice in America.* Ames, IA: Iowa State University Press.

Ravitch, D., & Finn, C.E., Jr. (1987). *What do our 17-year-olds know?* New York: HarperCollins.

Roper Organization. (1993, April 23). Holocaust awareness survey report. *New York Times,* p. A1.

Semmes, C.E. (1992). *Cultural hegemony and African American development*. New York: Praeger.

Sewell, G.T. (1988). American history textbooks: Where do we go from here? *Phi Delta Kappan, 70*(7), 552–558.

Wilson, S.M., & Wineburg, S.S. (1988). Peering at history from different lenses: The role of disciplinary perspectives in the teaching of American history. *Teachers College Record, 89*(4), 525–539.

Wineburg, S.S., & Wilson, S.M. (1988). Models of wisdom in the teaching of history. *Phi Delta Kappan, 70*(1), 50–58.

Yankelovich, D. (1991). *Coming to public judgment: Making democracy work in a complex world*. Syracuse, NY: Syracuse University Press.

Chapter 15

Teaching Evolution: Past and Present

Lawrence C. Scharmann

> The theory of evolution is the philosophical foundation for all secular thought today, from education to biology and from psychology through the social sciences. It is the platform from which socialism, communism, humanism, determinism, and one-worldism have been launched. Accepting man as animal, its advocates endorse animalistic behavior such as free love, situation ethics, drugs, divorce, abortion, and a host of other ideas that contribute to man's present futility and despair.... It has wrought havoc in the home, devastated morals, destroyed man's hope for a better world, and contributed to the political enslavement of a billion or more people (Morris, 1974, p. 5).

By the time Henry Morris, director of the Institute for Creation Research, penned these words, the revival of the creationist movement in the United States had begun (Nelkin, 1986). In a social environment increasingly receptive to ultraconservative religious views, Morris and other ICR representatives began to recommend more vigorous political activity intended to secure a place for creationism in school curricula. The nature of the activism, however, differed substantially from a similar movement in the 1920s: rather than attempt to legislate banning evolution instruction in the public schools, creationists promoted their views as an alternative scientific theory to evolution (Nelkin, 1982; Numbers, 1982). In fact, by 1981 balanced treatment of creation-science and evolution-science acts had been passed by

Arkansas and Louisiana; other states would soon attempt to pass similar bills. Although Arkansas's act was ultimately ruled unconstitutional, the publicity it generated continues to influence textbook writing, marketing, and adoption (Skoog, 1984, 1992) and local public school decisions and policies (Tatina, 1989; Van Koevering & Stiehl, 1989; Zimmerman, 1991).

It is fortunate that whenever creationists have attempted to impose overt censorship—through legislatures at the federal or state level—they have had either very limited or short-lived success; it is equally unfortunate that such overt efforts leave behind a legacy of a covert and very damaging form of censorship.

Initial Impressions of Evolution Theory

Charles Darwin's observations and conclusions about species, their origin, and their potential means for transformation over time are published in *On the Origin of Species*—a work that began the continuing controversy between creationism and evolution. Included in Darwin's findings were two theories—descent with modification and natural selection—that he saw as inseparable. Notions concerning common descent were not new at this time (Buffon, 1749; Lamarck, 1809). What was new in Darwin's explanations concerned the proposal of a mechanism by which common descent could occur—namely, natural selection. In fact, it was not descent with modification (the notion that all existing species have common ancestries) that created the initial debates about Darwin's work; this notion was actually fairly readily accepted by his fellow scientists. Instead, it was the lack of evidence for several of Darwin's major postulates of natural selection, which suggested how species became "improved forms," that raised questions (Gauld, 1992). Although disagreements are normal among scientists, especially in the case of theories, when these disagreements are made public they are often misinterpreted by nonscientists and thus serve as a weapon for the opportunistic individual or group choosing to refute a particular scientific stance.

Religious arguments against evolution were most vigorous from 1860 to the 1880s. Both scientific adversaries and theologians cited objections to evolution based on traditional Baconian scientific methods—the discovery of truth through induction.

The scientific community alleged that there was a lack of observable evidence, poor objectivity, and an inability to independently verify conclusions associated with natural selection; this component of Darwinism was suspect because it necessitated the use of "non-Baconian" subjective hypothesizing and theorizing. The theological community argued that evolution theory violated the notion of "doctrinal moralism"—a view that if an idea, concept, or theory implied immoral outcomes, as judged by the theologians' standards, then such a theory was simply untrue. These views from more than 120 years ago are still being echoed today in creationist writings and speeches.

By about 1880, however, creationists could identify only two notable U.S. biologists who had not come to accept some form of evolutionary theory (Numbers, 1982). In addition, with the advent of "the higher criticism" by biblical scholars, which subjected the Bible to the same forms of linguistic and historical analyses that were being applied to other documents, the mainline Christian churches slowly grew comfortable with the language of evolution (Kramer, 1986; Skehan, 1986):

> They took the position that religious and scientific knowledge are two different kinds of knowledge. Evolutionary theory, they said, is not a moral or religious doctrine; in turn, the Bible is not a scientific textbook...but it does tell us that God's creative act began and sustains the universe—a notion not contradicted by Darwinian evolutionism (Eve & Harrold, 1991, pp. 19–20).

In terms of educational policy, as early as 1895 the National Education Association recommended a zoology text that focused on evolution as a major theme; the book met with no vocal opposition (Nelkin, 1982). By 1916 secondary school textbooks presented evolution with confidence (Eve & Harrold, 1991). In other words, the evolution-creation battle appeared to be over a scant 30 years after the introduction of evolutionary theory. Scientists were quick to claim victory—too quick, in fact. The arguments for and against evolution up to this point had been performed within intellectual circles; in the late 19th and early 20th centuries, the public did not yet know enough about evolution to feel threatened by it.

Overt Censorship—Attempts to Outlaw Evolution

Eve and Harrold (1991) provide a delineation of the two major social and cultural factors leading up to the antievolutionism of the 1920s in the United States. The first was the tremendous growth in the numbers of students attending U.S. public high schools: in 1890 only about 7 percent of the 14 to 17 age group attended high schools; by 1920 about 32 percent of this group were in attendance; by 1930 over 50 percent were attending. It came as a surprise to parents, most of whom had not attained a high school diploma, that their children were being taught an increasingly secular worldview, one which included evolution theory. To a naive and scientifically uninformed public, evolutionary theory appeared to be contrary to religious beliefs. The fact that tax dollars were being spent to support such modernist instruction was disturbing to them, to say the least.

The second factor was a sense of cultural crisis that occurred after the end of World War I, a "morally lax" period that included drinking, dancing, and gambling—all of which conflicted with traditional conservative Protestantism. As some Protestant denominations adapted themselves to an increasingly secular world, conservatives became increasingly anxious—especially because their beliefs, once the consensus, were quickly becoming a minority point of view. This was especially true in the southern United States.

All that the creationist revival lacked to turn it into a movement with influence was a prominent figure: enter William Jennings Bryan, a three-time Democratic candidate for president of the United States, former secretary of state, and a conservative Presbyterian. After visiting college and university campuses and speaking with concerned citizen groups, Bryan became alarmed at the attitude of religious unbelief he encountered:

> He became convinced that the teaching of evolution as a fact instead of a theory caused the students to lose faith in the Bible— first, in the story of creation, and later in other doctrines, which underlie the Christian religion (Williams, 1936, p. 448).

In 1922 Bryan took up the creationist cause as spokesperson for traditional conservative Christian views. In fact, after hearing about a movement in Kentucky to ban the teaching of evolution, Bryan remarked, "The movement will sweep the country...and we will drive Darwinism from our schools" (Numbers, 1982, p. 538).

The antievolution movement of the 1920s reached its zenith at the Scopes trial of 1925. When the state of Tennessee enacted a law prohibiting the teaching of evolution, attorney Clarence Darrow defended John Scopes in what became a major turning point in the evolution controversy. The jury found Scopes guilty of violating the Tennessee law but also showcased the antievolution movement as ignorant, anachronistic, and intolerant of differing points of view. The legal defense and members of the press ridiculed Bryan unmercifully throughout the trial. When he died only a few days after the end of the trial, the antievolution cause lost a popular, powerful, and prominent leader whose reputation might have carried the cause into geographic regions beyond the South.

Covert Censorship—Aftermath I

Although antievolution bills were introduced after 1925—with Arkansas voters approving a referendum to abolish the teaching of evolution as late as 1928—most bills failed to gain support outside of the southern United States. The scientific community proclaimed victory, but once again far too quickly. Although the 1920s antievolution movement had very little impact on instruction in public colleges and universities, the same cannot be said for its effect on public secondary schools. The controversy surrounding evolution resulted in a subtle, persistent, covert censorship not only in the South but across the United States.

The dramatic change in the way evolution was emphasized in high school biology textbooks was staggering. In contrast to 1921, when Truman Moon had unabashedly displayed Charles Darwin as the opening photograph in his text *Biology for Beginners*, Nelkin (1982) reports,

> Textbooks published throughout the late 1920s ignored evolution-
> ary biology, and new editions of older volumes deleted the word

evolution and the name Darwin from their indexes. Some even added religious material. By the late 1930s some publishers were tentatively introducing evolution, but most, discouraged about market prospects and anxious to avoid controversy, avoided the topic, focusing largely on morphology and taxonomy (p. 33).

Thus, from 1925 until 1960, self-censorship in book publishing took place (Skoog, 1984). And because most secondary teachers make the majority of their curricular and instructional decisions based primarily (if not solely) on the textbook they use (Harms & Yager, 1981), as Allen explained in the previous chapter, this self-censorship extended to the classroom instructor as well.

How, when university biologists and science educators were well aware of the importance of evolutionary theory, could evolution have been so easily expunged? One reason is textbook authorship: secondary school biology textbooks during this time period were written by professional authors or secondary teachers (Eve & Harrold, 1991). And, because content integrity was not maintained and publishers faced market pressures and the fear of controversy, creationist tactics of the 1920s, while subject to ridicule, were amazingly effective.

The Launch of Sputnik

In the wake of the Soviet launching of the Sputnik satellite, the United States created the National Science Foundation to promote scientific research and examine the state of science and technology education. In regards to the latter, NSF established several curriculum study commissions to assess, develop, and implement programs for science instruction based on sound scientific and pedagogical principles. In 1960 the Biological Sciences Curriculum Study—represented by university biologists, university science educators, high school biology teachers, curriculum specialists, and educational psychologists—issued its assessment of the discrepancies between "what should be" and "what is" the status of biological science instruction in the United States. One key element was the lack of focus on evolution as an organizing theme in the secondary biology curriculum. BSCS resolved to inject evolutionary biology as a central theme back into the curriculum by producing new textbooks for use in the secondary classroom. Skoog (1984) reported that one of the 1963 books, for instance, devoted nearly 46,000 words to evolution and evolutionary themes compared with fewer than 9000 words in the 1963 edition of *Modern Biology*, the then-current version of *Biology for Beginners* (Moon, 1921).

The BSCS texts indirectly influenced the teaching of evolutionary thinking in 1965 when the Little Rock public schools attempted to adopt the books: Arkansas's antievolution law was eventually voided in 1968 by the U.S. Supreme Court on the grounds that it violated the First Amendment. Eve and Harrold (1991) state,

> By 1970 all other state antievolution laws had also been voided or repealed.... Thus in the 1960s, antievolutionists suffered a double blow: the re-emergence of evolution in the school curricula and the removal of laws protecting their children from exposure to it (p. 29).

Did the scientific community have cause to celebrate a victory this time? Yes, because it was no longer possible to completely forbid the teaching of evolution; no, because the creationist reaction to these events gave impetus to the more contemporary movement we still struggle against today.

Overt Censorship—Appeals to Legislate Equal Time

Antievolutionists of the late 1960s, perturbed by the fact it no longer seemed possible to make a strictly literal religious argument, were buoyed by a California Board of Education decision to grant equal time to creationist views (Nelkin, 1982). This decision was rendered as a result of efforts by two members of the Bible Science Association, who wanted to protect their children from beliefs offensive to their religious views. They used an argument similar to the 1961 decision of the U.S. Supreme Court that exempted atheist students from required school prayer (Bates, 1976). In 1970 the local BSA chapter merged with the Creation-Science Research Center, associated with Christian Heritage College. Joining them in the promotion of creationist views was the earlier quoted Henry Morris, who eventually established the Institute for Creation Research, which quickly became the dominant creationist organization (Nelkin, 1982). Morris employed a different tactic in promoting creationist views during the 1970s that other groups would emulate:

> Instead of trying to outlaw evolution, as they had done in the 1920s, antievolutionists now fought to give creation equal time. And instead of appealing to the authority of the Bible, as Morris and Whitcomb had done as recently as 1961, they consciously down-played the Genesis story in favor of what they called "scientific creationism."... In defending creation as a scientific alternative to evolution, creationists relied less on Francis Bacon and his conception of science and more on two new philosopher-heroes, Karl Popper and Thomas Kuhn. Popper required all scientific theories to be falsifiable; since evolution could not be falsified, argued the creationists, it was by definition not science. Kuhn described scientific progress in terms of competing models or paradigms rather than the accumulation of objective knowledge (Numbers, 1982, p. 543).

The ICR needed a contemporary William Jennings Bryan—a prominent spokesperson to promote their cause. And the ICR was certain they had found one in Ronald Reagan: he was open to positions espoused by the conservative Christian right and had a sympathy for the creationist point of view, demonstrated during his California governorship. As a candidate for president during the 1980 campaign, Reagan was asked his opinion concerning the teaching of evolution in public schools. Berra (1990) reports both Reagan's quote and his own comment about it afterward:

> "Well, it's a theory, it is a scientific theory only, and it has in recent years been challenged in the world of science and is not yet believed in the scientific community to be as infallible as it once was believed. But if it was going to be taught in the schools, then I think that also the biblical story of creation should also be taught." One must wonder where the President got his scientific advice. Here is ignorance (and pragmatic politics) celebrated at the highest level through an anti-intellectual appeal to a voting constituency (p. 123).

While Reagan may not have been as directly active in promoting antievolution as Bryan had been, the results were strikingly similar. By 1981, 20 states had introduced "equal time" bills. Most bills were defeated, but two states, Arkansas and Louisiana, actually passed and signed into law acts that required a balanced treatment of evolution science and creation science. The Arkansas law was declared unconstitutional by Judge Overton in 1982. In his statement, Overton made it apparent that creationism was not science and that the only real motive behind the Arkansas act was to advance a particular religious viewpoint (Nelkin, 1982). So decisive was his verdict that Arkansas state attorney general Steve Clark decided not to appeal and no further equal time bills were introduced in other states. The Louisiana law, although introduced with the same intent, was constructed more subtly and avoided much of the language that ultimately doomed the Arkansas act. As a result, challenges to the Louisiana law were more difficult and the defense better organized. However, after many years in the lower courts, Louisiana appealed to the Supreme Court, which declared the law unconstitutional in 1987.

In both the Arkansas and Louisiana cases, the antievolution cause was blunted. With the case decided by the Supreme Court, finally the scientific community could rest assured that victory had been won, couldn't they? Not at all, because, although the current antievolution camp is certainly convinced that the courts will not render judgments sympathetic to their cause, they recognize the influence they still have at the local level. The real question that might be asked is, are we winning the battles in the courts and losing the war at the local level?

Covert Censorship—Aftermath II

In the aftermath of the balanced treatment acts of Arkansas and Louisiana, creationists continue to influence textbook writing, editing, and eventual adoption policies at the local level (Skoog, 1992). But the scientific community's increased efforts to confront creationist tactics may prove more successful in defeating creationists than did past attempts. Rather than allowing the recent efforts of creationists to go unchallenged, groups such as the National Center for Science Education carefully monitor and challenge creationist activity at the local level. In addition, NCSE has established "Committees for Correspondence" in

46 U.S. states and 3 Canadian provinces to serve as expert witnesses, appear at public hearings, write letters to the editors of local newspapers, and send information to NCSE headquarters in Berkeley, California.

Victories in the federal courts, at public hearings, and even at the local level have certainly bolstered public and school-based policy concerning the teaching of evolution. However, if biology teachers are unwilling to provide direct instruction on evolution, policy means very little. Indeed, secondary biology teachers are a prominent target group for the current creationist movement. In 1993 in the southern United States, for example, teachers and their principals received a brochure encouraging them to attend a "Creation Science and the Scopes Evolution Trial" conference at William Jennings Bryan College in Dayton, Tennessee. A year earlier, biology teachers and principals in the midwestern United States were invited to attend one of several "Real Scientists Just Say No to Evolution" workshops sponsored by the Creation Science Association for Mid-America. Thus, although many individual biology teachers either dismiss or actively resist such creationist tactics, others, either through self-persuasion or pressure from their principal, avoid the potential controversy by simply not teaching evolution. In still other instances, individual biology teachers can be won over to the cause of the creationists by giving equal time to creationism. In any of these scenarios, some degree of self-censorship takes place. Creationists, therefore, feel that they have nothing to lose and everything to win. Occurrences and influence of these tactics have been recently reported in Kansas (Scharmann & Harris, 1992), Ohio (Zimmerman, 1991), South Dakota (Tatina, 1989), Texas (Eve & Dunn, 1990), and Wisconsin (Van Koevering & Stiehl, 1989). Covert censorship, through creationist activity, is on the increase (Scott, 1993).

Some Personal Observations

Many of my former students have reported experiencing frustration, challenge, and even outright criticism when they have presented evolution as an instructional unit in their classrooms. Evolution instruction can certainly be as sensitive an issue today as it ever has been, and continues to be the most significant facet of a larger effort concerned with enhancing an understanding of the nature of scientific knowledge among practicing teachers (Scharmann & Harris, 1992), undergraduate science education majors (Scharmann, 1993), and undergraduate general biology students (Scharmann, 1990). From my personal experiences, from formal coursework as a student to my current instruction and research, I am convinced of the need to address two major areas: (1) affective considerations impeding an understanding of the premises of evolutionary theory; and (2) instructional approaches to teaching evolutionary theory.

Affective Considerations

When secondary school students begin studying science, they come to class with personal assumptions, individual and family values, cultural influences, and past instructional experiences that have helped shape ideas they already have about the field, some of which are inaccurate. This can be especially troublesome when teachers attempt to provide instruction on evolution, especially if an individual perceives such instruction to be in conflict with his or her beliefs, values, and personal ideas. Thus, it is essential that teachers understand learners and what they bring to a course of study in biology. It has been my experience that once a perceived threat has been eliminated or (at the very least) reduced, a learner becomes more receptive to alternative ways of viewing the world. If the threat remains, even in implicit terms, little progress in conceptual change or shifts in worldview should be anticipated. This is true even when the best available instructors have the best of instructional intentions (Scharmann & Block, 1992).

Instructional Approaches

In my work with practicing teachers, I find that they use several approaches to evolution instruction. In an NSF-sponsored summer institute, teachers were given an open-ended questionnaire targeted to solicit their general impressions concerning evolution education. The results indicated that among teachers participating in the NSF institute,

1. 35 percent teach biological principles with no or only passing reference to the interdependence of such principles that can best be explained by evolutionary theory;
2. 56 percent teach evolutionary theory as "fact" (not based on fact); and
3. 9 percent present evolution and scientific creationism together and direct students to consider the "facts" offered by each theory in explaining the world.

One of the primary intentions of the summer institute was to examine each of these approaches. The first is scientifically inaccurate and without instructional integrity. It is, however, psychologically less troublesome for both students and teachers, although an implicit threat still remains for some students simply because the teacher avoids the subject. The second, in the view of the majority of biology teachers, is technically appealing; unfortunately, it is also psychologically more difficult for students who perceive a conflict because the conflict remains explicit. It is also scientifically misleading because it is incompatible with a strong foundational understanding of the nature of science in general and the nature of theories in particular. (It is, however, often resorted to by teachers as an overreaction to creationist pressure.) The third alternative is performed with the intent or hope that students will reject scientific creationism based on the evidence. However, this approach is scientifically irresponsible because it suggests that both theories are equally viable (even for scientists).

In each of these approaches to teaching evolution there are two common threads. First, it is easy to see that covert censorship has had an influence on a great many teachers. Second, it is also obvious that many biology teachers neither possess nor adequately communicate an understanding of the general nature of science, the nature of scientific theories, and the predictive power of such theories (Nelson, 1986; Scharmann, 1990). It is critical that such understandings be communicated to students and the public if we ever hope to defuse creationist appeals. Theories are the most powerful working tools of scientists: they explain patterns in evidence, predict consequences and events (which can be subjected to rigorous testing and verification), and establish research agendas (Kitcher, 1982). When two competing theories are proposed, the one that requires fewer assumptions (or is simplest) and offers the greater number of accurate predictions is usually adopted because it has great utility. Scientific creationism was said to be a theory that offered an alternative "explanation" to organic evolution: however, its advocates invoke supernatural explanations whenever anomalies are encountered. In addition, scientific creationism has never successfully predicted consequences or events without either invoking supernatural intervention or recognizing natural selection (microevolution). Natural selection is accepted by creationists as a mechanism, but only after creation has taken place. But simply explaining what theories are and how they work is often not sufficient to defuse creationists unless one already understands the nature of science and the instructional role of scientific theories.

Preparing a Rationale

If there is one philosophy I hope to impart to future teachers who will face instructional decisions, it is to be prepared to respond to the question, "Why do we have to know this stuff?" If a response to such a question does not have sufficient personal relevance, students simply dismiss the "stuff" as obviously not very important—something to be memorized and forgotten (at best), or something that scientists "believe" and the individual asking the question does not (at worst). Further, in the latter context, such a question is usually (perhaps purposely) asked in front of the entire class. Therefore, if the teacher is unprepared, the entire class can witness an inadequate response, which can undermine the teacher's instructional credibility and compromise future content integrity.

If the question is applied to a study of evolutionary theory it may be asked as "Why should I *believe* this stuff?" In this instance, the possibility exists that the student asking the question may have less than genuine motives. A response given by a teacher, especially when addressing the entire class, should perhaps mirror this one:

(You are right!) It doesn't much matter whether...the story of
Noah's Ark is true, or dinosaurs once lived. Believe what you will
of evolution in the past: but you had jolly well better believe it
will take place in the future if you hope to make political decisions
that will give your descendants a reasonable chance to exist
(Hardin, 1973, p. 15).

From a semantic point of view, I have never much cared
whether students "believe" in evolutionary theory. I have always
been very concerned, however, that students understand evolution to be the most powerful working tool at the disposal of every
biologist. In disease- and pest-control research, evolutionary theory is employed on a daily basis. What if every time a new dis-
ease were encountered, researchers did not assume common
ancestry with similar disease-producing bacteria, viruses, and
other pathogens? How much time would be wasted in beginning
a study of the organism from scratch, or in other words, from fiat
creationism? Or, when a field of crops is being destroyed by an
insect, which was formerly kept in check by a reliable pesticide,
how might an understanding of evolution help us make a good
decision about what to do? Finally, if a teacher attempts to make
points concerning the use (or abuse) of drugs, alcohol, or even
overuse of antibiotics in relation to evolutionary theory, generally
students begin to get the idea that evolution seems capable of
explaining a great deal; it seems to be one powerful idea—an
idea that changed the way biologists approach each and every
problem. An understanding and application of evolutionary principles, in fact, has already provided insights that may someday
contribute to the development of a cure for AIDS and other human
immune system afflictions (Cowley, 1993).

Once a strong rationale has been accomplished, it is important
to remember that the best approach to initiating a unit of study on
evolution is to appear neither too dogmatic nor overly teacher-
directed in presenting the scientific evidence. Dogmatism is easily perceived by students and leaves a teacher open to attack,
especially in situations where answers are not known or are
unclear. If students feel threatened by the information being provided, it is too easy to assume that the teacher is either against
them or that their views or beliefs are unimportant to the teacher.

Instead of making initial use of teacher-directed instruction, a more student-centered approach can make the initial lessons more acceptable. A peer discussion, for example, lends itself well to getting nonscience issues out in the open without students perceiving that the teacher agrees or disagrees with their individual views. The value of this approach has been further delineated by Nelson (1986), Scharmann (1990), Scharmann and Block (1992), and Scharmann and Harris (1992).

Instruction that is more holistic and diverse in nature is much more personally satisfying to students, especially those not interested in pursuing a career in biology. After all, it should be the intent of every biology teacher to develop scientific literacy, critical thinking, and logical reasoning, not at the expense of different points of view, but by encouraging a discussion of such differing viewpoints. In other words, instructional decisions should be made with less concern for getting students to think exactly the same way we do and more for getting students to think for themselves. If we accomplish that, then perhaps students and even the general public will not feel so threatened every time the topic of evolution arises in conversation, as Hardin (1973) said eloquently in this statement:

> Each new generation brings a fresh attack on the doctrine of evolution. Eternal vigilance is called for by biologists. Facts must be displayed once more; arguments must be explained. But this is not enough. The *beauty* of the evolutionary viewpoint must be made evident. It is not enough for teaching biologists to be good scientists in the narrow sense. They must be artists, as Darwin was. Looking back on the tortuous history of the acceptance of the theory of evolution, it seems to me that many biologists have not sufficiently appreciated the importance of esthetics in the act of affiliating with the past. Defending our position in a narrowly sectarian—that is, scientific—way, we have perhaps deserved the tactical defeats we have suffered. And we will continue to encounter defeat if we do not succeed in showing the supreme beauty of our views of the origin of the living world (p. 19).

A Look Toward the Future

Is the war almost over? Not in your most hope-filled dreams! We cannot simply assume that creationists have abandoned the courts as a venue to promote their views. When the current grass-roots efforts begin to achieve sufficient success, spread doubt, or sound persuasive, challenges to existing laws or the introduction of new legislation will not be far behind. Creationists are very hard at work in Vista, California, for example (Scott, 1993): they have succeeded in unseating a number of school board members and now have a 3–2 voting majority. Although the final elected member is an accountant for ICR, he says he is uninterested in a scientific creationism versus evolution debate because "creationism invokes a theological response in most people. That in itself is self-defeating in a science classroom" (p. 6). Instead, he is interested in promoting "intelligent design theory" as a scientific alternative to random mutation theory because "it's a random mutation theory that has a monopoly on science in our nation right now. I have a concern that this does not allow a scientific challenge to enhance (the development of) these critical thinking skills" (p. 6).

It does not take a genius to see through his ploy. Creationists will now replace evolution versus religion (of the 1920s) and evolution versus scientific creationism (of the 1980s) with intelligent design theory versus random mutational theory. If Kuhn's (1970) logic is correct, whenever a scientific revolution is about to occur, multiple working theories are necessary to challenge the current working paradigm. Educators should be warned: antievolutionists are not only making pronouncements concerning intelligent design theory (Davis & Kenyon, 1989; Thaxton, Bradley, & Olsen, 1984), they are also promoting abrupt appearance theory (Bennetta, 1988). Eve and Harrold (1991) provide this final caution:

> Advocates of the doctrine of abrupt appearance studiously avoid explicit references to supernaturalism and will not speak of any god, but instead will sometimes refer to a nebulous "intelligence" or "intelligent cause" or "intelligent design."... Even the term *creation science* itself will be increasingly avoided in the future. The new creationism has a generally calmer, less angry tone and is more willing to accept an old age for the earth. In other words, creationism is being sanitized, until it is no longer overtly recognizable as religious in origin (p. 187).

References

Bates, V.L. (1976). *Christian fundamentalists and the theory of evolution in public school education.* Unpublished doctoral dissertation, University of California, Davis, CA.

Bennetta, W.J. (1988). Telling a you-know-what for you-know-whom. *California Science Teacher's Journal, 18*(3), 10–12.

Berra, T.M. (1990). *Evolution and the myth of creationism.* Stanford, CA: Stanford University Press.

Buffon, G.L. (1749). *Histoire naturelle.* Paris: Imprimerie Royale.

Cowley, G. (1993, March 22). The future of AIDS. *Newsweek, 71*(12), 46–52.

Davis, P., & Kenyon, D.H. (1989). *Of pandas and people.* Dallas, TX: Haughton.

Eve, R.A., & Dunn, D. (1990). Psychic powers, astrology, and creationism in the classroom. *American Biology Teacher, 52*(1), 10–21.

Eve, R.A., & Harrold, F.B. (1991). *The creationist movement in modern America.* Boston, MA: Twayne.

Gauld, C. (1992). Wilberforce, Huxley & the use of history in teaching about evolution. *American Biology Teacher, 54*(7), 406–410.

Hardin, G. (1973). Ambivalent aspects of evolution. *American Biology Teacher, 35*(1), 15–19.

Harms, N.C., & Yager, R.E. (1981). *What research says to the science teacher* (Vol. 3). Washington, DC: National Science Teachers Association.

Kitcher, P. (1982). *Abusing science.* Cambridge, MA: MIT Press.

Kramer, W. (1986). *Evolution and creation.* Huntington, IN: Our Sunday Visitor.

Kuhn, T.S. (1970). *The structure of scientific revolutions* (2nd ed.). Chicago, IL: The University of Chicago Press.

Lamarck, J.B. (1809). *Philosophie zoologique* (Reprinted with a foreword by H.R. Englemann & J. Cramer, 1960). New York: Hafner.

Moon, T.J. (1921). *Biology for beginners.* New York: Henry Holt.

Morris, H. (1974). *The troubled waters of evolution.* San Diego, CA: Creation-Life.

Nelkin, D. (1982). *The creation controversy.* New York: Norton.

Nelkin, D. (1986). Science, rationality, and the creation/evolution dispute. In R.W. Hanson (Ed.), *Science and creation* (pp. 33–45). New York: Macmillan.

Nelson, C.E. (1986). Creation, evolution, or both? A multiple model approach. In R.W. Hanson (Ed.), *Science and creation* (pp. 128–159). New York: Macmillan.

Numbers, R.L. (1982). Creationism in 20th-century America. *Science*, *218*(4572), 538–544.

Scharmann, L.C. (1990). Enhancing an understanding of the premises of evolutionary theory: The influence of a diversified instructional strategy. *School Science and Mathematics*, *90*(2), 91–100.

Scharmann, L.C. (1993). Teaching evolution: Designing successful instruction. *American Biology Teacher*, *55*(8), 481–486.

Scharmann, L.C., & Block, T.D. (1992). Teaching evolution: Understanding, concerns, and instructional approach alternatives. *Kansas Biology Teacher*, *2*(1), 13–15.

Scharmann, L.C., & Harris, W.M., Jr. (1992). Teaching evolution: Understanding and applying the nature of science. *Journal of Research in Science Teaching*, *29*(4), 375–388.

Scott, E.C. (1993). Vista, CA district in turmoil over creationism. *National Center for Science Education Reports*, *13*(1), 1–6, 18.

Skehan, J.W. (1986). The age of the earth, of life, and of mankind: Geology and biblical theory versus creationism. In R.W. Hanson (Ed.), *Science and creation* (pp. 10–32). New York: Macmillan.

Skoog, G. (1984). The coverage of evolution in high school biology textbooks published in the 1980s. *Science Education*, *68*(2), 117–128.

Skoog, G. (1992). The coverage of evolution in secondary school biology textbooks, 1900–1989. In J. Herlihy (Ed.), *The textbook controversy* (pp. 71–88). Norwood, NJ: Ablex.

Tatina, R. (1989). South Dakota high school biology teachers & the teaching of evolution & creationism. *American Biology Teacher*, *51*(5), 275–280.

Thaxton, C.B., Bradley, W.L., & Olsen, R.L. (1984). *The mystery of life's origins: Reassessing current theories.* New York: Philosophical Library.

Van Koevering, T.E., & Stiehl, R.B. (1989). Evolution, creation, & Wisconsin teachers. *American Biology Teacher*, *51*(4), 200–202.

Williams, W.C. (1936). *William Jennings Bryan.* New York: Putnam.

Zimmerman, M. (1991). The evolution-creation controversy: Opinions of Ohio school board presidents. *Science Education*, *75*(2), 201–214.

Policy & Procedure

Some Plans for Action

" **A** stitch in time saves nine," "Forewarned is fore-armed," "An ounce of prevention is worth a pound of cure"—these proverbs hold true as the most effective strategies for dealing with would-be book banners. "Most effective," however, needs a bit of qualification, lest one think a cure for censorship has been discovered. Because many censors believe so strongly in their convictions, most attempts to appease or even negotiate with them are often ignored. And because most censorship confrontations pit two fundamental rights against each other—that of the local community to set educational policy against that of freedom of expression—such issues must be considered and resolved on a case-by-case basis.

The suggestions described in this final section for preparing for and fighting challenges to school materials represent the best the profession has to offer. For decades professional organizations have published documents that provide such advice. The American Library Association has been active in this area longer than any other, producing a number of highly practical arguments to be used by school personnel in responding to censors' attacks. In 1972 the National Council of Teachers of English first published the concise but pointed pamphlet "The Students' Right to Read." For over 20 years, teachers, principals, supervisors, and district school boards have been implementing sections of this pamphlet as a model for shaping their policies. In 1981 the Association of American Publishers issued another pamphlet, "Textbook Publishers and the Censorship Controversy," which outlines the extent of the issue and how it affects the publishing industry. In 1989 the National School Board Association developed a monograph, *Censorship: Managing the Controversy*—an extensive and thoughtful treatment of the matter from the perspective of elected school officials.

Probably the most recent statement of this kind was produced in 1993 by the National Council of Teachers of English and the International Reading Association Joint Task Force on Intellectual Freedom. Their publication, "Common Ground," is a strong position statement that provides strategies for fighting censorship at several levels and a concise bibliography for additional resources. It states,

> All students in public school classrooms have the right to materials and educational experiences that promote open inquiry, critical thinking, diversity in thought and expression, and respect for others. Denial or restriction of this right is an infringement of intellectual freedom.

In this section's lead essay, Sipe relies on her extensive background as a curriculum coordinator in recommending viable courses of action to a district office. She briefly summarizes the problems schools are up against and then offers ways in which to deal with each one. Agee also draws on his considerable experience to advise school administrators of their role in a controversy.

Small, another longtime advocate of the right to read, offers sound, immediately practical advice to novice teachers from his perspective as both a teacher and administrator.

Stern summarizes the responsibilities an English department chair must assume when a challenge is made to that program. He then explains the accepted and enforced guidelines promulgated by his school for dealing with complaints and challenges.

Penway articulates the philosophy of the American Library Association in her statement to school library media specialists; she suggests what to do in anticipation of attacks against a library's collection, how to deal with the attackers, and how librarians can follow up on any agreed-to courses of action after a controversy has ostensibly been arbitrated. She promotes the consistent implementation of the "Library Bill of Rights," a policy statement for libraries published by ALA, throughout any adversarial dialogue. As Grantham's essay title suggests, she is a veteran school board member who has been caught in the turbulence of a notorious censorship struggle. After cataloging the entire incident, which gained international media coverage, she details the step-by-step process her board followed in evolving a new policy for the school district. Readers will find this policy statement useful as they attempt to cope with censorship issues in their communities. Donelson completes this section and the anthology with his forceful review of "ten steps" for fighting school censorship.

Chapter 16

Negotiating the Narrow Path: Responding to Censorship in the 1990s

Rebecca Bowers Sipe

Few issues facing schools are as inflammatory as those relating to censorship. As the authors in Sections One and Two of this work have shown, the act of restricting access to information threatens the students' right to make judgments. In a democratic society, where each individual's right to make free and informed decisions has traditionally been treasured, the threat of censorship warrants concern and an urgent need to identify strategies to help educators meet the censors' challenges.

Both left- and right-wing political groups and parents look to the school curriculum to shape thinking in a manner that closely mirrors their own needs and wishes. As we have seen, when the schools fail to meet the needs of their communities, angry parents and community members fight back by waging war against offensive aspects of curriculum. In some cases tugs to move the curriculum beyond mainstream thought have proven divisive within schools and across communities. As part of the democratic process, various groups struggle to translate their values and beliefs into policy and regulation. In doing so the presence of their values is ensured even in the face of subsequent changes in power balance or personnel. Chubb and Moe (1990) describe the growth of bureaucracy within U.S. schools as the result of various power group attempts to "insulate themselves from subversion by opposing groups and officials who may gain hold of public authority in the future" (p. 167).

Some argue that schools censor with every instructional decision. While the assertion opens up an interesting debate, the role of intent must be examined. In selecting curriculum and teaching materials, educators attempt to match the scope and type of information presented to the developmental level of the students; this obviously means that some materials are omitted from the curriculum. Regardless of the content selected, it is the school's responsibility to provide as comprehensive a look at varying perspectives as possible. Those charged with making such curricular judgments must always question whether their decisions reflect an attempt to limit information in an effort to guide students' thinking within prescribed patterns. A narrow path exists between appropriate instructional placement and censorship. Educators must continually examine their choices and motives in all curricular decisions.

Censorship: The Noisy Storm and the Silent Tempest

Never before has society's agenda for schools been more confusing. Confronted with a baffling array of expectations, the English language arts teacher, for instance, may be asked to justify instructional decisions that are as basic as the rationale for including literature at the heart of the English curriculum. Literature is taught to help students gain a better understanding of themselves and others. Teachers search for literature that speaks to students individually while bridging the universal themes that connect us. Good literature deals with human drama and reflects author perspective and bias, which are interpreted differently by each student. When special interest groups or parents require an emphasis that differs from the established curriculum by excluding or including particular texts, teachers can quickly become embroiled in a censorship battle for which they are ill equipped. By understanding the current dimensions of censorship, educators will be better prepared to address challenges in a nonconfrontational, thoughtful manner.

In 1990 alone, more than 1000 books were banned in the United States in a series of well-publicized cases (*Anchorage Daily News*, 1990). The authors in Sections One and Two have stressed that these controversies leave communities in the throes of severe divisiveness while local district administrators and teachers re-evaluate the primary mission of the curriculum. These thunderous cases also cause a far more common form of censorship that silently alters curriculum: self-censorship that is shaped by fear in response to perceived threat. Like the eye of a storm, silent censorship grips the schools in an uneasy and dangerous calm, of which the authors in Section Two have warned, and sculpts the school curriculum with the tools of fear and doubt.

Review: Inclusion, Noninclusion, and Avoidance

As one response to a recognized need for a more inclusive curriculum, schools have attempted to infuse the English language arts program with multicultural literature (see Chapter 6 by Simmons). A heightened presence of works written by minority authors is clearly desirable. To ensure a quality program, it continues to be incumbent on school districts to maintain a clear focus as to why specific literature selections are made. To that end, literature-selection criteria must be fashioned through collaboration and discussion.

Curriculum revision efforts have occasionally prompted demands that selected literature present only positive portrayals of all cultural groups. But if this criterion is accepted at face value, a distorted picture of historical reality may emerge. Literature and history textbooks depicting African Americans as slaves in the last century certainly do not meet the criterion of positive portrayal; neither do those showing women as victims or in subservient roles. But these may be authentic historical portrayals that demonstrate the treatment and circumstances of people at a specific point in time. Books should never be eliminated because they fail to offer the vision of history we want. Instead, the use of literature and texts should be viewed as an opportunity to address our common past and to honestly discuss the situations and circumstances that we have inherited as a result of previous practice.

In the same sense, any attempt to control thinking through the presentation of literature representing only *one* perspective or group must be recognized as a dangerous form of censorship. Lack of inclusion or underrepresentation often fosters misinformation. Maxine Hill, a multicultural curriculum specialist in Alaska, expressed her concern about the characterization of black males in many contemporary literature classes: while stressing that books such as Alice Walker's *The Color Purple* are powerful and provocative selections, she urged teachers to think carefully of the need to provide students with positive role models as well because, as Simmons mentioned in Chapter 6, black males often criticize this and other works for their perceived negative portrayal of black men. History texts as well as literature survey and period literature classes must give careful attention to offering as inclusive a body of literature as possible.

Increasing numbers of teachers report a reluctance to introduce students to books and materials they fear are controversial. Titles such as *To Kill a Mockingbird* and *Black Like Me* are routinely dropped from the American literature curriculum, for example (see also Gallo, Chapter 12). Convinced of insufficient administrative support, teachers replace these titles with ones less likely to initiate parental objections. While it is entirely possible that the alternate titles have equivalent merit, it is of great concern when curricular changes are motivated by fear instead of thoughtful decision making.

The problems inherent in such a situation were clearly demonstrated in a large urban middle school during the 1991–92 school year. A highly qualified teacher possessing extensive knowledge of multicultural literature suddenly found herself under attack by a minority parent group for using Mildred Taylor's novel *Roll of Thunder, Hear My Cry* in her classroom. The novel was an approved text for the middle school level, and the teacher had a solid reputation for being both sensitive and effective in her use of multicultural literature. In a series of unpleasant meetings with a group of minority parents it was made clear that they believed the teacher to be unqualified to teach a book that included the word "nigger" because she was not African American. Unfortunately, the teacher walked away from the situation feeling inadequately supported by her district. She reports, "So, I don't teach that book anymore. I've had years of work in multicultural education and I really believe in this stuff. But I won't touch it again. I can't handle the personal attacks" (N. Alvey, personal communication, April 1993). Her words clearly illustrate why teachers in increasing numbers choose to eliminate portions of their curriculum rather than risk becoming targets of such attacks. Yet, if educators are not free to share outstanding literature that reflects human circumstances as they really exist, it is doubtful that young learners will gain the necessary insights to understand many contemporary situations. Curricula should not be shaped and reshaped as a result of fear; instead they should reflect the best thinking that the teacher, the school, and the community can muster.

Who May Judge?

In a recent literature-adoption process, the Anchorage, Alaska, School District struggled openly with questions about who might be qualified to judge the merits of literature representing a variety of cultural and ethnic groups. With over 46,000 students in a tremendously varied population (over 100 languages are spoken among the student body), the district had long recognized the need to provide literature representing a wide range of authorship. In the past, decisions about what constituted "good literature" for the program seemed simple enough: If the story was engaging, demonstrated good use of language, and fit the content parameters of the course, it generally was included.

Unfortunately, as local teachers began systematically to look for good literature that also provided authentic representation of cultural groups, the task took on new dimensions of difficulty. This struggle was spurred by controversies such as those related to the appropriateness of books such as *The Education of Little Tree* by Forest Carter and *Knots on a Counting Rope* by Bill Martin Jr. In each case, teachers were drawn to the books because of their lyrical use of language and strong appeal to students. Review committee members were shocked when they learned of concerns raised by the district's Indian Education Department. Though both books were beautifully written, questions about the authenticity of the cultural portrayal and cultural stereotypes in each case proved to be problematic. As a further shock, teachers learned that *The Education of Little Tree*, a charming book about the life of a young Cherokee boy, though voted by the American Booksellers Association in April 1991 as its favorite title to sell, was in fact written by a renowned segregationist and member of the Klu Klux Klan (*Newsweek*, 1991).

Circumstances such as these caused teachers to question their ability to select good multicultural literature and, in some cases, left teachers with the desire to abdicate that responsibility to others. In an effort to be as fair and accurate as possible, district administrators decided all pieces of minority literature must be reviewed *and* approved by persons from the ethnic or cultural groups represented. The motives for this decision were noble; the results left myriad questions unanswered.

In the attempt to ensure cultural authenticity and sensitivity in the literature curriculum, schools struggle to maintain footing on the narrow path that inches between genuine desire to provide this type of literature and pressure to surrender to censorship demands of special interest groups. As one male department chair lamented, "If I'm no longer qualified to select literature written from a Native American, Hispanic, or black perspective, does this mean that I'm no longer qualified to select literature that represents a female perspective either?" (G. Wright, personal communication, April, 1993). Such an approach to literature selection leads to factionalizing of staff and, potentially, to the abandonment of the established selection process. Literature selection should be as inclusive of diverse opinions as possible and should represent a high level of sensitivity to student needs. However, few literature classes are designed to provide a comprehensive cultural sampler. Instead, the magic of rich and diverse literature is that it gives students the ability to see themselves reflected across periods of time, across cultures, and across intensely varying personal circumstance.

Slipping from the Narrow Path: Abuse in the Library

Of all the places that should provide safe haven from the storms of censorship, the school library should be the most sacred. Yet stealthy censoring moves are reported by librarians on a continual basis (see also Chapter 20 by Penway). Under pressure from parents or community members, some school librarians report having to remove books from the collection and place them on special shelves elsewhere in the facility. In other cases, particular titles simply disappear without discussion or public decision making. Other reports tell of librarians—acting independently or with urging from administration—removing sections of periodicals that are deemed offensive for students to read.

Collection development provides many opportunities for subtle censorship. Librarians practice censorship when they do not purchase materials that reflect particular genres or perspectives in an effort to avoid controversy. One high school student reported that a local university library had hardly any information supporting an antiabortion position, in contrast to hundreds of sources supporting the opposing view. In an elementary school, the principal denied the librarian the right to order books by mystery writers such as Christopher Pike despite frequent student requests for these works.

With the advent of the age of computerized library services, a new and highly disturbing capability now lies in the hands of decision makers. Software applications allow for the "flagging" of items that may be viewed as controversial. Multiple fields permit different check-out policies to exist for individual students. Students whose parents approve all types of books could be granted one user code; others, whose parents choose to restrict their reading, would be granted a different code. In addition, books themselves could be coded to reflect "regular" or "restricted" circulation, requiring some special approval for a student to access the material. This type of software offers the option of restricting books for the entire district, at the local school site, or both. Proponents of such capability express satisfaction that libraries will be better able to address the needs of the community as a whole. Those who perceive the true censoring abilities of such a system are appalled at the prospect and express grave misgivings about surrendering the power to decide what is objectionable on moral, political, or other grounds to anyone other than the individual reader.

Being Prepared for Rocky Terrain: Establishing Policies and Procedures

If schools are adequately prepared, they need not respond with fear when censorship challenges knock at the door. All too often reactions—not decisions—characterize the initial responses to such challenges. Much administrative effort may be directed toward making the controversy, and its champions, go away. School districts that approach controversy ready for creative problem solving and genuine communication often open the door to collaboration and discussion, which leads to the development of policies that encourage inclusiveness in both decision making and perspectives.

Like any traveler venturing down a new and unpredictable road, it is critical that educators possess a good map for the journey. Such a map is developed through discussing and planning well before the trip—before a challenge develops. Establishing sound policies and procedures for selecting materials and addressing challenges will enable all participants in the process to understand the rules. Further, by aggressively pursuing staff education, which encourages professional self-reflection and sensitivity in methodologies, schools may do much to eliminate the insidious influences of silent censorship.

One of the best ways to be prepared for censorship challenges is for educators to know their community (Brown, 1987). We must try to understand the players, the philosophies, and the pressure points that simmer beneath the surface. By understanding the agendas of others, schools will be able to speak the protestors' language and hear their messages, both stated and implied. Sometimes challengers simply need to know they are being heard. When educators calmly and knowledgeably discuss the challengers' issues in their own terms, the door may be opened to fruitful communication.

Schools may find themselves most vulnerable to censorship challenges in two circumstances: when they fail to establish sound, equitable policies and procedures—in many cases because of an "it can't happen here" attitude, as Jenkinson warned—and when they fail to honor the procedures they do have. As the authors later in this section argue, policy should always be determined before storm clouds gather and procedure development should invite participation from all parties who will ultimately be affected by decisions. Good procedures protect all groups by ensuring equitable access. Guidelines should be formally adopted by the school board and should be included in official school district policy. At a minimum these should include philosophy and goals for the school system; goals and objectives for the instructional program; responsibility for selection of instructional materials; procedures for selection of instructional materials; and procedures for addressing challenges to materials (Van Horne, 1983).

Established policies and procedures should be adhered to by all. Once the first exception is granted, it will prove virtually impossible to refuse additional changes, making the viability of review processes questionable. Arbitrary changes initiated as "knee-jerk" reactions are almost guaranteed to bring unpleasant results. The following recommendations may prove helpful as policy and procedure development is undertaken.

Identify the participants and the steps in the processes for selecting materials and addressing challenges. Invite all voices into the process. Depending on the size of the district and the politics of the area, it may be advisable to identify the number of representatives from various segments of the population, including advisory groups, teachers, principals, students, community members, and program personnel.

Encourage clear communication and access to information throughout all processes. This may include the use of media, editorials, and community meetings. The more committees hear and reflect on the variety of community interests, the greater the likelihood that decisions will gain community support. It is imperative that procedures for selecting materials and for dealing with challenges be characterized by openness and accessibility.

Begin all processes with education. Review committees must always be provided with training to update them on the latest research in the field as well as on the current issues that may influence decisions. It is crucial that decision makers keep an eye toward the future and not limit decisions to past or current preference.

Seek agreement about the basic mission, goals, and objectives for programs being reviewed. If committee members can reach agreement on fundamental issues, those points can serve as anchors to all subsequent decisions. Whenever possible, seek consensus—even if consensus must mean "Can you live with this goal if I can live with that one?"

Keep an eye on the mission, goals, and objectives of the program when developing curriculum or selecting materials. At each decision-making juncture, revisit these basic tenets. They will help maintain a clear course throughout the process, making it less likely that attitudes will be defensive or entrenched when challenges arise.

Insist on written challenges. Written challenges require that complainants think through their concerns in order to articulate them in writing. According to Hopkins (1993), written challenges are far more likely to result in procedures being followed than are oral complaints. Important questions for complainants to consider may include the following: Have you read this material completely? To what specific aspects of the work do you object? What do you believe is the main idea of this material? What reviews of the material have you read? For what other age group might this be suitable? What action do you recommend that the school take on this material? What other materials do you recommend that would provide adequate information on the subject?

Maintain both integrity and goodwill. Curriculum decision making does not have to have winners and losers. By holding on to the principles of inclusiveness, honesty, and fairness in the face of challenge, many controversies can be defused. Most parents and community members are as eager as school staff members to create optimum learning situations for students.

Derailing Silent Censorship

In a recent secondary curriculum committee meeting that I facilitated, discussion focused on the question of why some teachers seemed to be able to teach almost *anything* without challenge while others encountered continual difficulty. Something was happening in those classrooms that allowed for potentially charged discussions without ensuing explosions: classrooms where teachers are able to deal with controversial issues and materials successfully are characterized by a strong sense of community. Community building begins on the first day of school. Everything about the class tells the students that they are valued and respected. The instructor demonstrates in many ways that the students' safety and security are of utmost importance. In such a nurturing environment, students allow the teacher to lead them into difficult reading and to engage them in challenging discussion because they *know* the teacher cares about them. In such classrooms there is no need to feel threatened; if and when a student begins to feel uncomfortable, there is security enough to talk with the teacher. Such reciprocal respect and sensitivity can only be developed over time. It cannot be feigned, nor can it be whisked together the day before a controversial book is introduced.

To create such a learning environment, teachers must truly know their students: their interests, their emotions, and their vulnerabilities. There must be a deep and abiding concern for each child's welfare that supersedes all other considerations. Too often pieces of literature are taught in classrooms because they have been included in the curriculum for decades. Enid Lee, a Canadian consultant on antiracist education, urges teachers to use responsive writing to find out how their students feel as specific pieces of literature are read and discussed. Regardless of the quality of the selection or its literary significance, its use cannot be defended if it damages students. By creating a safe learning community, such damage may be less of a possibility.

> *"Teachers who hold a firm rationale for what they do and why they do it are better prepared to provide information to parents or community members in a nondefensive manner when challenges do come."*

Successful teachers have carefully thought through their rationale for using the materials they have chosen. Teaching a selection just because it is in the curriculum is simply not adequate justification. Instead, instructors should answer questions for themselves regarding why they select particular titles and methods as opposed to others and how particular readings or discussions encourage cognitive development in students (see also Chapters 19 and 22). Teachers should never feel defensive when parents ask for rationale regarding specific units of study or assignments. Such requests for information should be viewed as opportunities to encourage parental involvement in their children's learning. Teachers who hold a firm rationale for what they do and why they do it are better prepared to provide information to parents or community members in a nondefensive manner when challenges do come. These teachers possess the freedom to shape their curriculum through professional reflection and attention to student needs.

Seeking Professional Development

Teachers, like other professionals, should pursue continuing education in their field. Language arts educators, for instance, often lament their lack of preparation for the teaching of literature. College courses engage future teachers in the analysis of literature, emphasizing the works of critics, but often fail to explore appropriate methods for helping young students connect and respond to the literature they are reading. This lack of preparation has led many English teachers to request additional learning opportunities as a part of inservice professional development.

Perhaps the most successful teacher education effort of this sort has been the summer institutes devoted to the exploration of strategies for the teaching of literature. Modeled on the format of the National Writing Project in the United States, these institutes focus in varying degrees on the reader response theory of Rosenblatt (1938; 1978). Teacher leaders attempt to model for participants an environment that mirrors Rosenblatt's theory. Fellows deal first with their own reading process, reading widely in a variety of genres for both professional growth and personal pleasure. Great efforts are made to develop a community of learners where teachers feel secure in sharing their responses to the works they are reading. Participants respond to literature in a variety of ways, always honoring the uniqueness of each individual's reading. Such experiences help teachers gain a deeper appreciation of the ways young readers feel in classrooms. In addition, teachers are encouraged to reflect on their own instructional beliefs and how these beliefs affect their classroom practice. Participants are invited to reflect on what they teach, why they make those selections, and how their lessons might be received by students. As a result of attending these institutes, teachers are better prepared to establish sensitive learning environments and experiences for students.

Keeping to the Narrow Path

The practice of censorship has never been more potent than it is now. By establishing and enforcing sound policies and procedures, schools can address many censorship attempts on equal grounds. By heightening sensitivity in instruction through quality professional development opportunities, the silent self-censorship that currently exists in schools may be eliminated. And by extending the circle of the community of learners, teachers, students, and parents may work together to negotiate the narrow path successfully.

References

Anchorage Daily News. (1990, September 20). Banned books: The victims of ignorance, prejudice.

Brown, J.E. (1987, November). Responding to the religious right. *Support for the Learning and Teaching of English, 12*(3), pp. 1–2.

Chubb, J.E., & Moe, T.M. (1990). *Politics, markets, and America's schools.* Washington, DC: Brookings Institution.

Hopkins, D.M. (1993, January). Put it in writing: What you should know about challenges to school library materials. *School Library Journal.*

Newsweek. (1991, October 14). New age fable from an old school bigot? The murky history of the best-selling 'Little Tree'.

Rosenblatt, L.M. (1938). *Literature as exploration.* New York: Modern Language Association of America.

Rosenblatt, L.M. (1978). *The reader, the text, the poem.* Carbondale, IL: Southern Illinois University Press.

Van Horne, G.T. (1983, February). Combatting censorship of instructional materials. *Support for the Learning and Teaching of English.*

Chapter 17

Advice for School Administrators

Hugh Agee

In the mid-1960s I was involved in an experimental curriculum development project for the middle grades that required seventh graders to read and study Anne Frank's *The Diary of a Young Girl*. During this part of the project I visited the schools and classrooms to observe instruction and confer with teachers. When I arrived one morning at a participating junior high school, one of the teachers informed me that the principal had decided that students should not read Anne Frank's *Diary*—on the basis of a mother's complaint that it was a "dirty" book.

I met with the principal to discuss the situation and learned that he had not read the book. The mother objected specifically to Anne's writing about looking at her body in a mirror—a natural act for a young woman. After I reasoned with the principal, he agreed that other students could read the book. The teacher, student, and parent (who accepted this alternative) would negotiate another selection for the student, and she would be excused from the classroom while *Diary* was being discussed.

This censorship episode was resolved without becoming a media event. The principal had made an arbitrary decision that, had he not reconsidered, would have deprived many students of the experience of reading and discussing a significant literary document. School administrators in the 1990s face many difficult decisions; they do not need the added burden of a censorship challenge. Yet increasing numbers of them are having to shoulder just such a burden.

This incident illustrates an administrator's hasty concession to a parent's objection, but sometimes an administrator may make the original complaint or challenge, as in the *Forever* case that Rosenblum described in Chapter 5. In the early 1970s I was teaching in a community where a local middle school principal had agreed to the purchase of new art books for students. The art teacher was very excited about the new text with its wonderful photographs and was looking forward to using it in class. However, when the books were delivered, the principal took a closer look at them and discovered a full-page photograph of Michelangelo's statue of David. The idea of middle graders seeing a nude male figure—albeit in marble—caused him to stop the teacher from distributing the books. The art teacher objected, and when support for the teacher's position grew within the school, the principal proposed excising that page from the book. When the story was published in the local press and the community showed its support for using the books unaltered, the principal relented.

A very recent incident (Berger, 1994) involves freedom of choice and freedom of expression. The book in question is Toni Morrison's *Song of Solomon,* which students in a 12th grade Advanced Placement English class had been reading. A parent who found an offensive passage in the book shared it with an assistant superintendent for instruction. Without a hearing as required in established procedures, the assistant superintendent sent a memorandum to all Advanced Placement teachers in the county that said that the book was not to be required reading or available for student to check out of the library. The incident was reported in the press, and many citizens became involved by expressing their feelings. The issue here, again, is whether or not one parent and one administrator should arbitrarily decide that students should be denied access to a book, even a book written by a winner of the Nobel Prize for Literature.

> **"School administrators hold strategic positions for maintaining a school environment where intellectual freedom should be the norm."**

An appropriate panel of educators did review *Song of Solomon* as required by school system guidelines and cleared it for use in schools. This decision is subject to appeal, as it should be, because the question of community standards was raised. However, to cite community standards as a rationale for action leaves one to question what those standards are and if they appropriately include diverse groups and perspectives.

These accounts have positive outcomes for the students, whose right to read was not restricted. In fairness to the school administrators involved, each no doubt acted or reacted in a way he or she thought appropriate to the situation without employing any supporting policies and procedures for selection and review of school materials. But each made judgments that clearly disregarded the broader prevailing issue—the right of students and teachers to learn and grow in a climate of free and open inquiry.

The responsibility of promoting and preserving intellectual freedom in schools is not solely that of school administrators: any charge this important should truly be a collaborative effort by students, teachers, librarians, parents, and all community members. Hentoff (1981) stresses the importance of the judgment of teachers, librarians, and administrators in censorship matters:

> Their ability to judge is at the core of their worth as educators in all matters—from knowing how to give a child the confidence to understand math to deciding on which books are to be chosen for the library. When educators allow their judgment to be denigrated by censors of any kind, they acquiesce in the erosion of their self-respect (p. 81).

However, school administrators are instructional leaders and act as liaisons among schools and school boards and the community. As such, they hold strategic positions for maintaining a school environment where intellectual freedom should be the norm. But not all school administrators are fully informed about censorship issues, as the earlier accounts suggest, nor are they always adequately prepared to deal with complaints or challenges. For school administrators to assist all learners in their goal of achieving full literacy, they must establish and support a sound rationale in defense of intellectual freedom and develop procedures in advance for dealing with censorship challenges as they arise.

A Rationale for Intellectual Freedom

The heart of any school program must be a fully articulated commitment to assisting students in achieving full literacy to the extent of their ability. This can never be realized as long as any impediment to freedom of speech, thought, and inquiry exists, which has been so adamantly stressed by the authors of this work. A free society that hopes to survive and flourish must support and defend without equivocation students' and teachers' right to pursue knowledge and read widely without the burden of censorship. Unfortunately, this is not always the situation in many school districts in the United States and in other countries. In fact, censorship has had a pronounced impact on how many teachers and students carry on the process of education in the classroom.

Textbooks in particular have come under fire in many communities when censors find a textbook's content in conflict with their own beliefs (see McClain's Chapter 9 on the Impressions series, for example). Craige (1986), in her article about a textbook trial in Alabama, suggests that any textbook presents the views of its authors, but students with the right of free inquiry and expert in critical thinking will examine text material intelligently and accept or reject ideas based on their own values. But as McClain emphasized, parents often express concerns that what their children read and experience in school is markedly different from what they remember. Craige's observation has merit:

> In granting academic freedom to scholars and teachers to pursue and impart knowledge without suffering coercion from partisan groups, we realize that our schools will be giving the young a different education from the education we adults received years ago. And in doing so we must accept a generation gap: the young will construct reality differently from their parents, and will, in fact, have different values. But in this dynamic exchange of ideas and criticism, in that endless change of what constitutes our culture's knowledge of the world, lies the health of our country's intellectual life. In that generation gap lies the hope of a better world than our own (p. 10-A).

Simmons noted in the introduction to this section that many professional organizations have published their positions on intellectual freedom and censorship. School administrators, teachers, parents, students, and other community members should read and study these as they formulate their own position on intellectual freedom.

Meeting the Challenges of Censorship

As a first step, then, school administrators should initiate the formulation of their schools' rationales and supporting policies on intellectual freedom. They would do well to make the National Council of Teachers of English and the International Reading Association Joint Task Force on Intellectual Freedom position statement as well as "The Students' Right to Read" and "The Students' Right to Know" published by the National Council of Teachers of English available to schools and school boards. In addition, not only must schools prepare in advance, they must review their position frequently. Administrators should also try to maintain open communication with the community to avoid an adversarial relationship.

Because young adult literature appears more and more on school reading lists—and on lists of most frequently censored works—administrators and schools should have a strong understanding of the nature of and purposes for teenage fiction. Gallo's Chapter 12 on YA literature and Cormier's Chapter 7 on his thoughts on being a much-censored writer earlier in this book are both good resources.

Young adult author Judy Blume, who may well be the most often censored writer in the United States, has voiced her opinion on the issue. As a member of a panel on sex, censorship, and social change at the 1986 Annual Conference of the American Library Association, Blume said:

> I believe that censorship grows out of fear.... And because fear is contagious, other parents are unsure about themselves and their relationships with their children are easily swayed by them [censors]. Book banning satisfies their need to feel in control of their children's lives.... If we really want to protect children, we'll educate them. We'll talk with them about everything on their minds,

including sexuality. We won't hide. We won't kill the messenger because we don't like the message (p. 144).

Administrators can encourage this type of constructive discourse by supporting community programs that bring parents and teenagers together to read and discuss openly what teens are reading and learning in school.

Many resources on dealing with censorship advocate having teachers write rationales to explain why they are using particular works in their classrooms (see Chapters 19 and 22 in this work and Davis, 1979; Shugert, 1983). Administrators can assist teachers in this endeavor by allowing them to use school time for research and writing. They should also support all teachers' reasonable classroom selections.

Administrators and teachers must be aware that even the most well-intentioned policies and procedures may be found wanting in a censorship crisis. As Pipkin (1993) discovered, procedures for reviewing instructional materials that are created after a challenge may be more advantageous to would-be censors than to schools. She describes her experiences that began with objections to two young adult novels and ended with many classics also being threatened. After, Pipkin realized,

> Democratic schooling is not a gift of the gods; it is hard won, and the struggle is continuous. If schools are to emerge as laboratories for the development of democracy, teachers [and administrators] must stand together against those who would dictate what we must read, write, say, think, and know in schools (p. 37).

Administrators for the Future

An administrator's positive, active leadership in defending intellectual freedom is absolutely essential. Having well-planned policies and procedures in place is a priority. Ongoing discussions or open forums on censorship issues are also helpful. When faced with a complaint or challenge, administrators should uphold the district's educational mission with strength and conviction.

The changing ethnic demographics in school populations in the future will have a major impact on education. Cultural diversity will demand that we re-examine instructional methods and materials. This will likely increase censorship incidents, and it definitely underscores the need to be prepared. The enlightened school administrator will be at the forefront of solutions to censorship problems. How else can schools fulfill their promise to our children and truly give them, as Craige said, "the hope of a better world than our own"?

References

Berger, M.D. (1994, February 17). Banned in Augusta. *The Metropolitan Spirit,* pp. 8–10.

Blume, J. (1986, September). Remarks. *Newsletter on Intellectual Freedom,* pp. 144, 176.

Burress, L., & Jenkinson, E.B. (1982). *The students' right to know.* Urbana, IL: National Council of Teachers of English.

Craige, B.J. (1986, November 6). On the issue of school book values. *The Athens Observer,* p. 10-A.

Davis, J.E. (Ed.). (1979). *Dealing with censorship.* Urbana, IL: National Council of Teachers of English.

Hentoff, N. (1981). Censorship in schools. *Learning, 9*(8), 78–81.

National Council of Teachers of English. (1982). *The students' right to read* (2nd ed.). Urbana, IL: Author.

Pipkin, G.T. (1993). Challenging the conventional wisdom on censorship. *The ALAN Review, 20*(2), 35–37.

Shugert, D.P. (Ed.). (1983). Rationales for commonly challenged books. *Connecticut English Journal, 15*(1).

Chapter 18

Preparing the New English Teacher to Deal with Censorship, or Will I Have to Face It Alone?

Robert C. Small, Jr.

College kids who want to be English teachers know absolutely nothing about censorship. More important, they also know censorship intimately. A contradiction? Well, if you were to tell my students about a group in a community calling itself "Concerned Citizens" demanding the removal of a textbook from a classroom or a novel from the school library, they would reply that nothing like that ever happened "at home." They remember no cases where their reading was censored by anyone outside the school; that is, they can remember nothing that affected their lives that was the kind of censorship that you and I worry so much about.

Censorship Type I: "I Know What's Best for You"

But ask them, "Did anyone ever try to keep you from reading what you wanted to read?" and they'll remember. And what they'll remember is insistence by English teachers that they read only certain books and stories, those books and stories chosen, of course, by their teachers. What they'll remember is insistence by school librarians that they "check out a better book than that" or

From *FOCUS*, *18*(1), pp. 74–77, 1991. Copyright © by Robert C. Small, Jr. Reprinted with permission from the author.

the librarians' sarcastic question, "Aren't you reading too much of *that sort of thing?*" What they'll remember is hiding a Judy Blume book from a teacher or not being able to take out a Norma Klein novel from the school library without a note from a parent. And some of them will remember their parents getting on them about what they were reading. They'll remember that the magazines that they wanted to read—*Seventeen* and *Building a Better Body,* for example—never satisfied any adult. They'll remember what I call the "I know what's best for you" censorship pressure that came at them from most of the adults in their lives.

Now, about to be teachers, they know little about *organized censorship.* Though most of these about-to-be teachers don't use these words, what they are saying to us English teachers is what Pogo said several decades ago: we—English teachers—truly "have met the enemy and he is us." Kids see us as the censors. We censor the reading that they do in their daily lives. Phyllis Schlafly and the Gablers are unknown to them. Fundamentalists objecting to what they see as anti-Christian elements in textbooks, blacks objecting to *Huckleberry Finn* as degrading to them, feminists objecting to the novels of Charles Dickens as demeaning to women—except in rare cases, none of these forces have touched their conscious lives. But we snatch away their comic books and their copies of *Forever.* Three or four years or more later, when they are preparing to be English language arts teachers, these former high school students identify us as the people who kept them from reading. Asked, "Who kept you from reading what you wanted to read?" they answer, "My English teacher." Less often, they answer, "The librarian." They also answer, "My parents," of course; but that's a problem beyond our reach.

Consequently, the first goal I have in this regard as I try to prepare these college students to be English language arts teachers is to help them see that English teachers shouldn't be in the business of keeping kids from reading what they want to read. As a preparer of English teachers, I try to be subtle in how I send it; but my message is, "Don't reject kids' reading. What they choose to read is what they are. Reject their reading, and you reject them."

I try to get this idea across: be glad they're reading. Show interest in it. Read some of the books yourself. Discuss your reading with them. Don't be a censor. Swap books. You don't need to pretend you liked a book you didn't. But value the enthusiasm of your students. So you hated a *Sweet Valley High* novel. That really isn't important. You probably were meant to hate it; and, anyway, your students wouldn't believe you liked it even if, by some odd happening, you really did. But what matters is the fact that some of your students loved it. They can respond to it. You can't. So who's missing the literary experience? Maybe they can help you respond.

The message is very hard to get across to English majors. I know. I was one. I've seen it from the inside, so to speak. I started my teaching of high school English after finishing a thesis— "James Joyce's *Ulysses* as a Comic Novel." You can imagine how helpful that was to me when I faced my two slow ninth grade and three slow eleventh grade classes.

English majors who plan to be school teachers are prime potential censors. You can almost hear them saying, "What! You're going to read another *Varsity Coach* novel for your book report? You can do better than that. Here, try *Pride and Prejudice*." The phrase that comes next—usually unstated but perfectly understood by both student and teacher—is "Or expect to receive an 'F' on your next book report."

I push at my teachers-to-be the idea of individualized reading programs. Now, I'm not even sure that there are any such programs out there in the schools anymore. But I keep trying. If I were head of education in the United States, I'd threaten, plead, and argue for individualized reading programs as one of the best counters to censorship. Why? First, because kids who have had happy experiences choosing their own books to read will, I feel sure, grow up to be parents who will want their children to have similar happy experiences and so will be less likely to be censors. And, second, because censorship by teachers and librarians will, by these programs, necessarily be reduced greatly in the lives of the current crop of students. And, third, because some of the current cadre of students will be the English teachers and school librarians of the future and will, from their own experiences with books, be much less likely to act the traditional teacher-censor role.

Though the term "role model" is now something of a cliché, the concept it embodies is a powerful one. I'm as sure as anything that the most powerful force acting on potential English language arts teachers is not the methods instructor nor even the supervising teacher during student teaching. No, prospective English teachers are most powerfully influenced by the tradition of English teaching that the 12 or more years they have experienced as English language arts students has established for them. Another cliché: we teach as we have been taught.

The long-range anticensorship goal for me as a teacher of English teachers is to change what teachers do from a controlling to an assisting act. Unfortunately, changing basic beliefs is very, very difficult. English majors want very much to be missionaries for "culture." Like E.D. Hirsch, they forget that literature is not something to know about but something to respond to, to be moved by, to be changed by. They forget that knowing that *Don Quixote* was written by Cervantes and that "tilting at windmills" comes from it are nothing but Trivial Pursuit board game information. They forget that the measure of our reading of a work of literature is how our response to that work changes us.

Censorship Type II: "I Wouldn't Do That If I Were You"

As potential English language arts teachers, my students will soon be out in the schools as timid, frightened, impressionable first-year teachers. They are likely to face a powerful but indirect force for censorship. Indeed, if I have done the other parts of my job well, they will encounter this force almost at once as they try to implement some of the teaching ideas I've suggested, ideas such as using personal narratives and keeping journals. Should they plan to ask their students to write about a personal experience and mention their plan to other teachers, they will encounter the force of "I wouldn't do that if I were you. Parents won't like it." If my ex-students decide to use one of the provocative novels they've read in my adolescent literature class—novels like *A Shadow Like a Leopard* and *Maniac Magee*—they'll hear from some of their more experienced colleagues, "I wouldn't use that if I were you. Parents won't like it."

This is the second kind of censorship that I try to prepare my students for—the pull toward self-censorship. In some ways, it's easier to alert them to this kind of censorship force than to help them understand the kind that I've called the "I know what's best for you" type. Most of the prospective English language arts teachers I've known become angry at the notion that someone would dare to question their judgment about literature or writing. They have a surprisingly high opinion of their own importance and abilities and wisdom considering that they are 20-year-olds who have never taught a class. But then, so did I when I was preparing to teach. At least, in discussing censorship, I am pretty sure that I can start with a strong—if uninformed—hostility on their part to the notion of outside censorship.

Still, I know how powerful is the influence of experienced colleagues on the new teacher. My students scorn self-censorship. They call it "wimpy" and claim that they will never yield to pressure from older teachers. But I know better. So, what I try to do is to make them realize that they will face three kinds of powerful pressures to change their instructional plans. If they can distinguish among the three and figure out how to deal with each, then, I hope, they have a chance of resisting pressures for self-censorship.

Wise advice. First, they need to be able to detect wise advice when it is given to them. Sometimes the "I wouldn't use that if I were you" advice is educationally sound: "I wouldn't use *Moby Dick* with that slow ninth grade class if I were you." I consider that sound advice based on educational knowledge and experience. *Moby Dick,* great though it may be as an artistic creation, is not a work of literature that those slow ninth grade students will be able to respond to. The new teacher is being told, "Don't ask them to read something they can't understand." "Good advice!" I say.

Wimpy advice. On the other hand, a colleague might say, "I wouldn't use that novel if I were you. Parents won't like it. Stick to something safe." That seems to me to be wimpy advice based on fear and a general unwillingness to take risks. I don't consider that sound advice.

Ambiguous advice. Unfortunately, life rarely falls neatly into two classes, the good and the bad. So, there is a third kind of "I wouldn't do that if I were you" advice that I consider sound but that has the ring of the wimpy, self-censorship kind. No teacher should want to create a community uproar unnecessarily. And parents have a right—indeed, a responsibility—to protect their children from harm. New, inexperienced teachers straight from a university campus sometimes have been known to select a novel or a story or piece of nonfiction that is bound to offend most parents and lots of students. In that case, the "I wouldn't use that" advice might be wise, even though it is suggesting self-censorship. Maybe teaching *Forever* to a whole class or using the latest hit gay novel from Christopher Street or some such isn't such a good idea. It's sometimes hard to distinguish between wimpiness and accepting community standards; but I believe that my students need to think about the differences.

When I'm suggesting to my students ways that they should go about deciding what literature to use in their classes, the first place I send them is to the school librarian. No one in the school knows more about what students are reading. What they like. What they object to. And what their parents won't want them to read. And no one in the school has a better sense of what books have caused concerned parents—in the good sense—to raise, not objections, but questions: "Is this really good for Jane to read?" "Will that rough language influence Joe? I've tried to encourage him not to use that kind of talk." No one in the school will know more about the various review publications that can serve as a source of information about the quality, popularity, and problems with works of literature under consideration.

Censorship Type III: "Don't You Dare Teach That Filth to My Children"

I also try to prepare by students for the possibility that they will face a censorship effort mounted by people outside the school. As I said earlier, they almost never remember experiencing this kind of censorship, although some of them come from school systems that I know have been the targets of planned, organized efforts to remove textbooks from classes and books from the school library. But high school students live in their own world, and Beverly La Haye is rarely a part of that world.

Indeed, troubling as it is to concede, I have to admit that many of the university students that I encounter seem only vaguely to realize that people in the United States want to censor the books that children and teenagers read, as well as the books and magazines they themselves can buy. They haven't heard of Anne Frank's *Diary of a Young Girl* accused of being subversive to religious values. They haven't been accused of "teaching filth to my children" when they suggested *I Know Why the Caged Bird Sings* for individualized reading to a group of students. When my students read about such cases—as I have them do—and discuss the reasons why parents and others might come to the school with complaints about books, they usually react by saying that kids should have the right to read what they want to, that forbidding a certain book will only make it more attractive to teenagers, and that kids aren't going to be hurt by reading a book, certainly not the kinds of books that seem to be the targets of organized censors. In other words, they say more or less what I would say.

In fact, I find myself having to take the other side of the issue in order to force them to think about what they are saying rather than merely reciting absolute truths. It's an odd role for me to play, though probably good for me to have to carry out. I've found these preservice teachers I work with hold their views on censorship simplistically, mostly without having thought much about them. "Censorship is bad, right?" "Freedom is good, right?" "Censorship is un-American, right?" "Censors are kooks, right?" "I have the right to lead my life the way I want to, right?" So, first, I try to deepen their understanding of why people might want to censor children's reading and of the rights of the various individuals involved in censorship situations. Doing so seems to me to be an important part of my larger effort to prepare them to deal with a censorship situation if they find themselves in the midst of one (see Small, 1979). We talk about book selection policies and procedures for English departments and school systems in general. We consider the mood and frame of mind of a parent who shows up in a school to protest the use of a piece of literature in class. We consider how to deal with such a parent, what approaches will be helpful, and which will make the situa-

---

tion worse. We consider policies and procedures that a school system might establish to deal with a complaint (see Small, 1989).

I ask them to read model selection policies and procedures for dealing with objections to literary selections. I use materials from the National Council of Teachers of English, American Library Association, and the International Reading Association; and I try to help them see that the school librarian faces exactly the same problems that they will as language arts teachers: if *The Wizard of Oz* is objectionable to some parents when parts of it are included in a reader or literature textbook, it will nearly as quickly become objectionable when those same parents find that the entire book is in the school library and on lists of "books you might enjoy." If Anne Frank's diary is irreligious when it is assigned in English class, it will soon follow that it should be on a restricted shelf in the library.

Conclusion

There is only so much that preservice teachers can absorb about censorship or anything else. With no experience and, while they are student teaching, with daily survival their main concern, they quite wisely discard much detailed information that would only confuse them and make decisive action impossible. At this beginning point in their careers, the attitudes with which they approach teaching and its many problems are, I believe, more significant than any particular knowledge they may have about such matters as censorship. Positive attitudes about kids and their reading, cautious attitudes about advice not to try something new, open but questioning attitudes about individuals and groups that want to remove books from the school will, I believe, equip my students to meet censorship challenges with confidence in themselves.

References

Small, R. (1979). Censorship and English: Some things we don't seem to think about very often (but should). In J. Davis (Ed.), *Dealing with censorship* (pp. 54–62). Urbana, IL: National Council of Teachers of English.

Small, R. (1989, Spring). So what do we do now? A case of censorship. *FOCUS: Teaching English Language Arts, 15*(2) 82–87.

Chapter 19

A Plan of Action for Secondary English Teachers

Malcolm E. Stern

"Scratch anyone deeply enough and you'll find a censor," says Judith Krug (personal communication, April 25, 1994), director of the American Library Association's Office for Intellectual Freedom. High school teachers throughout the United States are finding, unfortunately, that even minor scratches are revealing many censors. Over the last decade the number of challenges to literature taught in high schools has risen dramatically as the authors in this work have learned. Some attacks are rather mild complaints about a specific title being taught, while others are actual book burnings as in Warsaw, Indiana, described by Jenkinson in Chapter 3.

English teachers must be ever vigilant regarding challenges to the curriculum. The National Council of Teachers of English has issued a pamphlet on "The Students' Right to Read" (1982) mentioned earlier in this section. In it the teacher's purpose for educating students and using diverse literature—free from censorship—in the classroom is clearly articulated:

> The right to read, like all rights guaranteed or implied within our constitutional tradition, can be used wisely or foolishly. In many ways, education is an effort to improve the quality of choices open to all students. But to deny the freedom of choice in fear that it may be unwisely used is to destroy the freedom itself. For this reason, we respect the right of individuals to be selective in their own

reading. But for the same reason, we oppose efforts of individuals or groups to limit the freedom of choice of others or to impose their own standards or tastes upon the community at large.

The right of any individual not just to read but to read whatever he or she wants to read is basic to a democratic society. This right is based on an assumption that the educated possess judgment and understanding and can be trusted with the determination of their own actions. In effect, the reader is freed from the bonds of chance. The reader is not limited by birth, geographic location, or time, since reading allows meeting people, debating philosophies, and experiencing events far beyond the narrow confines of an individual's own existence.

In selecting books for reading by young people, English teachers consider the contribution which each work may make to the education of the reader, its aesthetic value, its honesty, its readability for a particular group of students, and its appeal to adolescents. English teachers, however, may use different works for different purposes.... But the teacher selects, not censors, books. Selection implies that a teacher is free to choose this or that work, depending upon the purpose to be achieved and the student or class in question, but a book selected this year may be ignored next year, and the reverse. Censorship implies that certain works are not open to selection, this year or any year.

How does an English teacher fight censorship? The first step is to follow the motto "be prepared," as Simmons stressed in this section's introduction. Donelson (1974), author of Chapter 22 in this work, suggests that each English department should consider doing the following before complaints or challenges arise:

1. Develop a rationale for teaching literature.
2. Establish a committee that recommends books for possible use to the department.
3. Work on community support of academic freedom.
4. Communicate with the community about the English program.
5. Implement a formal policy to handle attempted censorship.
6. Write rationales for each book taught in any class.

A 1993 censorship survey of 97 English departments was conducted by the Illinois Association of Teachers of English. The results suggested that many districts need to consider seriously Donelson's suggestions: only 43 percent have a formal written policy regarding censorship; only 27 percent keep rationales for teaching controversial texts; and only 48 percent require that a complaint be in written form. Nearly half reported they had received challenges to reading materials, 27 percent said they had complaints about specific writing assignments, and 21 percent reported attacks on a particular method of teaching. Donelson also cites similar findings in Chapter 22. Hopkins reported in the January 1992 *Newsletter on Intellectual Freedom* that she found if a written policy existed for the district, if there was a formal complaint process, and if the teachers had administrative support, challenged material was more likely to remain in the curriculum. The message is clear. Donelson's suggestions will take time and energy to implement, but much agony can be spared if policies and procedures are in place when a challenge comes.

As a guide and a place to start, I have written a sample rationale for *Slaughterhouse-Five* by Kurt Vonnegut.

> *Slaughterhouse-Five* is an excellent novel for high school seniors to study; it was written by Kurt Vonnegut, a contemporary author. Far too often the high school curriculum ignores the contributions of living, working writers. This is a good novel to bridge the gap from long deceased writers to vibrant, living ones.
>
> This novel is based on Vonnegut's experiences as a prisoner of war in Dresden, Germany, during the fire bombing on February 13, 1945. In this attack on an open city over 135,000 people died. This represents more casualties than were incurred in the bombing of Hiroshima where *only* 71,000 were killed. *Slaughterhouse-Five* is Vonnegut's response to this experience.
>
> *Slaughterhouse-Five* does not glorify war: Billy Pilgrim, the main character, is not a much-decorated war hero; he is a chaplain's assistant. In fact, Vonnegut promises that this book will have no role for John Wayne or Frank Sinatra; he has kept his word. This novel addresses a part of our history that is presented to the reader in a very nonhistorical manner.
>
> This novel does indeed debunk several myths about war, but it does much, much more. It illustrates how materialism can destroy culture; how people deal with stress; how people in high positions

make decisions without regard for human life; how important a sense of humor is to survival; and how war can destroy buildings, art, and countries but not the human spirit. Discussions on this novel can be about censorship, war, time travel, satire, humor, secret files, style, and so on.

The style of this novel is unconventional. Whereas most novels progress in a linear manner, *Slaughterhouse-Five* does not. It meanders forward, backward, circular, and into other galaxies. Characters are clearly drawn, and readers can empathize with them. The novel deftly mixes fiction and nonfiction. A discussion of style of this novel can be challenging and stimulating.

Many parents may attack the novel because of the language Vonnegut uses. It is true there are obscenities and vulgar language in places; however, they add an air of realism to a novel about World War II. Vonnegut is most judicious in his use of profanity. Where it helps establish a mood or tone, he uses it. When literature reflects the dynamic nature of language, we need to include that in our students' education. The language in this novel certainly is not included to stir the prurient interests of our students. To focus on the language of the novel is to miss his major point: war is the obscenity, not words.

Our students should be exposed to a wide range of literature both in content and style. *Slaughterhouse-Five* is a different and important experience for our students to have. This multifaceted novel is too frequently dismissed as mere science fiction. The fact is, it presents our students with some serious philosophical issues to contemplate and discuss.

This novel has been attacked and even burned since it first appeared in 1969 in the United States. This is an unfortunate fate for such a powerful book in a country that prizes freedom. When his novel was banned and burned in a school in Drake, North Dakota, Vonnegut (1981) wrote a letter to the board of education and said, "those words really don't damage children much. It was evil deeds and lying that hurt us." He concludes by noting, "You have insulted me, and I am a good citizen, and I am real." He is, indeed, as real as his book. All of us need the challenge of a thoughtful novel, and *Slaughterhouse-Five* certainly provides us with that.

Literature-Selection Procedures

A rather effective method of sharing the responsibility for the selection of the literature in an English program is to develop a selection process that involves several different communities. The local board of education should have a clear policy, procedures, and criteria for selection of instructional materials. In my district, we developed the following "Selection of Instructional Materials Policy" in 1981–82 (see also Grantham's Chapter 21 for a more detailed discussion):

Selection of Instructional Materials Policy

The board of education recognizes that academic freedom is basic to the survival of a democratic society and that the faculty has the right and responsibility to select instructional materials for board approval. The district shall provide a wide range of instructional materials at varying levels of difficulty, with diversity of appeal, and with presentation of different points of view to meet the needs of students as expressed in the philosophy, goals, and objectives of the high school.

Procedures for Implementation

I. Objectives

In order to ensure that the instructional materials selected will implement and support the educational programs of the school, the following selection objectives are adopted:

- to provide materials that will enrich and support the curriculum, taking into consideration the varied interests, abilities, maturity levels, and learning patterns of the students

- to provide materials that will stimulate growth in factual knowledge, literary appreciation, aesthetic values, and ethical standards

- to provide background of information which will enable students to make intelligent judgments in their daily lives

- to provide materials on opposing sides of controversial issues so that young citizens may have an opportunity to develop under guidance the skills of critical analysis

- to provide a collection of instructional materials reflecting a range of views promoting the student's positive self-image and depicting a pluralistic society which reflects the contributions of our ethnic heritage

- to place principle above personal opinion and reason above prejudice in the selection of materials of the highest quality in order to ensure a comprehensive collection appropriate to the school community

II. Definition of Instructional Materials

Instructional materials include textbooks, library books, supplementary reading, information materials, charts, dioramas, filmstrips, flash cards, games, globes, kits, machine readable data files, maps, microfilms, models, motion pictures, musical scores, pamphlets, periodicals, pictures, slides, sound recordings, transparencies, video recordings. Materials may be commercially acquired or locally produced.

III. Responsibility for Selection of Instructional Materials

The board of education is legally responsible for all matters relating to the operation of the high school and its instructional program. It delegates to the administration the selection of materials in accordance with the objectives listed above. The administration acts on the recommendations of the faculty based on the following criteria:

- educational significance of the material
- contribution of the material to the curriculum and interests of the students
- favorable reviews found in standard selection sources
- favorable recommendations based on preview and examination of the materials by professional personnel
- reputation and significance of the author, artist, composer, producer, or publisher
- accuracy, authoritativeness, and appropriateness of the material
- contribution of the material to the breadth of representative viewpoints on controversial issues
- readability and degree of student appeal
- appropriate artistic and literary quality
- compliance with district standards on racism and sexism
- reflective of the pluralistic character and culture of people in the United States
- timeliness and permanence of the material
- acceptable technical quality and durable format
- cost-effectiveness of the material

IV. Selection of Textbooks and Supplementary Materials

Individual teachers utilizing the stated selection criteria and the school's Recommendation for Adoption of Instructional Materials form will evaluate materials. Their recommendation will be presented to departmental grade level committees for discussion and approval. The department chairperson will review and approve the grade level committee's recommendations and forward them to the administrator responsible for action regarding instructional materials. A committee will review all materials requests and will make recommendations to the superintendent. The final decisions concerning adoptions will be made by the board of education.

V. Selection of Instructional Materials Housed in the Library and Resource Centers

When recommending materials for the library, audiovisual center, and resource centers, the certified library/media personnel will evaluate the existing collection; assess curricula and recreational needs; examine materials; and consult reputable, professionally prepared selection aids. Suggestions for acquisition will be solicited from administrators, faculty, and students. All materials will be judged by the criteria outlined above and will be accepted or rejected by those criteria. Selection is an ongoing process which will include the removal of dated materials and the replacement of lost and/or worn items retaining education value. Recommendations for selection and removal will be forwarded to the administration for approval.

Source: Evanston Township High School, Evanston, Illinois

Once a selection policy has been set, each English department should establish a textbook selection committee to read, discuss, and recommend titles to the department chair. First, this committee completes a form similar to the one in Figure 1. Second, the school should have a curriculum council comprising school administrators and department chairs to review the titles as well. A curriculum forum could also be established that would include some school personnel, parents, and students who could voice their opinions about the books. Finally, recommendations from these committees would be sent to the superintendent and board of education for final approval. Once approved, the literature becomes part of the curriculum.

Figure 1 Recommendation for Adoption of Textbooks and Supplementary Materials for Classroom Use

Submit a separate form for each textbook adoption to the chair of the curriculum council by _____ (date)

Title_____Hardcover_____Softcover_____

Author, editor, or compiler_____

Type of material _____

Publisher or producer _____

Publication date _____

List price_____

Recommended for use in grade _____

subject area _____

How Do These Materials Rate?

1. To what extent is the material suitable for the ability level?

2. What is the readability level?

3. To what extent is the readability appropriate for the ability level?

4. To what extent does the material meet the school's guidelines on sexism?

5. To what extent does the material meet the school's guidelines on minority representation?

6. To what extent does the material meet the school's guidelines on metric education?

7. To what extent is the material up to date?

8. To what extent is the format attractive and pleasing?

This process does indeed take time, but it offers many advantages. Several groups are involved in the decision: students, parents, teachers, department chairs, administrators, and board members. These groups share the responsibility for the decision, so if a challenge is made, no single teacher bears the brunt of the attack. The teacher has, in writing, the support of these other communities.

Reconsideration of Materials

Another effective tool in fighting censorship is to have in board policy a formal process for the reconsideration of instructional materials. My district developed the following policy:

Reconsideration of Instructional Material Policy

The board of education supports the principles of intellectual freedom protected by the First Amendment of the United States Constitution and encourages the free expression of opinions. The right of dissent also protected by the First Amendment allows objections to instructional materials to be raised. Any resident or employee of the school district, therefore, may formally challenge instructional resources used in the district's educational programs.

Procedures for Implementation

I. Request for Informal Reconsideration

The school, upon receiving a complaint regarding an instructional material, shall try to resolve the issue informally. The department chairperson or other appropriate administrator or staff member shall explain to the objector the school's selection procedure and criteria, as well as the qualifications of those persons selecting the material. The department chairperson or other appropriate staff member shall explain the particular place the questioned material occupies in the educational program and its intended educational usefulness. If the objector wishes to file a formal challenge, a copy of the district's Selection of Instructional Materials Policy and a Request for Reconsideration of Instructional Materials form shall be provided to the party concerned.

II. Request for Formal Reconsideration

All formal objections to instructional materials shall be made on a Request for Reconsideration of Instructional Materials form. The form shall be signed by the objector and filed with the superinten-

Figure 2 Request for Reconsideration of Instructional Materials

Title_____

Author, Editor, Compiler_____Type of material _____

Publisher_____

Request initiated by _____

Address _____

City _____Phone _____

Do you represent

_____ yourself

_____ an organization (name)

_____ other group (name)

1. To what in the material do you object? (Please be specific: cite page, frames in a filmstrip, film sequence, band number on a record, or other information.)

2. What do you feel might be the result of a student becoming involved with this material in a learning situation?

3. For what age group would you recommend this material?

4. Is there anything good about this material?

5. Did you read the entire book, see the entire film, listen to the entire recording, use the entire kit or evaluate component parts of the kit? What parts?

6. Are you aware of the judgment of this material in any printed reviews?

7. What do you believe is the theme of this material?

8. Are you aware of the teacher's purpose in using this material?

9. What would you like your school to do about this material?

_____Do not assign or lend to my child

_____Request it be re-evaluated by a reconsideration committee

_____Other (explain)

10. In its place, what other print or nonprint material would you recommend that would convey as valuable a picture and perspective of the subject treated and would be of equal value to the instruction program?

Signature _____

Adapted from the National Council of Teachers of English, "The Students' Right to Read" (1982).

It is also important to recognize and acknowledge that, in expressing their opinions and concerns, censors are exercising the same rights librarians seek to protect when they confront censorship. Complaints and criticism are forms of expression that are protected in the same way as the rights of those who create and disseminate "objectionable" material. But censors do not just complain: they ask that the material they find objectionable be removed, and as mentioned earlier, this is *not* their right.

Policy, Policy, Policy

What do you do if someone complains and demands that school library resources be removed or restricted? For years, the Office for Intellectual Freedom has been urging librarians to have written materials-selection and -reconsideration policies in place, similar to those recommended for school boards and English departments in previous chapters. While having a procedure for dealing with complaints does not reduce the number of challenges received, it does greatly increase the percentage of challenges that are resolved with retaining the materials (McAffee, 1992). The materials-selection policy should incorporate a statement on intellectual freedom that refers to or appends a statement such as the Library Bill of Rights or the Freedom to Read Statement, both published by the American Library Association. These serve as fundamental statements of principle on how the library will conduct itself in selecting materials and evaluating the collection.

The procedure by which library or school boards adopt the Library Bill of Rights or the Freedom to Read Statement is purely local—in the United States, almost all determinations about library or school operation rest with the local governing body, usually the library or school board. The Office for Intellectual Freedom simply encourages such bodies to adopt the Library Bill of Rights and the Freedom to Read Statement as the best expressions of intellectual freedom principles under which the board, school district, or library will operate. There is no identified procedure for adopting these documents. Ordinarily, the local school or library board simply adopts a policy that says that its operations and procedures will be consistent with the principles expressed in those documents and appends the documents.

Endorsement of these documents is a separate issue. International organizations of librarians, educators, booksellers, or publishers, through their own governing bodies, could endorse these statements. If they plan to do so, they should inform the American Library Association of their intent. The statements are copyrighted documents of the American Library Association; other organizations wishing to reprint them generally seek permission to do so from the ALA by writing a letter of request.

An essential corollary to a selection policy is a written reconsideration policy, which provides a vehicle for parents or library patrons to express their concerns to the school library's management. Reconsideration policies typically set up a three-level procedure. The first level involves the patron issuing a written complaint by filling out a Patron Request for Reconsideration form. *Written* complaints launch the procedure. It is not at all unusual to resolve initial verbal complaints informally in the librarian's office by explaining the philosophy, mission, and operation of the library. Many complainants—when given the form at the close of such a talk—elect not to go through the process after all. On the other hand, some patrons may attempt to *bypass* procedures and go straight to the school board, the local press, or a politically well-situated friend. Libraries should insist their procedures be followed. If the complainant goes to the board first, the appropriate response is to inform that person of the procedures, give him or her the form to fill out, and wait for the form to be returned. Under most policies, unless and until there is a written complaint, the process cannot be started.

If the complainant does return the form, the librarian—after a careful review of the materials—responds in writing, explaining the mission of the library and the criteria for selection. If the librarian concludes that the materials meet the selection criteria (which is usually the case), the letter should explain exactly how this is so. If the complainant is not satisfied with the librarian's response, a reconsideration committee is formed. (Sometimes policies skip the first step and form a committee directly.) The composition of these committees varies from community to community; ordinarily they involve the librarian, and in larger libraries, the appropriate library staff (such as the children's or young adult librarian), a member of the community who is not affiliated with either the library or the complainant, and some other designated persons either in the town government or other profession. Some school policies require that a teacher, member of the Parent-Teacher Association, or lawyer and a student representative be members of such a committee. In any case, the committee should be composed of a diverse group of individuals who can render an objective evaluation of the challenged material. It is, of course, *not* advisable to allow the complainant to sit on such a committee.

Each member of the committee reviews the material under question *in its entirety* and weighs it against the materials-selection criteria. With smaller libraries, it is sometimes difficult to do this because there may be a limited number of copies of the material under question, and all the reconsideration committee members need to read them. Often complainants focus on a word or one or two pages of a book. The selection criteria and reconsideration policy should make it clear that materials will be judged *as a whole*: materials that meet the selection criteria will *not* be removed due to controversial content. Also, ALA's policy on "Challenged Materials" says that no materials that have been the subject of complaints shall be removed from circulation unless and until a final decision has been reached through an adversary process—either a school board meeting or litigation.

> *"The selection criteria and reconsideration policy of a library should make it clear that materials will be judged as a whole."*

Other information can certainly be part of the reconsideration process, including reviews, information about the author, information about how many other libraries maintain the same materials in the collections (this can be a double-edged sword—see the discussion of how pressure groups use this technique against libraries in the next section), information about the demand for the materials within the community, and any policy that may apply to the specific complaint. For example, if the complainant feels that books of scary poetry are inappropriate for elementary level students and objects to the fact that they are available to children of all ages in the library, you might want to consult ALA's policies on "Access to Resources and Services in the School Library Media Program" and "Free Access to Libraries for Minors," both interpretations of the Library Bill of Rights. Also, when the challenge is first received, the librarian should contact the Office for Intellectual Freedom. The office provides a "case support" service, gathering the necessary reviews and ALA policies that will support the defense of the library's position on intellectual freedom and aid the committee in its review. (The case support service of the Office for Intellectual Freedom is primarily a service for librarians in the United States. We do, of course, provide information about censorship in U.S. libraries to international callers and occasionally field calls from the international press. However, we are not equipped to take on servicing case support calls internationally, not only because we do not have enough staff, but because the people calling may live in countries that do not have legal protections similar to the U.S. First Amendment. Within the United States, state library association intellectual freedom committees should be contacted for support in addition to the Office for Intellectual Freedom. Related organizations maintain similar resources for educators.)

Give the committee time enough to undertake its process in a thoughtful manner. It is a good idea for policies to include time limits: how many days after receipt of a complaint a response shall be issued; how many days after that the complainant has to appeal and ask that a reconsideration committee be formed; and how many days or weeks after that the committee must be formed and render its decision (see Grantham's following chapter).

When the reconsideration committee has completed its deliberations, it should notify the complainant in writing. If the complainant is not satisfied with the recommendation of the committee, then the complainant can appeal to the school board. The librarian or others who support intellectual freedom should also have an opportunity to appeal. The fact that the board will consider the issue should be widely announced, and all persons wishing to speak should be encouraged to attend the meeting. There will most likely be people in the audience prepared to testify against the challenged book. Be smart: make sure a network of supportive parents is available to be called upon to speak in favor of intellectual freedom. Those who attend should be handed a copy of the materials-selection policy and reconsideration procedures, if possible. Working within whatever rules are set by law and policy, ask those who wish to speak to sign in and set a time limit for each speech. No one should speak twice until everyone who wants to speak has had a chance. The rules of operation of the meeting should be announced at the start by the chair, which helps control the high emotions often involved in a censorship controversy.

At such a meeting, the community has an opportunity to see the democratic process of citizens voicing their opinions and debating the issues: they can come to recognize that the preservation of their right to voice those views depends on the preservation of the rights of others to dissent and to disagree; they may come to appreciate that this right is a protection of individual liberty against government abuse, of individuals with controversial ideas against the mainstream forces that attempt to silence them. It is actually possible to come out of such a meeting with new and committed friends of the library and supporters of intellectual freedom. The most important strategy is sticking to policy. Insist it be followed, even when someone has tried to go around it and has created a public stir before filing a complaint. Get policies together, urge the board to pass them, and publicize that the board supports the library and will stand by those policies.

How Pressure Groups Try to Use Policy Against Libraries

Failure to follow policy and procedures provides potent ammunition for challenge to any official action. Censors realize this and often attempt to pressure local school boards to remove the key elements of the policy—namely, the Library Bill of Rights and the Freedom to Read Statement. Censors seem to harbor the facile belief that removing these documents will "free" the board to commit censorship with impunity (as if their obligations suddenly disappeared).

Librarians in the United States should fight for the retention of these documents in policy because they are the most effective expressions of how First Amendment principles should be applied in the library context. They also provide an invaluable policy perspective on intellectual freedom, which can help answer many questions about how libraries should operate. In response to a move to delete the Library Bill of Rights and the Freedom to Read Statement from policy in Nevada, the Office for Intellectual Freedom prepared a statement on the importance and centrality of these documents to library policy and operation. The statement observes in part,

> To delete them from operational standards, guidelines, and poli-cies would be to cut school librarians and school boards adrift without their most trusted guiding star. These essential statements of principle have been proven more valuable than any others in guiding librarians and school boards through controversy and helping them to fulfill their constitutional obligation to uphold the freedom to read for students. The patent motivation of those who would call for the removal of these essential statements of princi-ple...is to create a loophole for engaging in censorship. The Library Bill of Rights and Freedom to Read Statement stand as bulwarks not only against censorship, but also against the inevitable consequences of censorship: intolerance, closed-mindedness, orthodoxy, and sometimes litigation.

Library or school boards that have adopted the Library Bill of Rights or the Freedom to Read Statement would violate their own policies by voting to remove or restrict books, which otherwise meet selection criteria, on the grounds they are offensive, not age appropriate, or controversial. Pressure groups *know* this, and that is why they have launched campaigns to remove these statements of principle from library policy. Often they attack the reconsidera-tion procedure, saying it is a meaningless exercise with a foregone conclusion. Libraries should not be coy about the fact that removal of materials under reconsideration is highly unlikely; the procedure is there for persons who feel strongly that materials do not meet selection criteria, *not* to facilitate censorship.

Be aware that censors who encounter firm resolve at the outset will sometimes challenge selection criteria next, attempting to insert various restrictions, most of which would be at least arguably unconstitutional. They may present a list of *words,* the mere presence of which anywhere in any book will disqualify those books from selection in the censors' eyes. But materials should be judged as a whole, and library policy should say so. They may ask that the library rigidly enforce "age appropriateness standards." These deny the individuality of students, their different levels of maturity, background, and ability—which do not uniformly correspond to their chronological age or grade level—by categorizing them as "fourth grade" or "ages 10 and up," as if there are no younger students mature enough for or older ones interested in the material. Your policy should say that you do not restrict materials based on age or grade level.

Pressure groups may accuse you of censoring everything not selected. This is nonsense, as Sipe pointed out in Chapter 16. Obviously, no library has the budget or the space to purchase all the materials the librarian would like to provide. Some censors have realized this too, and they may argue that because the library has limitations, surely it could make better use of its resources than choosing *this* book! Rarely do they have suggestions for alternative titles that would fill the same niche in the collection, or if they do, they may suggest materials that are not equivalent but present sectarian or partisan views opposite to those in the challenged material (views that should already be represented in the collection). The answer to these attacks is that, within its limitations, the library strives to provide a diversity of materials and does not exclude materials just because they may be controversial or offensive to some people. Selection is an inclusive process; censorship is an exclusive process.

If protesters are not accusing the library of censoring through selection, then they may say that the collection is biased and underrepresents their point of view. Do not legitimize this attack: make sure your collection adequately provides a diversity of views.

If the library makes a strong statement in support of intellectual freedom, censors may say, "So you're saying anything goes? There are no standards?" Still more nonsense. Of course there are standards, right there in the selection policy. But there is also a statement that the library will not exclude appropriate materials just because they contain controversial depictions, words, or explicit material, when, taken as a whole, they meet selection criteria and serve the needs of library users.

In the current atmosphere of intense intimidation and pressure, pressure groups have learned to pit weak librarians against strong ones by comparing their collections. This is why gathering information about how many other libraries have the challenged title can be damaging if school librarians in your area have failed to stand together to defend access to controversial books. If there is only one librarian in the area who has supported intellectual freedom, the collection overseen by that librarian will probably reflect his or her commitment. But the groups will use the selection decision of that librarian's colleagues against other libraries: "Yours is the only school library in our district that has this book! You are obviously out of line and out of touch with community standards," they may say. This accusation ignores what may be legitimate differences in selection criteria that exist based on varying community needs and disregards the library's mission to serve all of its users, not just the most vocal. When censors cry "community standards" they usually imply that the only community that *counts* is the one they represent. So do not become a weapon to be used against colleagues—resist self-censorship because the impulse to protect yourself will only result in grief for a fellow member of the library profession later.

Remember the Library's Mission

It should be obvious that the active communication of the school library media center's essential mission—to provide choice among a diversity of materials that supplement and go beyond the curriculum—must be a priority. Censors forget that selection is not endorsement: it is the library doing its job as a neutral provider of information. They also often forget that books are precious and wonderful to children. Books offer secret places of joy and understanding, the love of which makes lifetime readers out of children. School librarians are uniquely situated to communicate by example the precious and fragile nature of the freedom to read.

Reference
McAffee, D.H. (1992, January). Why school book challenges succeed or fail. *Newsletter on Intellectual Freedom*, p. 1.

classrooms. Individual teachers selected these books with the approval of the department chair; classroom sets of the YA novels were purchased by the school with the approval of the principal. This literary genre represented a unique problem for our school board. Not only was it classified as "supplementary materials," but it was unfamiliar to most citizens in our community; they did not view YA novels as "classics"—well-established works broadly recognized as worthy of required study. Moreover, because most of the novels appearing in the classrooms had been only recently published, teachers who used them did not have a comfortable fund of literary scholarship with which to defend them when challenged by a parent or concerned citizen.

Superintendents: Varied Personalities

Bay County elects a school superintendent every four years. An appointed superintendent can be removed from office if his or her performance is not in accordance with the collective will of the school board, whereas an elected superintendent is in office for four years, regardless of the board's inclination. Thus the lines of authority have never been well defined between the school board and the superintendent. Because the nature of the superintendent's office changes every four years—as determined by the personality of the individual elected—the school board must "shift gears" in the way it coordinates policy prerogatives with each new superintendent. It is much more difficult to establish mutually acceptable policy between school boards and elected superintendents.

"It is much more difficult to establish mutually acceptable policy between school boards and *elected* superintendents."

The "new" superintendent in 1984 was Leonard Hall. He ran for office on a platform that promised to "get Christian values back in our schools," and he did not have formal education in school administration. When an elected superintendent has particular views of morality and authority that conflict with those of many community members, it is not difficult to predict that some of the superintendent's decisions might be unpopular. Under such potentially confrontational circumstances, the school board's role becomes complex.

A Problem Grows and Intensifies

In the early 1980s, Mowat Junior High School in Panama City had recruited an English language arts faculty distinguished by its members' youth and the recency of their graduate training. Within this department, the teachers sought to invest current ideas into their curriculum, including the study of young adult literature.

Gloria Pipkin, the chair of the department, was an outstanding, experienced teacher and a dynamic leader. Both the students in her classes and the other English teachers responded enthusiastically to her and produced exceptional work. The majority of the teachers in the department were fiercely loyal to Pipkin. Most had been students of a newly established graduate program in English education on the Panama City campus of Florida State University, where teacher education programs were well respected. During the early 1980s, these young English teachers enjoyed the heady feeling that they were really making a difference in the lives of their students. They were rewarded for their efforts when, in 1985, Mowat was the only junior high school in Florida to receive a "Center for Excellence" award from the National Council of Teachers of English.

The teachers had just begun to savor their success when they became embroiled in a heated controversy. A parent expressed concern that the book *I Am the Cheese* by Robert Cormier (an author in this work) was being taught to her daughter's class. This parent did not approve of the book's profanities, its depressing theme, and its subversive (to her) message that government agents are capable of becoming involved in murder.

Previous to this incident, Mowat teachers had dealt with complaints by assigning alternative books to individual students. This parent, however, rejected that option. She was afraid her daughter would become the object of ridicule or be ostracized if she were set apart from other students by reading a different novel. Soon the parent filed a formal challenge with the county against both *I Am the Cheese* and *About David* by Susan B. Pfeffer,

ferences is extremely demanding, and the solutions are not always perfect. However, citizens in a democracy continue to grope for a means to reach a consensus on difficult issues such as these.

Out of the conflict, the distrust, and the bitterness evoked by the challenge to the Mowat program there has emerged a set of guidelines that—at least for now—are acceptable to all parties and comprehensive enough to cover all types of curricular materials. The difficult lesson we learned and suggest that other school boards heed is that a policy covering all possible teaching materials must be created. Such a policy allows the board to control the introduction or exclusion of all materials and, at the same time, allows concerned citizens and parents to make responsible complaints.

Appendix: Bay County School Board Policy (1991) Review of Classroom Instruction Materials

The following process and procedures shall be followed by any parent or parents who object to the use of specific material in a classroom.

A. All textbooks, instructional aids, supplementary materials, and classroom library materials used in the classroom shall be subject to review under this procedure.

B. There shall be created in each school in the district an instructional material review committee. It shall be made up of five citizens selected by the school board who reside in the particular school zone, two teachers selected by the superintendent from the particular school, and two teachers selected by the principal from the particular school. Each committee member shall be selected for a one-year term.

C. Parents or citizens who object to the use of specific material should make their objections explicitly known to the teacher and principal and attempt to resolve the problem at that level. If their objections cannot be resolved at that level, a request for Reconsideration of Instructional Material form shall be filed with the school instructional material review committee. Within 10 working days of such filing, parents of other students in the class(es) involved or potentially affected in that school shall be notified in writing by the principal that a challenge has been initiated.

D. Based on a parent or citizen's written complaint, each school instructional material review committee is authorized to conduct a review of the textbook(s), instructional aid(s), or supplemental material(s) challenged. If the complainant is a member of the review committee, he or she shall not participate in a review of the challenged material.

E. The school instructional material review committee shall meet and shall make written recommendations to the individual principal within 30 working days of the filing of a complaint. The committee recommendations shall address whether the challenged material is consistent with the selection criteria outlined in the selection policy. The committee shall have no authority to determine curriculum. The principal shall take into account these recommendations when making his or her decision as to whether the material should be retained or removed.

F. Within 10 working days of receiving the recommendations of the school instructional material review committee, the principal shall make a decision whether to retain the material or remove the material.

G. If the principal determines that the challenged material be retained, the complainant shall be notified in writing within 5 working days. The complainant shall be given a copy of the decision of the school instructional material review committee and a copy of the procedures for filing an appeal. If the principal determines that the challenged material be removed, then the complainant, the teacher(s), the students in the class, and the parents of the students in the class where the complaint was initiated, shall be notified in writing within 5 working days of the decision. At the same time the decision will be referred to the district instructional material review committee.

H. An appeal of a principal's determination to retain challenged material must be filed with the principal within 5 working days of notification of that determination and shall include a specific statement of the complainant's grounds for disagreement with the principal's determination. Copies of the appeal shall be furnished to the teacher(s) and the parents of the students in the class where the complaint was initiated within 5 working days of the filing of the appeal.

I. The superintendent shall appoint a district instructional material review committee to hear appeals from decisions made at the school level. The committee shall be composed of the following 15 members. All but 4. and 6. below shall be appointed for one-year terms. In the event the challenge originates at the same school at which a member of the committee works then the superintendent shall substitute another individual from the same category:

1. *Two lay persons.* One of whom shall be a district school advisory council member and one of whom shall be a member of and approved by the public library board.

2. *Three principals.* One principal shall be appointed from each level (elementary, middle, and high school). However, only one principal from the same level as the school at which the challenge originates shall serve on the review panel for the particular material.

3. *Two instructional staff members.* Two shall be appointed by name.

4. *Grade level instructional staff member.* One instructional staff member who is a department head, grade level chair, or team leader from the same level (elementary, middle, or high school) at which the challenge originates.

5. *District level instructional staff member.* One shall be appointed by name.

6. *District level coordinator.* A coordinator of the level or special area where the material has been challenged.

7. *Four parents.* One shall be a parent of an elementary school student, one shall be a parent of a middle school student, and two shall be the parents of high school students.

8. *One instructional staff member designated by the* ABCE.

J. This district instructional material review committee shall make recommendations to the superintendent as to whether challenged material is appropriate under the criteria set forth in the selection policy. The superintendent shall take into account the recommendations of the committee when making the decision as to whether or not the challenged material should be removed.

K. The district instructional material review committee shall have 30 working days from the date of the complaint to file its written decision with the superintendent, who shall then have 10 working days from that date to make a written decision and distribute it to the complainant, the teacher, the principal of the school involved, and the school board.

L. If the superintendent recommends removal of the material, the school board shall act on the recommendation within 45 working days. Should the superintendent decide not to recommend removal, that decision shall be final unless the complainant appeals in writing directly to the school board within 10 working days of the decision. The school board shall act upon the appeal within 45 working days.

M. The school board shall notify the complainant and teacher(s) seeking to use the challenged material of the date and time of the school board's consideration of the recommendation to remove or the appeal of the recommendation not to remove. The school board shall furnish the complainant and the teacher(s) seeking to use the challenged material an opportunity to be heard prior to the board's making a decision on the approval or rejection of the material challenged. The teacher(s) shall be granted a temporary duty assignment for the purposes of attending the meeting.

N. A decision by the principal or the superintendent to remove the instructional material shall result in an automatic appeal to the next level. If the school instructional material review committee or the district ad hoc committee fails to act within the time specified, the principal or superintendent shall then make the decision without committee input.

O. During the review process, the material shall not be removed from use.

don't win them all, and that makes most of us more willing to prepare for the next battle. What we sometimes forgot was that not all secondary schools were prepared to face the censors. A recent survey of 421 California school districts by Louise Adler (of California State University at Fullerton)—autumn 1988 through spring 1990—found that nearly one-fourth of these school districts lacked formal policies to handle objections to books or other teaching materials. This is especially important for middle and junior high schools to undertake. Their curricula tend to be broader and more integrated. More important, they are schools more likely to include young adult literature, a body of materials much less familiar to school personnel and the community.

The ten steps following are mostly intended for those schools and school districts without clear-cut policies for handling censorship, though it's remotely possible that schools with formal policies in place might want to consider a few changes. I'd like to suggest also that some current procedures in some schools leave out significant steps (for example, they begin with the writing of a library selection policy or they ignore what ought to happen to the book under attack during the attack). Some suggestions may strike educators as impractical or visionary. They ought to consider the suggestions before discarding them.

First, the school board and superintendent should prepare an honest and succinct statement of the school's educational philosophy. The statement should be readable and even worth reading, in other words devoid of jargon, those ugly garbage words and phrases that lack meaning but sound impressive to the uneducated or the easily confused, for example,

> facilitate, meaningful, viable, relevant, change agents, bottom line, coping strategies, interacting, output (input or any kind of put), optimize, decision making, dialoguing, conferencing, interpersonal, parameter (leave that to the mathematicians), impact or impacted as a verb, as in "The thrust of his argument impacted me" (leave that word to the dentists), thrust (as a noun, as in "The thrust of his argument impacted me"), role-model, prioritize, goal-oriented, feedback, on the firing line, actualization (or that other barbarism, self-actualization), or any such psychopsychotic, sociosociopathic babble.

The purpose of this one–two page statement (and no one willingly reads more than two pages of educational philosophy) is to make clear what the school stands for and particularly where it stands on *indoctrination* and *education.* Those terms are not synonymous, nor are they compatible, no matter how some strange educators play with language and pretend that the two can exist side by side without damage to a school. *Education* implies the right of students to explore ideas and issues without interference from anyone, parent or teacher or administrator. *Indoctrination* implies the right of those in charge of students to force onto students certain values determined by what purports to be the dominant culture. Deviations from the norm are possible in a system that proposes to educate. Not so in a system that proposes to indoctrinate. Banning books or screening out "dangerous" issues or "controversial" ideas from classroom discussion typifies a school dedicated to indoctrination. And when the rights to inquire and question and even doubt are denied young people, education inevitably degenerates into indoctrination. Parents have a right to assume their kids will get an education, not an indoctrination into someone else's set of values or beliefs.

The brief statement of educational philosophy should make clear what the school proposes to be and to do. Since the statement is clearly not carved out of mosaic stone, it should be periodically examined and revised to take into account new educational ideas and practices and changing social conditions. The statement must reflect the realities of the school, the community, and the world and the educational dreams of the board, the administration, the teachers, and the students.

Second, with that statement in place, a series of statements by the several academic departments and the library should be forthcoming. A statement from the English department need not always be first, but as the department most certain to use controversial books and to consider dangerous ideas and issues, it logically should develop a rationale for studying English, particularly why literature is worth teaching and recommending and reading, maybe even worth enjoying. The rationale ought to announce a well-reasoned excitement about the joys and vitality of literature. It ought to emphasize that there is no one way of getting at any literary work and there are many kinds of literature worth reading. What I'd like to see is beautifully summed by poet and businessman Wallace Stevens. "Literature," he wrote, "is the better part of life. To this it seems inevitably necessary to add, provided life is the better part of literature." Teachers who use young adult literature, and librarians who include it in their acquisitions, need to include the distinctive place of that genre in their curriculum.

Other departments would add their rationales, for example the social sciences and science departments. Certainly, no three departments are so likely to become embroiled in censorship battles as these three—English, social studies, and science.

Once these statements are in place, the school librarian has a sound base for developing a book-selection policy. It will reflect the educational, intellectual, and emotional needs of students, the educational dreams of the school board, the administration, the teachers, and the community, and our heritage of freedom to read and inquire and think. Obviously, the school librarian can examine policies of other schools, but, while schools may have much in common, no two are the same. Similarly, no two book-selection policies will be identical.

A sound policy will help in fighting censorship, but in any community someone is certain to be disturbed by an author or a book. Indeed, the first law of censorship is that anything is potentially censorable by someone, some place, some time, for some reason. The second law is the more recent the work, the more likely the censorship. And the third law is that no one can guess what authors or books will come under attack next. The perennial *Catch-22* or *Catcher in the Rye* or *Adventures of Huckleberry Finn*? Classic targets like *Romeo and Juliet* or *Oedipus Rex* or *Lysistrata*? Surprises like Emily Dickinson's poetry or a short story by Bernard Malamud or William Saroyan? Or no surprises at all—anything by Judy Blume or Norma Klein or John Steinbeck.

Some books challenge us, make us think, make us wonder, make us doubt. That's the danger of reading, just as it's the rationale for reading. And some books will inevitably offend. Dorothy Broderick (1984), formerly a librarian and now editor of *Voice of Youth Advocates,* one of those essential magazines, wrote about a librarian's responsibilities:

As individuals, we must be willing to unite with others who share our values; as librarians, we must be willing to provide the materials that allow us and our patrons access to ideas we love and ideas we loathe. "This library has something offensive to everyone" (p. 14).

And because the library must protect its carefully selected books and because the several departments must be free to read and discuss ideas and follow them wherever they lead, the school's educators must recommend to the school board a policy and procedure to handle objections or attempted censorship. The most obvious sources for help are the *Intellectual Freedom Manual*, second edition from the ALA and "The Students' Right to Read," third edition from the NCTE. Both have practical suggestions, and the Citizen's Request for Reconsideration of a Work in the NCTE pamphlet is widely, and deservedly, used. (It is adapted in Chapter 19 of this work.)

Third, the school board, urged on by the academic departments and library and the administration, should accept the statements above, particularly the policy and procedure on objections to teaching materials. Every year at the beginning of the school year, the board should officially go on record sustaining both policy and procedure again and explaining in the board's minutes why it subscribes, particularly for new members of the board. A school that has no such clear policy or procedure is an accident waiting to happen. Given the change in school board personnel over several years, it is vital that the board reaffirm its approval of the policy and procedure each year.

Fourth, the school board should go on record reminding the school's educators to accept their disciplines and their professional organizations. Ignorant or lazy teachers aid and abet censors. Good educators take their responsibilities seriously and can—do—explain to parents why certain books or teaching materials are valuable for an entire class, why other books are appropriate for small groups, and why yet other books are worthwhile for individual students. Parents often know, or can guess, what is going on in school, but they usually are ignorant of why it's going on. Good teachers want parents to know *what*, *why*, and even *how*.

Fifth, the school board should request that teachers justify their teaching and materials. I'd take that one step further and insist that teachers prepare a rationale of a page or so explaining/justifying the use of any long work in class—any class use of a novel or play or book length nonfiction. Such a rationale should be written whether the work is new or old. In fact, I'd be more curious about a justification for *Silas Marner* or *Macbeth* or *A Tale of Two Cities* or any number of literary warhorses than I would a rationale for *A Hero Ain't Nothin' but a Sandwich* or *To Kill a Mockingbird* or *Invisible Man*, though rationales need to be written for all works read in common. I'd wonder why any teacher would want to inflict Eliot's *Four Quartets* or Hardy's *Jude the Obscure* or Shakespeare's *Titus Andronicus* or Twain's *The Mysterious Stranger* on young adults, but having done even wilder things myself with high school kids, I'd not be antagonistic, only curious. I'd like to read those rationales, partly to learn about the reasoning of challenging English teachers, partly to discover again the simple joy of reading good, clear English prose.

What would I want answered in those rationales? Answers to four questions:

1. Why would you want to use this work with this class at this time?
2. How do you believe this work will meet your announced objectives?
3. What problems of style, texture, tone, and theme exist for students in reading this work, and how will you meet those problems?
4. Assuming that the objectives are met, how will the class and the students be different for having read and discussed this work?

In James E. Davis's collection, *Dealing with Censorship* (1979), Diane Shugert's "How to Write a Rationale in Defense of a Book" provides helpful details on the problems of writing rationales. (See also Stern's Chapter 19 in this work for an example of a rationale.)

While I didn't recognize it at first, one of the best rationales for writing rationales was that they forced teachers to write and have their writing made available to the public. I suspect that most parents would like to know whether their children's teachers can write clear and forceful prose.

Sixth, after the censor arrives—and it's almost always a surprise—school personnel should remember all they've prepared for this occasion and avoid losing their wits, tempting as it is in moments of crisis. In many schools, censors can count on immediate panic, and they can count on rash promises being made in the midst of chaos. Three points do need to be remembered. The policy and procedure apply to everyone alike, whether it's the school board president or the most shiftless member of the community. The objector, no matter who it is, should be treated tactfully and speedily. And most important, and often forgotten—the fact that someone has questioned a book or an idea does not mean that censorship has arrived. Parents and any citizens have a right to question our teaching materials or methods whenever they wish, and sometimes we may even quietly, or secretly, agree that it's about time Mrs. X or Mr. Y was questioned about the way she or he wastes time doing Task A or Task B in senior English or sophomore biology. Challenging a book or debating the virtue of discussing a particular idea does not imply the beginning of the battle between the powers of light (us) and darkness (them), *though it may*. We can't be sure, and that's reason enough to watch carefully.

Seventh, the protester must be willing to talk with the offending teacher or librarian before any further steps can be taken. The meeting may not solve the problem, but the parties must have the chance to work matters out on their own. Educators need to remember that if they dread meeting parents, parents may be even more uneasy about facing teachers or librarians. That can translate into parental anger. Parents may assume there's nothing to be gained by a meeting. They may fear teachers, a residue from youth when no one voluntarily met any teacher for any reason. Parents may worry that teachers will look down on them because of their lack of formal education. But it's amazing how often parents interject a comment like one of these early in the discussion—"But that's not what Bob said you wanted" or "I wish she'd told us that you'd given them two weeks to write that paper" or "He said everyone in the class had to read that book."

Parents may come to the meeting angry or cowed or humiliated or whatever. It's our best chance for public relations although we may not think of it precisely in those terms. Teachers who use YA literary selections need to prepare for such conferences with great care. Without an abundance of ponderous literary criticism to support their choices, it is the teachers themselves who must offer cogent argument for what they ask their students to read and study.

Eighth, if the objector wishes to pursue the matter even after meeting with the teacher or librarian, the parent should be politely told that a form must be completed, preferably one mentioned earlier, the Citizen's Request for Reconsideration of a Work in NCTE's "The Students' Right to Read." The form asks for some obvious information—the objector's name, whether the person represents herself or himself or a group—and brief answers to 14 questions, among them:

1. Have you been able to discuss this work with the teacher or librarian who ordered it or used it?

4. What do you think is the general purpose of the author in this book?

5. In what ways do you think a work of this nature is not suitable for the use the teacher or librarian wishes to carry out?

10. Do you have negative reviews of this book?

12. What would you like your library/school to do about this work?
 ___ Do not assign/lend it to my child.
 ___ Return it to the staff selection committee/department for re-evaluation.
 ___ Other—please explain.

13. In its place, what work would you recommend that would convey as valuable a picture and perspective of the subject treated?

The form is simple and rapidly completed, and it allows objectors (or censors) to get the bile out of their systems. Sometimes, that's all that's needed—a few nasty words written down, the form wadded up, and the parent can victoriously basketball the form into the nearest wastebasket. The form encourages a cooling-down time. It's one thing to complain about the schools, the easy and immoral books they use today and not the difficult and immoral classics we read back in the good-old days when education was run right. That's part of the United States' love affair with nostalgia. It's a popular U.S. sport beloved of parents and editors and university professors who haven't been near a real classroom in years. Facing that form forces critics to put their objections in specific answers, and that's difficult. Many critics find it impossible.

Please don't misunderstand me. I edited the second edition of the NCTE pamphlet in 1972, and I've had friends compliment me for devising something that got rid of censors, or stalled them. But I don't want to get rid of censors, at least not that way. The Citizen's Request for Reconsideration form wasn't created to stall parents, and I hate to see it praised for doing that. It's not all that difficult to get rid of objectors if we want to play the condescending snob, but if we do that, objectors almost invariably come back to haunt us, and they should.

I'd much prefer having critics complete the form so we can listen to the objections. Stifling parents and preventing them from speaking is a dangerously temporary nonsolution to a problem. Almost inevitably, the problems get worse and the objectors get more demanding.

Ninth, if nothing has worked thus far and if the form is completed and the objection is now filed, a standing (not ad hoc) committee established for just this purpose should be convened. The committee will receive the completed Request for Reconsideration form and the rationale written for the book—or a justification written specifically for the committee—and will set a mutually agreed upon time for the committee to meet to hear both sides. At that time, the objector and his or her supporters and those defending the book will advance their cases followed by questions from the committee. While the meeting may easily become heated, the chair of the committee—probably an ex-officio member and an administrator appointed to represent the school board and its interests—should be chosen to keep the business moving and as unemotional as possible. That is clearly no easy task. I would want everyone on whatever side to have all the time needed to advance any and all points, but since students are waiting to get back to work and the town is certain to be curious (or alarmed) and the town paper needs to go to press, the committee should avoid unnecessary delays in the committee's actions.

I need to add something here that I once assumed but no longer do. The book in question will be kept on the shelves or in the classroom until the matter is adjudicated, as Penway stressed in Chapter 20. Some districts have given in to a mob rule and pulled the book out and put it somewhere safe until it's no longer regarded as contaminated. I realize a book is not a person (it might not be difficult to prove that most books are better than most people and will endure longer), but we've been taught to assume that one is innocent until proved guilty. It's odd that educators who revere books don't insist on the same treatment for books under attack. Maybe it's because we think books can't talk. Maybe it's because we don't want to hear what books have to say.

This permanent committee should be representative of the school, but it must be small enough to be efficient. Anyone who's been on a committee larger than ten people knows that the major task of the committee is finding a time to meet. The committee should be chaired by an administrator, likely an assistant principal with guts who knows how to work with the public, who will remain ex-officio. Voting members should include an English teacher and a librarian, partly because their fields are most likely to be attacked, mostly because they're likely to be readers and to know sources of help in time of trouble. Other members should include a teacher in another discipline, a parent representing a parents-teachers association or boosters group, and the president or delegate of the local American Federation of Teachers or National Education Association, whichever is the bargaining agent with the school board. That is a five-member group that could meet and act speedily. That is essential for everyone involved.

Other members might include a carefully chosen student or the president of the local Rotary, but whatever democratic impulse leads to adding members will almost certainly make committee deliberations more difficult. Members may find deliberations already frustratingly difficult, and the work may be emotionally draining if the battle is fierce. People will likely not fight to get on this committee, and they must be chosen carefully. This is one committee that almost certainly will not want or accept parents or other citizens anxious to volunteer their services.

Tenth, after the committee has read the objection and the rationale and has heard the contentions of both sides, the committee will need time to talk and deliberate, guaranteeing that everything said is confidential. Once they have gathered again (soon—perhaps a few hours later), and reached a decision, both objector and the educator involved should be notified at the same time the decision is relayed to the school board. The precise details of how all this is handled may vary from school to school, but the structure of the deliberations should not vary. The committee is to hear arguments from both sides speedily and politely and to determine the fate of the book in question speedily.

I would assume, as I believe most educators would, that in the majority of cases, books, and teachers and librarians will be vindicated. As in a criminal case, the objectors must prove guilt beyond a shadow of a doubt. But I assume also that sometimes a good teacher will be shown to have exercised bad judgment. Anyone who's been in schools more than a few days knows that some teachers act days before they think. But whatever the decision of the committee, it should be reached in an honest and impartial manner. I would hope that the community believes that, but it is essential that educators and school personnel believe it. Where indicated in the curricula using YA literature, the English teachers need to take the initiative in supplying the committee with well-documented critical material on the value and quality of such texts. It is unreasonable to expect committee members to be knowledgeable in this area.

These then are my ten recommendations for schools or districts seeking guidelines to protect books and educators.

References
American Library Association. (1983). *Intellectual freedom manual* (2nd ed.). Chicago, IL: Author.

Broderick, D. (1984, February). *Serendipity at work. Show-Me Libraries.* MO: Missouri State Library, p. 14.

Lindgren, K. (1990, December 7). Complaints about texts reported about average. *Los Angeles Times,* p. A-24.

Morris, S.F. (1957). "Adagia" in Wallace Stevens' *Opus posthumous.* New York: Knopf.

National Council of Teachers of English. (1982). *The students' right to read.* Urbana, IL: Author.

Shugert, D. (1979). How to write a rationale in defense of a book. In J.E. Davis (Ed.), *Dealing with censorship* (pp. 187–201). Urbana, IL: National Council of Teachers of English.

Note: Two fine collections of rationales are "Rationales for Commonly Challenged Taught Books" in the *Connecticut English Journal* (1983, Fall) and N.J. Karolides and L. Burress (Eds.) (1985), *Celebrating Censored Books,* Wisconsin Council of Teachers of English.

Bibliography

American Library Association. (annual report). *Banned books, 19: Celebrating censored books.* Chicago, IL: Author.

American Library Association. (1983). *Intellectual freedom manual* (2nd ed.). Chicago, IL: Author.

Aronowitz, S., & Giroux, H. (1983). *Education under siege: The conservative, liberal and radical debate over schooling.* Gransby, MA: Bergin & Garvey.

Burress, L. (1989). *The battle of the books: Literary censorship in the public schools.* Metuchen, NJ: Scarecrow.

Delfattore, J. (1992). *What Johnny shouldn't read: Textbook censorship in America.* New Haven, CT: Yale University Press.

Demac, D.A. (1988). *Liberty denied: The current rise of censorship in America.* New York: PEN American Center.

Donelson, K., & Nilsen, A. (1993). *Literature for today's young adults* (4th ed.). Glenview, IL: Scott, Foresman.

Haight, A.L. (1970). *Banned books: Informal notes on some books banned for various reasons at various times and in various places* (3rd ed.). New York: Bowker.

Hoffmann, F. (1989). *Intellectual freedom and censorship.* Metuchen, NJ: Scarecrow.

Hulsizer, D. (1989) *Protecting the freedom to learn: A citizen's guide.* Washington, DC: People for the American Way.

Karolides, N., Burress, C., & Kean, J. (1993). *Censored books: Critical viewpoints.* Metuchen, NJ: Scarecrow.

National Coalition Against Censorship. *Censorship News.* New York: Author.

National School Board Association. (1990). *Censorship: Managing the controversy.* Washington, DC: Author.

People for the American Way. *Attacks on the freedom to learn: Annual reports.* Washington, DC: Author.

Provenzo, E.F., Jr. (1990). *Religious fundamentalism and American education.* Albany, NY: State University of New York Press.

Schlechty, P.C. (1990). *Schools for the 21st century*. San Francisco, CA: Jossey-Bass.

Simmons, J.S. (Ed.). (1993, Winter). *Censored: ALAN Review*. Urbana, IL: National Council of Teachers of English.

Thomas, C. (1983). *Book burning*. Westchester, IL: Crossway.

West, M.J. (1988). *Voices against censorship in children's literature*. New York: Neal-Schuman.

Young Adult Services Division Intellectual Freedom Committee. (1989). *Hit list: Frequently challenged young adult titles: References to defend them*. Chicago, IL: American Library Association.

Author Index

Note: An "f" following a page number indicates that the reference may be found in a figure; an "n" that it may be found in a note; a "t" that it may be found in a table.

A

Adams, M.J., 83, 84
Adler, L., 87, 91, 93
Agency for Instructional Technology, 141, 144
Alexander, F., 107, 112
Altick, R.D., 3, 11
Altwerger, B., 80, 85
American Library Association, 231, 235, 241. *See also* Young Adult Services Division
Anchorage Daily News, 172, 182
Anderson, M., 105, 106
Anderson, R., 107, 113
Anti-Defamation League of B'nai B'rith, 142, 144
Apple, M.W., 135, 140, 144
Arizona Daily Star, 105, 106
Arizona Range News, 104, 106
Arizona Republic, 97, 106
Asante, M.K., 143, 144
Ashley, L.F., 109t, 112

B

Baer, R.N., 41, 42, 44
Bailey, R.W., 85
Barchas, S.E., 109t, 112
Barish, E., 111, 112
Batchelor, J.E., 137, 145
Bates, V.L., 154, 164
Beale, H.K., 139, 144

Beck, I.C., 135, 145
Bennetta, W.J., 163, 164
Berger, M.D., 184, 189
Berra, T.M., 155, 164
Beta Upsilon Chapter, Pi Lambda Theta, 109t, 113
Beyer, B.K., 19, 27
Block, T.D., 158, 162, 165
Bloome, D., 79, 84
Blume, J., 187, 189
Board of Education, Island Trees (N.Y.) Union Free School District No. 26 v. Pico, 20, 21, 27
Boyd, W.L., 138, 145
Bradley, W.L., 163, 165
Breen, T.H., 145
Brent, D., 80, 84
Brinkley, E., 81, 84
Broderick, D., 234, 241
Brown, J.E., 177, 182
Bruner, J.S., 23, 24, 27
Buffon, G.L., 149, 164
Burress, L., 95, 106, 189, 242n

C

Campbell, P.J., 118, 122
Carlson, K., 124, 133, 138, 145
Carroll, J.D., 135, 145
Cherryholmes, C.H., 136, 138, 145

Nelson, C.E., 159, 162, 164
Nelson, J.L., 124, 125, 128, 130, 133, 138, 139, 146
Newsweek, 175, 182
Noebel, D.A., 41, 44
Numbers, R.L., 148, 150, 152, 155, 165

O

Ochoa, A.S., 35, 128, 132, 133
O'Hara, M., 41, 44
Olson, R.L., 163, 165
Orcutt, S., 137, 146

P

Palmer, B.C., 4, 12
Palonsky, S., 124, 133
Parker, F., 30, 36
Parker, W., 125, 126, 133
Patrick, J.J., 135, 146
Pattison, R., 77, 85
Peck, R., 118, 122
People for the American Way, 86, 94
Perlmutter, P., 142, 146
Pi Lambda Theta. *See* Beta Upsilon Chapter, Pi Lambda Theta
Pinar, W.F., 27
Pipkin, G.T., 188, 189
Postman, N., 9, 12

R

Raburn, J., 111, 114
Raphael, T.E., 113
Ravitch, D., 27, 128, 133, 134, 146
Richards, I.A., 5, 12
Roberts, G., Jr., 139, 146
Roberts, P.H., 27
Robertson, P., 39, 40, 41, 42, 44
Roper Organization, 142, 146

Rosenblatt, L.M., 5, 12, 80, 85, 181, 182
Russell, B., 124, 133

S

Saloman, G., 79, 85
Saperstein, D., 37, 44
Scharmann, L.C., 157, 158, 162, 165
Schlafly, P., 33
Schlessinger, J.H., 111, 114
Scott, E.C., 157, 163, 165
Semmes, C.E., 143, 147
Sewell, G.T., 134, 147
Shafer, R.E., 80, 85
Shaver, J.P., 133, 145, 146
Shugert, D.P., 188, 189, 236, 242
Shupe, A., 38, 44
Simmons, J.S., 4, 12, 55, 57, 61
Simonds, R., 40, 44
Skehan, J.W., 150, 165
Skoog, G., 149, 153, 154, 156, 165
Small, R., 196, 197
Smith, K., 80, 85
Snow, S., 46, 54
Staab, C., 80, 85
Sternberg, R., 125, 133
Stiehl, R.B., 149, 157, 165
Strassman, P.A., 78, 85
Suhor, C., 117, 118, 122

T

Tatina, R., 149, 157, 165
Taylor, R., 210
Tell City (Ind.) *News*, 32, 36
Thaxton, C.B., 163, 165
Thorndike, R.L., 109t, 114
Tuman, M.C., 77, 85
Turlington, R.D., 4, 12
Turnbell, M., 89–90, 94

Subject Index

Note: An "f" following a page number indicates that the reference may be found in a figure; a "t" that it may be found in a table.

A

Literature, selection of; Textbooks, selection of); student-selected, 192; student-written, 102; written rationales for, 199–200, 236–237, 239, 241. *See also* Anthologies; Literature; Novels; Paperbacks; Textbooks; YA (young adult) literature

C

DRAKE, N.D.: 201

DRESDEN, GERMANY: 200

DROWNING OF STEPHAN JONES, THE (Greene): 117

DRUGS: as classroom topic, 33, 95, 128; evolution theory relevance to, 148, 161; as textbook no-no, 57

DUNGEONS AND DRAGONS (game): 32

E

EAGLE FORUM: 4, 17, 82, 118; affiliates of, 34. *See also* Schlafly, Phyllis

ECONOMICS (field of study): 127; as sensitive classroom topic, 140; in social studies purview, 131

EDGERTON, CLYDE: 46

EDUCATION: 14; censor mistrust of, 25; censor theory of, 19–20; and indoctrination contrasted, 233; nature of, 233; on 19th century plains, 137; purpose of, 10, 198; Rehnquist on, 20. *See also* Classrooms; Curricula; Literacy; Physical education; Schools; Special education; Students; Teachers; Textbooks; Training; Values education; Vocational education

EDUCATIONAL RESEARCH ANALYSTS: 4, 16; international character of, 30. *See also* Gabler, Mel; Gabler, Norma

EDUCATION OF LITTLE TREE, THE (Carter): 174–175

EFFECT OF GAMMA RAYS ON MAN-IN-THE-MOON MARIGOLDS, THE (Zindel): 117

E.J. HALE AND SON: 139

ELDERLY: CIBC solicitude for, 142

ELECTIVE(S): sex education as, 32; as Warsaw (Ind.), HS problem, 31–32

ELEMENTARY SCHOOL: censor focus on, 95–106

ELLISON, RALPH: 59

EMIG, J.: 79, 80

ENGLISH: achievement standards for, 83; censor focus on, 233, 234; as literacy element, 79; teaching of, 190–193, 198–200, 209, 241 (*see also* National Council of Teachers of English). *See also* Black English

ENVIRONMENTALISM: 56; as social studies issue, 126; as textbook-writer desideratum, 57

ESP (extrasensory perception): New Age and, 41

ESSAYS: social studies–related, 126

ETHNOMETHODOLOGY: 79

EUROPE: growing pains in contemporary, ix

EVALUATIVE THINKING: 125

EVANSTON, ILL.: 204–209

EVOLUTION, THEORY OF: 15; banning from schools of, 148; BSCS on, 153; centrality to science of, 161; creationism vs., x, 8, 15–16, 76, 139, 148–157, 160, 162–163; criticism of, 149–151 (*see also* Evolution, theory of; creationism vs.); development of, 149–150; legacy of, 148; M. Gabler vs., 32; Reagan on, 155; student resistance to, 157–158, 160–162; teaching techniques re, 157–162. *See also* Natural selection

F

HENTOFF, NAT: 121
HERESY: in 17th century Boston, 139
HERO AIN'T NOTHIN' BUT A SANDWICH, A (Childress): 21, 24, 26, 236
HERSEY, JOHN: 5
HIDDEN DANGERS OF THE RAINBOW, THE (Cumbey): 41
HIGH SCHOOLS: population explosion in U.S., 151
HILL, MAXINE: 173
HILLSVILLE, VA.: 45–47, 51–53
HINTON, S.E.: 115, 118, 119
HIROSHIMA, JAPAN: 200
HIROSHIMA (Hersey): 5
HIRSCH, E.D., JR.: 58, 78, 193
HISTORY: 127; politically correct revision of, 59; right-wing defense of
    traditional, 128; teaching of, 130, 134, 138–139, 140–144 (*see also*
    Textbooks, history)
HOBBIES: books on, 109t
HOLISM, GLOBAL: religious right suspicion of, 81. *See also* "One world"
HOLOCAUST: as nonevent, xi, 142, 143. See also *Diary of a Young Girl, The*
HOLT, RINEHART AND WINSTON: 86. *See also* Impressions reading series
HOMESTEADERS: history-text approach to, 136–137
HOMOSEXUALITY: 58; CIBC and, 142; as classroom topic, 95; "promotion"
    of, x, 91; as social studies concern, 126; as story subject, x, 117
"HOORAY FOR THREE" (Impressions series story): 91
HORROR STORIES: 107–109t
"HOUR OF DELIVERANCE" (radio show): 45
HUCKLEBERRY FINN. See *Adventures of Huckleberry Finn, The*
HUGHES, LANGSTON: 22, 59
HUMANISM: 40; censors vs., 16, 32, 38, 39, 225; evolution theory and, 148
"HUMAN POTENTIAL" MOVEMENT: New Age and, 43
HUMILITY: persuasion through specious, 9
HUMOR: popularity of literary, 109t; *See also* Comic books
HUNDREDTH MONKEY, THE (Keyes): 42
HUNT, M.P.: 139
HUXLEY, ALDOUS: 115
HYDRICK, C. JANE: 75, 111, 138
HYPNOSIS: religious right fear of student, 50

I

I AM THE CHEESE (Cormier): 5, 63, 223, 224
I KNOW WHY THE CAGED BIRD SINGS (Angleou): 196
ILLINOIS: book-selection/retention guidelines in, 202–209; censorship
    efforts in, 56, 200

LEE, HARPER: x, 116. See also *To Kill a Mockingbird*

L'ENGLE, MADELEINE: 100, 110, 111, 117

LESBIANISM. *See* Homosexuality

LESSING, DORIS: 59

LETTERS (missives): class-to-librarian, 99

LETTERS (symbols): phonics and, 83

LEWELLING (Kansas governor): 137

LIBERTY FOUNDATION: 4

LIBRARIANS, SCHOOL: book selection by, 204, 234; censorship by, 190–192 (*see also* Librarians, school; self-censorship by); "parental notes" solicited by, 191; and parents, 237–238; responsibilities of, 234–235; self-censorship by, 131; student pressure on, 99; as teacher allies, 195. *See also* Media specialists, school library

LIBRARIES: public, x, 104 (*see also* Bookmobile); school (*see* Librarians, school; School libraries)

"LIBRARY BILL OF RIGHTS": 169, 212–213, 215–217, 231

LIFE (mag.): 42

LIGHT IN THE ATTIC, A (Silverstein): 115

LIGHTWEIS, PATRICIA: 53

LINEBERRY, J.B.: 45–47, 51–53

LINGUISTICS: literacy and, 79; as sensitive area, 60–61. *See also* Metalinguistics; Sociolinguistics

LITERACY: crisis in, 78; defined, 25–26, 77–79; functional, 77; media, 78–79; mindless, 14, 17–19; new approaches to, 77–80, 83–84 (*see also* Reading, new approaches to; Whole language); "real," 23–25, 27; scientific, 16. *See also* Communication, verbal; Critical literacy; Reading; Writing

LITERATURE: adoption forms for selecting, 205f; African American, 31, 59–60; antiwar, 200–201; as basal-reader alternative, 80; joys of, 233–234; nature of, 193; protest, 34f, 35; selection of classroom, 172–175, 180–181, 194–196, 199, 201–206, 209, 212–219, 221–222, 234–235 (*see also* Books, student-selected; Literature, adoption forms for selecting; Media specialists, school library; Textbooks, selection of); teaching of, 171, 181; as whole language element, 80; young adult (*see* YA literature). *See also* Anthologies; Biography; Novels; Poetry; Stories

LITERATURE AS EXPLORATION (Rosenblatt): 5

LITERATURE LOGS: 99

"LITTLE RED RIDING HOOD": 6

LITTLE ROCK, ARK.: 154

LOGIC: students introduced to, 9

LOGS, STUDENT. *See* Journals, student; Literature logs

MINORITIES: and censorship, 21–22, 57; in language arts programs, 172; oppression of, 56; textbook representation of, 4, 205f. *See also* African Americans; Asians, U.S.; Elderly; Handicapped; Homosexuality; Latinos; Native Americans

MOBY DICK (Melville): 194

MOFFETT, JAMES: 31, 83, 84

MOON, TRUMAN: 152

MOORE, ALICE: 30

MORALISM, DOCTRINAL: 150

MORALITY: as sensitive classroom issue, 140

MORAL MAJORITY: 4

MORRIS, HENRY: 148, 154–155

MORRISON, TONI: 59–60, 184

MOWAT JUNIOR HIGH SCHOOL: 223–224

MULTICULTURALISM: 43; as book-selection consideration, 202, 203; as *Impressions* series theme, 87; religious right fear of, 81. *See also* Language arts, multicultural enhancement of

"MUMMIES MADE IN EGYPT" (Impressions series story): 92

MUPPETS: in religious right sights, 43

MURDER: as sensitive literary subject, 224

MUSIC: as whole language element, 80

MYERS, WALTER DEAN: 115, 119

MYSTERIOUS STRANGER, THE (Twain): 236

MYSTERY STORIES: 107–109t

N

NACOGDOCHES, TEX.: 5

NASHUA, N.H.: 97–98

NATIONAL ASSOCIATION FOR THE ADVANCEMENT OF COLORED PEOPLE: 56

NATIONAL BROADCASTING COMPANY (NBC): 42

NATIONAL CENTER FOR SCIENCE EDUCATION: 156–157

NATIONAL COALITION AGAINST CENSORSHIP: 2, 45, 47, 48, 51, 72

NATIONAL COUNCIL OF TEACHERS OF ENGLISH: 187; and censorship, 168, 197, 198, 231 (*see also* "Students' Right to Read, The"); and language question, 60; Mowat JHS honored by, 223; and whole language, 80

NATIONAL COUNCIL OF TEACHERS OF ENGLISH AND THE INTERNATIONAL READING ASSOCIATION JOINT TASK FORCE ON INTELLECTUAL FREEDOM: 168, 187

NATIONAL COUNCIL OF TEACHERS OF MATHEMATICS: 18

NATIONAL EDUCATION ASSOCIATION: as bargaining agent, 240; and evolution theory, 150; Simonds vs., 88; teacher guidelines from, 139

NATIONAL GEOGRAPHIC (mag.): 98
NATIONALITY: censorship and, 55; textbook writer sensitivity to, 57
NATIONAL ORGANIZATION FOR WOMEN: 57
NATIONAL SCHOOL BOARD ASSOCIATION: 168
NATIONAL SCIENCE FOUNDATION: 153; and MACOS, 129
NATIONAL WRITING PROJECT: 79, 181
NATIVE AMERICANS: and censorship, 57, 174–175; popular image of, 60; social studies role-playing as, 127; teaching about, 141. *See also* Lakota Sioux
NATURAL SELECTION: 149–150, 160
NELSON, JACK L.: 76, 134, 135, 138
NETWORKING: religious right suspicion of, 43
NEVADA: censorship efforts in, 217
NEW AGE: 2, 50; literature of, 42; literature opposing, 41; religious right vs., 39–43, 53, 81
NEW AGE CULTS AND RELIGIONS (Marrs): 41
NEW AGE MASQUERADE, THE: THE HIDDEN AGENDA IN YOUR CHILD'S CLASS-ROOM (Buehrer): 34f
NEWBERY AWARD: 100, 110
NEW DEAL: xi
NEW HAMPSHIRE: censorship efforts in, 97–98
NEW JERSEY: censorship efforts in, 129–131
NEW MILLENNIUM, THE (Robertson): 41
NEW SCIENCE OF LIFE (Sheldrake): 42
NEWSPAPERS: as censor forum, 33, 52; censorship of student, 129–130
NEWSWEEK (mag.): 129
NEW YORK (state): censorship efforts in, 20, 21
NEW ZEALAND: whole language theory in, 86
"NIGGER JIM" (*The Adventures of Huckleberry Finn*): 56
1984 (Orwell): 115
NORTH DAKOTA: book burning in, 201
NOVELS: mission of, 65. *See also* Paperbacks; YA literature
NUCLEAR POWER: as classroom topic, 141
NUDITY: in books, 96, 183 (*see also* David, Michelangelo statue of); in puzzles, 98

O

OCONEE COUNTY, S.C.: 50–52
OCONEE COUNTY CITIZENS AGAINST CENSORSHIP: 50–51
O'CONNOR, FLANNERY: 59
OEDIPUS REX (Sophocles): 234
OF MICE AND MEN (Steinbeck): 32

O'HARA, M.: 41, 42

OHIO: censorship efforts in, 88–91, 157

ONE DAY IN THE LIFE OF IVAN DENISOVICH (Solzhenitzyn): 115, 131,

O'NEILL, THOMAS P., JR.: 64

"ONE WORLD": evolution theory and, 148; as subversive concept, 16, 32, 33

ON THE ORIGIN OF SPECIES (Darwin): 149

ORCUTT, SUSAN: 137

OREGON: censorship efforts in, 87

ORWELL, GEORGE: 115

OSBORN, JEAN: 83

OUT ON A LIMB (MacLaine): 42

OUTSIDERS, THE (Hinton): 115, 117, 118

OVERTON (Arkansas jurist): 156

P

PACIFISM: censors vs., 16

PANAMA CANAL: 141

PANAMA CITY, FLA.: 5, 221

PAPERBACKS: 119; censors vs., x

PARENTS: as anticensorship resource, 215; librarians and, 237–238; nurturing responsibilities of, 104; teachers and, 181, 235, 237–238

PARENT-TEACHER ASSOCIATIONS: 214

PARKS, RAMON: 48, 52, 53

PATERSON, KATHERINE: 100, 101, 115

PATRIOTISM: Madison Avenue–packaged, 9; NEA deference to, 139; right wing affinity for, 4, 55, 128, 139; as sensitive classroom issue, 140; social studies focus on, 130, 131

"PAUL" (*Fade*): 69–70

PECK, RICHARD: 118, 119

PECK, ROBERT NEWTON: 115

PENNSYLVANIA: censorship efforts in, 56–57

PENWAY, ANNE L.: 169, 221, 240

PEOPLE FOR THE AMERICAN WAY: ix, 88

PERIODICALS: librarian "cleansing" of, 176. *See also* Newspapers

PETERSON, PAUL: 47–49, 52

PETITION(S): censor-originated, 33, 52; pro-*Forever*, 49

PFEFFER, SUSAN, B.: 223

PHOENIX, ARIZ.: 80

PHONICS: censor promotion of, 87, 91; federal support for, 83; and whole language theory, 91

PHYSICAL EDUCATION: critical thinking and, 124

R

RACISM: book selection and, 203, 205f; censorship and, x, 4, 21–22, 31, 55–57, 59–60, CIBC focus on, 142; NEA uneasiness with, 139; as sensitive classroom issue, 140; as social studies issue, 127

RADIO: as censor forum, 33, 53, 118, 119

RAND, AYN: 11

RANDOM MUTATION(AL) THEORY: 163

RAPE: in classroom text, 100–101

RATIONALES, BOOK. *See* Books, written rationales for

READABILITY: as textbook desideratum, 205f

READALOUDS: 97, 99, 100, 106

READER: constructive responsibilities of, *See* Meaning, reader-derived

READER RESPONSE THEORY: 5–7, 80, 106, 181. *See also* Critical reading

READING: affective vs. cognitive, 6; behaviorist approach to, 80; and critical reading contrasted, 3; new approaches to, 81; skepticism inspired by, 9–10; voluntary, 107; whole language theory and, 81; writing and, 79–80. *See also* Critical reading; Literature

REAGAN, RONALD: 155

REBECCA CAUDILL YOUNG READER'S AWARD: 108

RECITATION, CLASSROOM: 134; censor endorsement of, 88

RECONSIDERATION COMMITTEES: 208, 209, 213–216, 235, 239–241; forms for, 238–239. *See also* Instructional material review committees

RECONSTRUCTIONISM: Christian, 38–39

RECORDINGS: objections to, 207

REHNQUIST, WILLIAM: 20

REINCARNATION: as New Age tenet, 41

RELIGION: censorship and, x, 55 (*see also* Evolution theory, creationism vs.); as classroom topic, 140; NEA uneasiness with, 139; science and (*see* Creationism; Evolution, theory of); as social studies issue, 126, 131; textbook writer sensitivity to, 57. *See also* Atheism; Bible; Christianity; Creationism; God; Islam; Judaism; New Age; Sacrilege; Schools; prayer in

RELIGION OF SECULAR HUMANISM AND THE PUBLIC SCHOOLS, THE (Duncan): 34f

REPORTS: Hayakawa on, 7

REPRODUCTIVE SYSTEM, HUMAN: second grade approach to, 102

RESOURCE BOOKS: teacher, 92

RESOURCE CENTERS: school, 204

RESPONSE THEORY. *See* Reader response theory

REVISION: of reflexive writing, 79

RIB LAKE, WIS.: 47–50, 52, 53

"RICHARD CORY" (Robinson): 82
RICHARDS, I.A.: 5
ROBERTSON, PAT: 4, 39, 40
ROBINSON, EDWIN ARLINGTON: 82
ROLE PLAYING, CLASSROOM: 126; Schlafly vs., 17
ROLL OF THUNDER, HEAR MY CRY (Taylor): 173
ROMANCE NOVELS: 109t
ROMEO AND JULIET (Shakespeare): 117, 234
ROOSEVELT, FRANKLIN D.: xi
ROOSEVELT, THEODORE: 141
ROSENBLATT, L.M.: 5, 80, 181
ROSENBLUM, MARC R.: 2, 119, 184
ROTE LEARNING: 124. *See also* Memorization
RUSHDIE, SALMAN: 1
RUSSIA: censor focus on, 128
RUTHERFORD INSTITUTE: 82

S
SACRILEGE: censor sensitivity to, 118
SALINGER, J.D.: 115, 116. See also *Catcher in the Rye, The*
SAROYAN, WILLIAM: 234
SATANIC VERSES, THE (Rushdie): 1
SATANISM: x; censors vs., 32, 38, 110, 111; in Impressions series, 87, 88. *See also* New Age, religious right vs.
"SAVE THE WHALES" MOVEMENT: religious right mistrust of, 42
SCHARMANN, LAWRENCE C.: 76
SCHLAFLY, PHYLLIS: 4, 17, 33, 118, 191; vs. student journals, 82
SCHOOL BOARD(S): of Bay County, Fla., 221, 222, 224–226, 229–230; and censorship issue, 169, 220, 225–226, 232–236, 239–241
SCHOOL LIBRARIES: access to, 215; accession standards for, 204; age-related restrictions on, 218; censor focus on, 169, 175–176, 211–219, 221; check-out procedures in, 176; litigation against, 214, 217; solidarity among intercommunity, 219. *See also* Librarians, school
SCHOOLS: dynamiting of W.Va., 29; educational policy statements for, 232–233; New Age "invasion" of, 40; prayer in, 34, 154; responsibilities of, 124; superintendents of (*see* Superintendents of schools). *See also* Classrooms; Curricula; Education; Elementary school; High schools; School boards; School libraries; Students; Superintendents of schools; Teachers
SCIENCE(S): books on, 109t; critical thinking and, 124; teaching of, 76, 234. *See also* Biology; Social sciences

TENNESSEE: censorship efforts in, 16; Scopes trial in, 152

TERM PAPERS: history, 134

TESTIMONIAL: persuasion through tendentious, 9

TESTS: censor focus on, 82; textbook-bound, 134

TEXAS: censorship efforts in, 5, 117, 157; as Gabler country, 35

"TEXTBOOK PUBLISHERS AND THE CENSORSHIP CONTROVERSY" (Association of American Publishers): 168

TEXTBOOKS: biology, 152–154; censorship of, 135, 139–140, 142–144; Darwin expunged from U.S., 152–153; Dixie-slanted, 139; errors in, 35; history, 76, 134–144, 173; Japanese, 143; reconsideration of in-use, 206–209, 213–217; selection of, 221 (*see also* Literature, selection of); social studies, 138; student criticism of, 10. *See also* Books; Publishers, textbook

THEORIES: importance of scientific, 159–160

TIME (mag.): 129

TITUS ANDRONICUS (Shakespeare): 236

TOBACCO: as classroom-discussion taboo, 57, 117

TO KILL A MOCKINGBIRD (Lee): x, 116, 173, 236

TOMLINSON, CARL M.: 75, 92, 99

TRADITIONAL VALUES COALITION: 88

TRAINING: industrial, 78. *See also* Vocational education

TUNNELL, MICHAEL O.: 75, 92, 99

TURLINGTON, RALPH D.: 4

TURNING POINT, THE (Capra): 42

TWAIN, MARK (Samuel L. Clemens): 57, 115. See also *Adventures of Huckleberry Finn, The*

TWAYNE PUBLISHERS: Young Adult Author series of, 118–119

TYLER, ANNE: 59

U

UNDERSTANDING THE TIMES (Noebel): 41

UNITED KINGDOM: censorship in, ix

UNITED NATIONS: religious right mistrust of, 43

UNITED STATES: antievolution legislation in, 148–149, 154, 156 (*see also* Arkansas, creationism certified in; California, creationism certified in; Louisiana, creationism in); censorship in, ix–xi, 4, 107–108, 129, 139, 183–186, 188–189, 211. *See also* Congress, U.S.; Department of Education, U.S.; Supreme Court, U.S.; *and individual states by name*

UNITED STATES JUSTICE FOUNDATION: 82

UNMASKING THE NEW AGE (Groothuis): 41

UP FROM EDEN (Wilbur): 42

V

W

Also available from IRA...

Common Ground: The National Council of Teachers of English and the International Reading Association Speak with One Voice on Intellectual Freedom and the Defense of It

Prepared by the NCTE/IRA Joint Task Force on Intellectual Freedom, this informative pamphlet outlines four principles of intellectual freedom in education and provides action plans and strategies for teachers, administrators, and parents on the local, state/provincial, national, and international levels.

Single copies are available free for a self-addressed no. 10 envelope stamped with first-class postage for one ounce. (Outside the U.S., send only a self-addressed envelope.) Bulk quantities are available at 100 copies for US$7.00.

Send orders to the International Reading Association, 800 Barksdale Road, PO Box 8139, Newark, Delaware 19714-8139, United States.